Learn on the C++ Macintosh®

INCLUDES
SPECIAL VERSION
OF SYMANTEC C++
FOR MACINTOSH

Dave Mark

Addison-Wesley Publishing Company
Reading, Massachusetts • Menlo Park, California • New York
Don Mills, Ontario • Wokingham, England • Amsterdam
Bonn • Sydney • Singapore • Tokyo • Madrid • San Juan
Paris • Seoul • Milan • Mexico City • Taipei

Library of Congress Cataloging-in-Publication Data

Mark, Dave.
    Learn C++ on the Macintosh : includes a special version of
Symantec's C++ compiler / Dave Mark.
       p. cm.
    Includes bibliographical references and index.
    ISBN 0-201-62204-1
    1. Macintosh (Computer)--Programming.   2. C++ (Computer program
language) I. Title.
QA76.8.M3M36772   1993
005.26'2--dc20   93-61
                                                 CIP

Sponsoring Editor: Keith Wollman
Project Editor: Elizabeth G. Rogalin
Production Coordinator: Gail McDonald Jordan
Cover design: Jean Seal
Icons in book designed by Crystal Sarno, Graphic Perspectives, Inc.
Set in 11 point Palatino by Rob Mauhar and Lenity Himburg, CIP

1 2 3 4 5 6 7 8 9 -MA- 9796959493
First printing, June 1993

To the rest of the quadrangle:

Daniel, Deneen, and Stu.

See you all New Year's Eve!

Contents

Preface   *ix*

Acknowledgments   *xi*

Chapter 1   Welcome Aboard   1

What's in the Package?   3

Why Learn C++?   4

What Should I Know to Get Started?   4

What Equipment Do I Need?   5

The Lay of the Land   5

Strap Yourself In...   8

Chapter 2   Installing THIN C++   9

Installing THIN C++   12

Testing THIN C++   13

Features of THIN C++   16

Summary   19

Chapter 3   Remembering C   21

Literal Constants   24

Variables   28

Operators   37

Statements   42

Functions   43
Preprocessor Directives   44
Comments   45
Summary   45

Chapter 4   Introducing C++   47

Getting C Code to Run under C++   50
New Features of C++   54
The // Comment Marker   54
Handling Input and Output   55
Default Argument Initializers   64
Reference Variables   68
Function Name Overloading   75
The new and delete Operators   79
The Scope Operator   85
Inline Functions   88
Summary   91

Chapter 5   Object Programming Basics   93

The Organizational Power of the Struct   96
Bundling Data and Functions   97
Creating an Object   98
Accessing an Object's Data Members
     and Member Functions   100
Deleting an Object   103
Writing Class Functions   104
Access Priveleges   111
Bringing It All Together   114
The friends Mechanism   119
Summary   126

Chapter 6   Derived Classes   131

Inheritance   134
Derivation, Constructors, and Destructors   141
Base Classes and Constructors with Parameters   147
Overriding Member Functions   154
Summary   158

Chapter 7   Operator Overloading   161

The Operator Overloading Alternative   165
A Few Restrictions   173
Covering All the Bases   174
Special Cases   183
Summary   204

Chapter 8   Inside iostream   205

The Character-Based Interface   208
The iostream Classes   208
Working with Files   216
The iostream State Bits   220
More File Info   226
Customizing iostream   228
Formatting Your Output   234
Using Manipulators   240
istrstream and ostrstream   241
Summary   244

Chapter 9   C++ Potpourri   245

Templates   248
The Templates Approach   249

Multiple Inheritance   260
Resolving Ambiguities   270
Initialization Versus Assignment   280
Memberwise Initialization   284
Summary   292

Chapter 10   Moving On   293

The User Interface   295
The Macintosh Toolbox   297
Class Libraries   299
Books and Other Reference Material   301
Go Get 'Em...   305

Appendices

Appendix A   Glossary   307
Appendix B   Source Code Listings   313
Appendix C   fstream.h   351
Appendix D   iomanip.h   359
Appendix E   iostream.h   361
Appendix F   strstrea.h   385
Appendix G   Unoffical C++ Style Guide   391
Appendix H   The Complete Symantec C++
**   Development Environment   429**
Appendix I   Bibliography   439

Preface

Some time ago, back in 1988 or 1989, I remember reading an article written by someone at Apple Computer. The article was addressed to all Macintosh programmers, and spoke to the future of Macintosh software development. Back then, the vast majority of Macintosh programs were written in either C or Pascal. Sure, there might have been a little Basic here, and a little C++ there, but those languages were viewed as the fringe—a definite minority.

Anyway, this article went on to describe the wonders of object programming and of C++ in particular. Normally, I would have turned the page, since I was perfectly happy programming in C and Pascal, my personal languages of choice. But this article quickly captured my attention. As I read, I began to realize something basic was happening. This article wasn't just an interesting discussion of an alternative development methodology. It was a warning shot across my bow. Apple was making a real commitment to object programming and to C++. At development conferences, the message was also becoming clear. Apple expected all Macintosh software developers not just to understand, but to embrace object programming.

Pay attention to this message: Object programming is the future, and C++ is the language for object programming. Why C++? Apple rewrote MacApp (their object development library) entirely in C++. Apple rewrote much of their operating system in C++. When Symantec and Apple announced their joint cross-platform development library, Bedrock, they made it clear that Bedrock would be written entirely in C++.

Once you've made the commitment to learn about object programming and C++, you're ready to take the next step. Bring this book home with you (pay for it first) and start reading. *Learn C++ on the Macintosh* will do the rest.

By the way, if you feel like getting in touch, I'd love to hear from you. Get on CompuServe, type **GO MACDEV**, and leave a message in the *Learn Programming* section (section 11). In the meantime, let's get started...

D.M.
Arlington, Virginia

Acknowledgments

I'd like to take a few moments to thank all the people who made this book possible. First and foremost, I'd like to thank my good friend Steve Baker. His programming experience and C++ expertise provided invaluable assistance. Steve put in a lot of long hours helping to put this book together. Whether he was fine tuning the table of contents or tinkering with one of my C++ sample programs, Steve's heart and soul were poured into this book. By the way, thanks also to Steve's family, Kelly, Michael, and Matthew, for patience and understanding above and beyond the call of duty.

Thanks to Elizabeth Rogalin, my friend, confidante, and project editor, for seeing this book through. Thanks, Elizabeth!

Thanks to Steve Bushell and Jaime Jouris at Symantec for putting together THIN C++ and for answering all my questions.

Thanks to Dan Weston, C++ guru extraordinaire, for his awesome tech review. Dan helped keep this book on the straight and narrow path to C++ correctness.

Thanks to my old pal Julie Stillman up in Vermont. Happy birthday to you! Wish I could have been there.

Thanks to Crystal Sarno for her excellent artwork. Crystal designed the icons sprinkled throughout the book.

Thanks to Jean Peck for an incredible job copyediting the book.

Thanks to Carlos Derr for guidance and friendship.

Finally, thanks to Deneen Joanne Melander, for companionship, love, and understanding. LFUEMISOK?

Chapter 1

Welcome
Aboard

Interested in learning how to program in C++? Well, you've come to the right place. Grab your Mac, hop into your most comfortable chair, and read on...

1

This Chapter at a Glance

What's in the Package?
Why Learn C++?
What Should I Know to Get Started?
What Equipment Do I Need?
The Lay of the Land
    The Chapters and Appendices
    The Conventions Used in This Book
Strap Yourself In...

WELCOME! BY PURCHASING THIS BOOK/DISK PACKAGE, you've taken the first step toward learning the C++ programming language. As you make your way through the book, you'll learn one of the most popular and powerful programming languages in the world today—you've definitely made a wise investment.

Before we start programming, we first need to address a few questions.

What's in the Package?

Learn C++ on the Macintosh is a book/disk package. The book is filled with interesting facts, figures, and programming examples, all of which are designed to teach you how to program in C++.

In the back of the book is a Macintosh floppy disk that contains all the software you'll need to run each of the book's programming examples on your own computer. Included on this disk is THIN C++, a customized version of the leading Macintosh programming environment, written especially for this book. The disk also includes each of the programs presented in the book so that you don't have to type the examples yourself. Such a deal!

Why Learn C++?

There are a lot of reasons for learning C++. Perhaps the biggest reason is the popularity of C++ as a programming language. Go to your local technical bookstore and count the books dedicated to each programming language. Ten years ago, you would have found that the most popular language out there was Pascal. Five years ago, the pendulum shifted and C became the most popular language. Now, the move is toward C++.

Apple recently began rewriting the majority of the Macintosh operating system in C++. Apple and Symantec recently announced Bedrock, a cross-platform development vehicle written completely in C++. You'll find support for C++ everywhere. There are C++ compilers for Unix, Windows, DOS, and, of course, the Macintosh. The number of C++ programming texts is growing by leaps and bounds. Opportunities for a good C++ programmer are endless.

The bottom line is this: C++ is *the* language of the nineties. Major computer companies like Apple, Microsoft, and Sun are basing their future operating system designs around C++. Knowledge of C or Pascal just isn't enough anymore. In my opinion, C++ is a must!

What Should I Know to Get Started?

There are two prerequisites to using this book. First, you must have a basic knowledge of the Macintosh. Do you know how to double-click on an application to start it up? Does the scrolling list in Figure 1.1 look familiar to you? Do you know how to use a word processor like MacWrite or Microsoft Word? If you can use the Macintosh to run programs and edit documents, you're halfway there.

Second, you should have a working knowledge of C. If you're just getting started with programming or if your language of choice is a language other than C, you might want to pick up a copy of my book *Learn C on the Macintosh*. If you just need a quick C refresher course, check out Chapter 3 of this book. Once you have a handle on both C and the Macintosh, you're ready to tackle C++.

FIGURE 1.1
Scrolling through a list of folders.

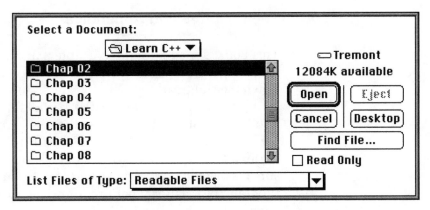

What Equipment Do I Need?

While it is possible to learn C++ just by reading a book, you'll get the most out of this book if you run each example program as you read and discover how it works. To do this, you need a Macintosh. If you don't have one, borrow one from a friend. You'll need a Macintosh with at least 2 megabytes of memory. THIN C++ will run with most Macintosh system software, from System 6.05 on up through the various versions of System 7.

If you can, upgrade your Mac to the latest version of System 7. At the same time, see whether you can get a couple of extra megabytes to bring your Mac up to 4 megs or more. The extra breathing room will help.

The Lay of the Land

This book was designed with several different readers in mind. If you're new to programming, you'll want to read each and every chapter. Try not to skip over material that seems fuzzy. If you get stuck, find a C++ programmer who can answer your questions. Most C++ programmers are friendly and are usually more than glad to help someone just getting started. Make a commitment to finish this book. You can do it!

If you're a C master, you might want to skip the C review in Chapter 3. Do *not* skip Chapter 2, however. Chapter 2 walks you through the THIN C++ installation process and ensures that you copy all the sample code to the right spot on your hard drive.

The Chapters and Appendices

This book is made up of ten chapters and nine appendices. This chapter provides an overview of the book and gets you started down the right path.

Chapter 2 introduces the disk part of this book/disk package. You'll learn about THIN C++, the C++ programming environment designed especially for use with this book. You'll install THIN C++ on your hard drive and test out the software to make sure it's installed properly. In Chapter 2, you'll run your first C++ program. No matter what programming experience you already have, don't skip Chapter 2!

Chapter 3 contains a refresher course in C. Even if you're a seasoned C programmer, you might want to take a quick look through this chapter just to make sure everything in it looks familiar.

Chapter 4 introduces the basic syntax of C++. It covers topics ranging from C++ operators and keywords to reference types and function name overloading.

Chapter 5 introduces you to the basics of object programming, the heart and soul of C++. You'll learn all about classes and objects and the C++ functions that allow you to create objects of your very own.

Chapter 6 takes the concept of classes one step further. It shows you how to use one class as the basis for a new, derived class. Derived classes play a critical role in extending an existing set of C++ classes.

Chapter 7 introduces the concept of operator overloading. C++ allows you to overload its built-in operators, customizing them to work with objects you define. For example, you might overload the + operator, enabling you to add two arrays together.

Chapter 8 introduces `iostream`, C++'s equivalent of C's `stdio` library. Just as routines such as `printf()` and `scanf()` allow you to build a portable user interface in C, the `iostream` functions allow you to build a portable C++ interface.

Chapter 9 takes you down the homestretch by exploring a potpourri of miscellaneous C++ topics. When you finish this chapter, you'll have completed the first phase of your C++ education.

Chapter 10 wraps things up. It prepares you for the next step on your programming path. You'll learn about class libraries like Bedrock, MacApp, and the THINK Class Library. You'll take a look at several Macintosh C++ development environments and choose the one that's right for you. Finally, you'll read about some of the books and reference materials that you'll want by your side as you start your own C++ development efforts.

Appendix A is a glossary of the technical terms used in this book.

Appendix B contains a complete listing of all the examples used in this book. This section will come in handy as a reference, as you write your own C++ programs. Need an example of an overloaded operator? Turn to the examples in Appendix B.

Appendices C, D, E, and F contain listings of the files `<iostream.h>`, `<fstream.h>`, `<strstrea.h>`, and `<iomanip.h>`, respectively. These files are all critical parts of the `iostream` library. If you'll be using `iostream` in your own applications, you'll find these appendices helpful.

Appendix G contains a reprint of an article that appeared in the April 1990 issue of Apple's excellent programming magazine *develop*. The article is titled "Unofficial C++ Style Guide." Take the time to read the style guide. It is packed with extremely useful information that every C++ programmer should have.

Appendix H describes Symantec C++ for Macintosh, the full version of the development environment used in this book.

Appendix I is a bibliography of useful programming titles.

The Conventions Used in This Book

As you read this book, you'll encounter a few standard conventions that make the book easier to read. For example, technical terms appearing for the first time are displayed in **boldface**. (You'll find most of these terms in the glossary in Appendix A.)

All of the source code examples in this book are presented using a special font, known as the `code font`. This includes source code fragments that appear in the middle of running text. Menu items, or items you'll click on, appear in **Chicago font**.

def'ə nish' ən

Occasionally, you'll come across a block of text set off in a box, like this. These blocks are called *tech blocks* and are intended to add technical detail to the subject currently being discussed. Each tech block will fit into one of five categories: "By the Way," "Style," "Detail," "Definition," and "Warning." Each category has its own special icon, which will appear to the left of the tech block. As the names imply, "By the Way" tech blocks are intended to be informative but not crucial. "Style" tech blocks contain information relating to your C++ programming style. "Detail" tech blocks offer more detailed information about the current topic. "Definition" tech blocks contain the definition of an important C++ term. "Warning" tech blocks are usually trying to caution you about some potential programming problem, so pay attention!

Strap Yourself In...

That's about it. Let's get started!

Chapter 2

Installing THIN C++

Before you get into the details of C++ programming, you need to install the C++ development environment included with this book. This chapter takes you step-by-step through the THIN C++ installation process.

This Chapter at a Glance

Installing THIN C++
Testing THIN C++
    Opening the hello++ Project
    Running hello++.π
Features of THIN C++
Summary

TUCKED INTO THE BACK OF *LEARN C++ ON THE MACINTOSH* is a floppy disk containing THIN C++, a sort of swiss army knife for programmers. THIN C++ provides you with all the tools you'll need to work with the programming examples presented in the book.

THIN C++ was created especially for this book by Symantec. In Macintosh programming circles, Symantec is known best as the maker of THINK C and Symantec C++ for Macintosh, the programmer's choice among Macintosh development environments.

THIN C++'s built-in text editor allows you to edit the source code included with each of the sample programs. The THIN C++ compiler is fast and efficient, making short work of the book's largest programs. Once your code is compiled, THIN C++ will even run your program for you.

Installing THIN C++

Before you do anything else, make a backup copy of the THIN C++ disk and place the original disk in a safe place. From now on, only work with the backup copy of THIN C++. That way, when your dog uses your backup disk as a teething ring, you'll still have the original tucked away to make a new backup from.

Next, insert the THIN C++ backup disk (you did make a backup, didn't you?) into your floppy drive. The disk contains a single file named THIN C++.sea. That file is a self-extracting archive. It contains the files that make up THIN C++ as well as the examples from this book, all rolled together in a special compressed format.

To decompress the archive, double-click on the THIN C++.sea icon. A dialog box, like the one shown in Figure 2.1, will appear and ask you to select a location for all the THIN C++ files. Navigate to the top level of your hard drive (so that the name of your hard drive appears on the pop-up menu label), and then press the **Extract** button.

FIGURE 2.1
Selecting a location for the THIN C++ files.

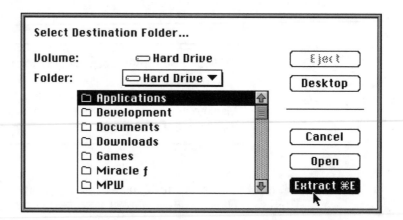

When you press the **Extract** button, don't worry if one of the files or folders in the scrolling list is highlighted. The THIN C++ files will be stored in the folder whose name appears in the dialog box's pop-up label.

Once you press the **Extract** button, the extraction software will start to decompress the THIN C++ files. All the files from the archive are stored in a folder called `THIN C++ Development`. Within this folder, the THIN C++ compiler and its related files are stored in a folder called `THIN C++ Folder`. Also within `THIN C++ Development`, the examples from the book are stored in a folder called `THIN C++ Projects`.

Testing THIN C++

Now that you've installed THIN C++, you're ready to take it for a test drive. On your hard drive, open the folder `THIN C++ Development` and then open the folder `THIN C++ Projects`. Inside `THIN C++ Projects`, you'll find a subfolder for every sample program in the book. Notice that the subfolders are in numerical order, sorted by chapter number. Open the first subfolder in the list, `Chap 02.01 - hello++`.

Figure 2.2 shows the files in `Chap 02.01 - hello++`. One file is named `hello++.cp`; the other, `hello++.π`. Each of these files is necessary to run the example program called `hello++`.

FIGURE 2.2
The `hello++` *subfolder.*

The file `hello++.cp` contains the `hello++` source code. The file `hello++.π` is known as a **project file**. A project file holds information about a program, including the list of the program's source code files, as well as the object code generated when these source code files are compiled. Together, these two files make up the `hello++` **project**.

All of the sample programs in this book are presented in project form. THIN C++'s older sibling, Symantec C++ for Macintosh, is also based on the project concept. The term *project* is not part of C++, however. Outside the Symantec development universe, use the term *program* instead.

Opening the hello++ Project

Just to make sure THIN C++ is installed properly, let's take the `hello++` project for a spin. Double-click on the icon for the project file `hello++.π`. A program called the `THIN Project Manager` will start running. As its name implies, the `THIN Project Manager` manages your project files and takes care of tasks like calling the compiler and running your projects once they're compiled.

If the Finder has trouble locating the `THIN Project Manager` when you double-click on the `hello++.π` icon, don't panic. You'll need to rebuild your Mac's desktop file. To do this, restart your Macintosh while holding down both the option and command keys (the command key is the one with the ⌘ symbol on it). Keep holding down these keys until your Mac asks you if it's alright to rebuild the desktop file. Click on the **OK** button and, when you get back to the finder, double-click on the `hello++.π` icon again.

If you don't want to rebuild your desktop file, you can also solve this problem by launching the `THIN Project Manager` directly. You'll find the `THIN Project Manager` in the `THIN C++ Development` folder, inside the `THIN C++ Folder`. When the `THIN C++ Project Manager` prompts you for a project to open, go back to the `THIN C++ Projects` folder and open the `hello++.π` project.

Once the THIN Project Manager starts up, the hello++ **project window** will appear (see Figure 2.3). The project window is the focal point for the project. Its title reflects the name of the project file, in this case, hello++.π.

FIGURE 2.3

The hello++ *project window.*

Name	obj size
CPlusLib	0
hello++.cp	0
ANSI++	0
IOStreams	0

Inside the project window is a list of the files that make up the project. The project file hello++.π makes use of four files: The files CPlusLib, ANSI++, and IOStreams are libraries that contain various C++ support functions; the file hello++.cp contains the source code for the project.

Wheel your mouse over to the project window and double-click on the name hello++.cp. The first click causes the name hello++.cp to be highlighted. The second click opens an editing window showing the source code contained in the file hello++.cp. You can use the standard Macintosh text-editing techniques (clicking, dragging, and typing) to edit the source code in this window. You'll have plenty of editing opportunities later in the book. For now, close the source code window, leaving the source code as you found it.

As the more adventurous of you may have already discovered, the rest of the files in the project are not source code files. For example, if you double-click on the name ANSI++ in the project window, nothing happens. THIN C++ allows you to edit source code only, not libraries.

Running hello++.π

Now try running the program whose source code you just looked at. Select **Run** from the **Project** menu. THIN C++ will first compile and then run your program. A new window will appear on the screen, similar to the one shown in Figure 2.4. Hit the return key to exit the program. If you encounter problems running hello++.π, try recopying the files from the original floppy disk.

FIGURE 2.4
Running hello++.π.

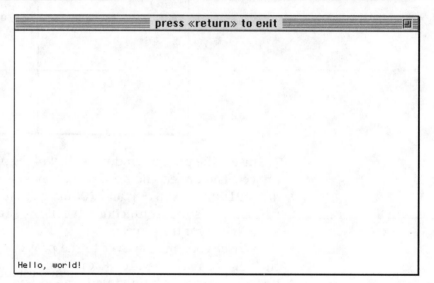

Features of THIN C++

A few features of THIN C++ are worth mentioning at this point. Most of these features are accessed via THIN C++'s pull-down menus. Look at the **File** menu (as shown in Figure 2.5). By selecting **New**, **Open...**, or **Close**, you create, open, or close a text file. For the most part, the only text files you'll work with are the project source code files. Since these files already exist, you probably won't have much need for the **New** command. Since you can open a source code file by double-clicking its name in the project window and can close the file by clicking on the window's close box, you also probably won't have much need for **Open...** or **Close**. On the other hand, it's nice to know these options are avialable.

FIGURE 2.5
THIN C++'s **File** *menu.*

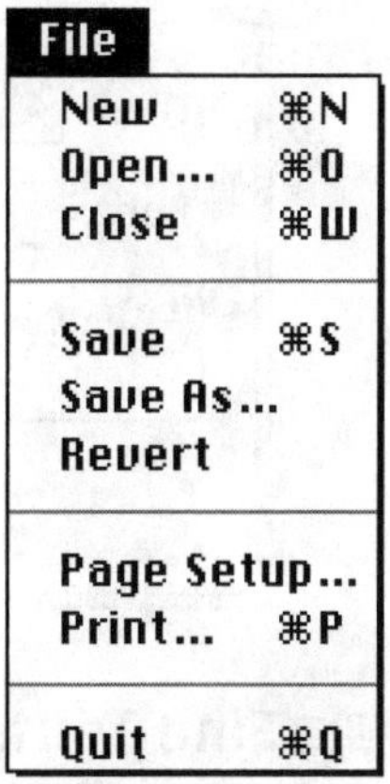

File	
New	⌘N
Open...	⌘O
Close	⌘W
Save	⌘S
Save As...	
Revert	
Page Setup...	
Print...	⌘P
Quit	⌘Q

The rest of the **File** menu is fairly straightforward. **Save** and **Save As...** are useful for saving your source code once you've made changes to it. **Revert** reverts the open file back to the last saved version. **Page Setup...** and **Print...** are useful for printing a copy of your source code. **Quit** exits THIN C++.

The **Edit** menu (Figure 2.6) starts with the Macintosh standards **Undo**, **Cut**, **Copy**, **Paste**, and **Clear**. The **Set Tabs & Font...** item brings up a dialog box (Figure 2.7) that allows you to set the tabs and font for the currently open source code file. The number in the **Tabs** field determines how many characters wide a tab character is; the **Font** pop-up menus establish the font and font size for the source code file.

FIGURE 2.6
The **Edit** *menu.*

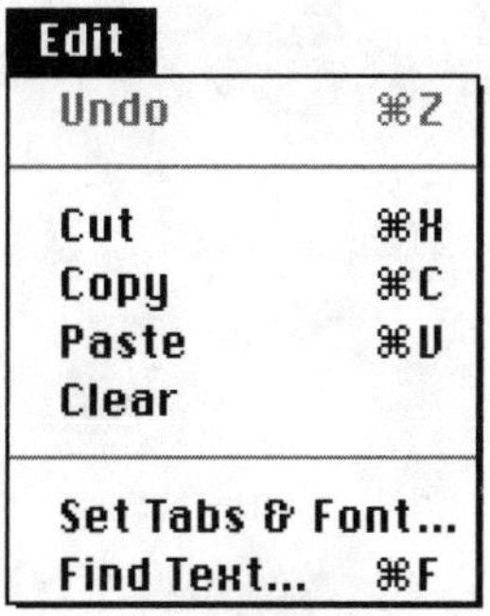

Edit	
Undo	⌘Z
Cut	⌘X
Copy	⌘C
Paste	⌘V
Clear	
Set Tabs & Font...	
Find Text...	⌘F

FIGURE 2.7
The **Set Tabs &
Font...** *dialog box.*

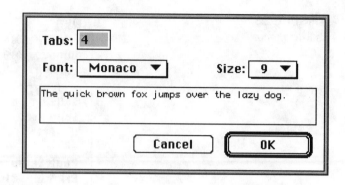

The **Find Text...**item brings up a dialog box (Figure 2.8) that lets you search through your source code for a specific text string.

FIGURE 2.8
The **Find Text...**
dialog box.

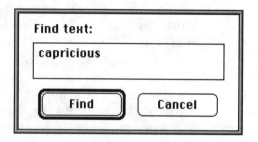

The **Project** menu (Figure 2.9) is perhaps the most used menu in THIN C++. If no project is open, the **Open Project...** item prompts you for a project to open. **Close Project** closes the currently open project and then prompts you for a project to open.

FIGURE 2.9
The **Project** *menu.*

Remove Objects is useful for compacting project files (and therefore saving disk space). When THIN C++ compiles your source code, it saves the newly created machine code (also known as object code) inside the project file. This makes the project file bigger, taking up precious disk space. **Remove Objects** deletes the object code from the project file, saving you some disk space.

Normally, once you've compiled a project, you can run the project again and again without recompiling. Two things will force THIN C++ to recompile your code: making a change to your source code or performing a **Remove Objects.**

Since **Remove Objects** does save you disk space, it's a good idea to **Remove Objects** once you finish exploring a project.

The final item on the **Project** menu is by far the most useful. Selecting **Run** asks THIN C++ to run your program for you.

Summary   That's about it for our THIN C++ intro. Are you ready to get started? Get comfortable, and turn the page. Here we go!

Chapter 3

Remembering C

One of the basic assumptions made in this book is that you are already acquainted with the C programming language. This chapter contains a quick refresher course in C. Even if you're a seasoned C programmer, you might want to take a few moments to look over this material.

This Chapter
at a Glance

Literal Constants
    Integral Constants
    Floating-Point Constants
    Character Constants
    String Constants
    Enumerations
Variables
    Arrays
    Automatic Initialization
    Structs
    Unions
    Typedefs
    Automatic Type Conversion
    Typecasting
    The const Qualifier
    Storage-Class Specifiers
    Pointers
Operators
    Arithmetic Operators
    Assignment Operators
    Bitwise Logical Operators
    The Conditional Operator
    Increment and Decrement Operators
    Logical Operators
    Relational Operators
    The Comma Operator
    The sizeof() Operator
    Operator Precedence
Statements
Functions
    The Ellipsis
Preprocessor Directives
Comments
Summary

BEFORE WE GET STARTED WITH C++, IT'S IMPORTANT that you have a good handle on the C programming language. This chapter offers a review of the primary features of C. Since C is a subset of C++, you'll want to make sure you feel comfortable with all the material covered here. As you read through the chapter, build yourself a checklist of the C features you need to bone up on. Then grab your favorite C reference and plug away.

Literal Constants

This section covers the various forms you can use to represent a constant in C.

Integral Constants

Integral constants (constants that represent mathematical integers) can be represented in decimal, octal, or hexadecimal format. Decimal constants appear as plain numbers. Octal (base 8) constants always start with a leading zero. Hexadecimal (base 16) constants always start with the two characters `0x`.

The size in bytes of an octal or a hex constant is determined by the number of characters that appear in the constant. For example, since there are two characters to every hex byte, this constant is 4 bytes long:

```
0x00FF00FF
```

Decimal constants default to the size of an `int`.

Interestingly, an `int` can vary in size from compiler to compiler. Typically, your compiler will feature either a 2-byte or a 4-byte `int`. If portability is your goal, this fluctuation can be a real problem.

The solution is simple enough. Avoid `int`s. Don't use them. Ever. When you need to represent an integral type, select between a `char`, a `short`, or a `long`. There's nothing to gain by playing the `int`-size guessing game.

To represent a decimal constant as a `long`, tack an `L` (in either upper or lower case) at the end:

```
205L
```

To represent a decimal constant as an `unsigned int`, tack a `U` (in either upper or lower case) at the end:

```
205U
```

The characters `UL` (in either upper or lower case) are used to denote a decimal constant of type `unsigned long`:

```
205UL
```

The characters `U` and `L` can also be used at the end of octal and hexadecimal constants.

Floating-Point Constants

Floating-point constants represent signed, real numbers. A complete floating-point constant consists of an integer portion (to the left of the decimal point), a fractional portion (to the right of the decimal point), and an exponent. For example the constant

```
103.75e2
```

represents 103.75 times 10 to the second power, or 10,375.

To qualify as a floating-point constant, either the decimal point or the exponent (or both) must be present. All of the following are legal constants:

```
100.e2
.5e2
100.5
.5
100e5
```

Normally, floating-point constants are represented as a `double`. To represent a floating-point constant as a `float`, tack an `F` at the end:

`125.7F`

To represent a floating-point constant as a `long double`, tack an `L` at the end:

`125.7L`

`float`, `double`, and `long double` are the three floating-point types offered by C. For more information on these types, read the section on variables a few pages down the road.

Character Constants

Single-byte character constants are represented by enclosing a character in single quotes, like this:

`'a'`

The \ character (backslash) is used to create special single-byte character constants. If the first character following the \ is a zero, the remainder of the constant is interpreted as an octal ASCII character code. If the first character following the \ is an x, the remainder of the constant is interpreted as a hexadecimal ASCII character code. For example, both of the following constants represent the ASCII bell character:

`'\007'`
`'\x7'`

In addition, there are 12 backslash combinations that represent single-byte characters (Figure 3.1). For example, the constant `'\a'` represents the ASCII bell character.

FIGURE 3.1
Single-byte backslash characters.

Constant	Meaning
\a	Bell
\b	Backspace
\f	Formfeed
\n	Newline
\r	Return
\t	Horizontal tab
\v	Vertical tab
\\	Backslash
\?	Question mark
\'	Single quote
\"	Double quote

The most frequently used backslash sequence is the newline character, represented by the sequence '\n'. When placed at the end of a string sent to the console, the newline character forces the cursor to the beginning of the next line of output.

Finally, the constant '\0' represents a single byte with a value of 0. This constant is also known as the NULL constant and is frequently used as a terminator for C character strings.

String Constants

String constants are formed when a set of zero or more characters is surrounded by double quotes, like this:

```
char   *nickname = "Apple dumpling";
```

Each character in the string consumes 1 byte of memory. A NULL byte ('\0') is automatically placed at the end of the string.

The \ combinations presented in the previous section are particularly useful when placed inside a string constant.

Enumerations

Enumerations are types declared using the enum keyword and a list of enumeration constants. These constants provide an alternative to the #define mechanism (described later in the chapter) by allowing you to declare a series of constants with a single statement. Here's an example:

```
enum  weekDays { monday = 2, tuesday, wednesday,
    thursday, friday }
```

By default, the first constant starts with a value of 0, and following constants increase in value by 1. Any or all of these constants can be initialized automatically. In the example just given, monday is initialized to 2, tuesday to 3, wednesday to 4, and so on.

Variables   Variables can be defined within any block of code. The basic variable types are char, int, and float. All three of these can be defined as signed or unsigned. A signed variable can represent either a positive or a negative number, while an unsigned variable is limited to nonnegative numbers. For example, a signed char can hold values ranging from –128 to 127 and an unsigned char can hold values from 0 to 255.

In addition to signed and unsigned, an int can be defined using the qualifier short or long, as in these examples:

```
long int    myLong;
short int   myShort;
```

Most programmers prefer the shorthand notation, using long for long int and short for short int:

```
long    myLong;
short   myShort;
```

As pointed out earlier, the ANSI standard does not specify the size of the `int` data type, leaving that decision up to the development environment.

> I know I brought this up earlier, but it really is worth repeating. If you want your code to be portable, don't use `int` for your integral data. If you need the extra range, use `long`. If you're really squeezed for space, and you know your data will stay in range, use `char`. In general, however, `short` should fit the bill just fine.

Just as `char`, `short`, and `long` represent a steadily increasing sequence of integral types, `float`, `double`, and `long double` are a steadily increasing sequence of floating-point types.

According to the ANSI standard, a `double` is at least as large as a `float`, and a `long double` is at least as large as a `double`. Typically, a `float` is four bytes long, and a `double`, appropriately enough, is 8 bytes long. On most machines, a `long double` is the same size as a `double`.

Arrays

Any variable data type can form the basis of an array definition. Array definitions consist of a *type*, an *identifier*, and a *dimension*, as in the following:

```
short myShortArray[ 10 ];
```

Arrays can be multidimensional. For example, the code

```
unsigned char bytes[ 10 ][ 20 ];
```

defines an array named `bytes` that totals 200 bytes in size. `bytes` is actually an array of 10 arrays, each of which is 20 bytes in length.

In real life, multidimensional arrays are rarely used. In most cases, an array of pointers serves the same purpose and allows the size of each "row" to be specified independently, as opposed to the fixed row size of a multidimensional array.

Automatic Initialization

Variables and arrays can be initialized automatically. Here are a few examples:

```
char     firstLetter = 'a';
char     *name = "Dave Mark";
short    value = 0xFFAA;
float    numbers[ 5 ] = { 10.0, 20.0, 35.0, 6.7, .2 };
```

Structs

Structs allow you to group a set of variables under a single name and are declared using the **struct** keyword. The individual variables in a struct are known as *fields*. To access a struct field, use the **.** operator, as shown in the following example:

```
struct
{
  short   myFirstField;
  float   mySecondField;
} myStruct, *myStructPtr;

myStruct.myFirstField = 20;
```

To access a struct using a pointer, use the **->** operator as follows:

```
myStructPtr = &myStruct;

myStructPtr->myFirstField = 20;
```

Unions

Unions allow you to interpret the same block of memory in more than one way. Unions are declared using the same format as a struct declaration, but the `union` keyword is substituted for the `struct` keyword. In a union, however, enough memory is allocated to hold the largest of the declared fields. The contents of the union are interpreted based on the field you reference. Here's an example:

```
union short_or_long
{
   short    myShort;
   long     myLong;
}

union short_or_long myUnion;
```

The union declaration just given merges a `short` and a `long` into a single entity. If you refer to

```
myUnion.myShort
```

the first 2 bytes of the union will be interpreted as a `short`. If you refer to

```
myUnion.myLong
```

all 4 bytes of the union will be used as a `long`. The size of the union is determined by the largest of the union's fields.

Typedefs

Typedefs are used to create new variable types from existing types. For example, the `typedef` statement

```
typedef short    MyType;
```

creates a new type called `MyType`, which can be used in future variable definitions, such as the following:

```
MyType   myVariable;
```

Typedefs are frequently used in combination with struct and union declarations. Here's a struct example:

```
typedef struct
{
  short shortField;
  long  longField;
} MyStructType;

MyStructType  myStruct;

myStruct.shortField = 20;
```

The `typedef` statement in this example creates a new symbol with the name `MyStructType`, which can then be used to define a struct variable called `myStruct`.

Automatic Type Conversion

When an operator joins two operands of differing data types, the operands are converted to a common type before the operation is performed. Here's an example:

```
short    myShort = 20;
long     myLong = 10;
long     result;

result = myLong + myShort;
```

In this code, the + operator joins a `short` (2 bytes) and a `long` (4 bytes). Since the `long` is larger than the `short`, the `short` is converted to a `long` before the addition is performed, producing a `long` as a result.

This example typifies C's approach toward automatic type conversion. In general, a small type will always be converted to a larger type, rather than the other way around. In this way, no information is lost by truncating a value.

If the two operands linking an operator are both built-in C data types (one of `char`, `short`, `int`, `long`, `unsigned`, `unsigned long`, `float`, `double`, or `long double`), the following rules are used to guide the automatic type conversion:

- First, if either of the operands is a `char` or a `short`, that operand is converted to an `int`.
- Next, if the operands are of different types, the shorter of the two operands is converted to the longer of the two.

For example, if the operator was joining an `int` and a `double`, the `int` would be promoted to a `double` before the operation was performed. A comparison between a `float` and a `char` would first see the promotion of the `char` to an `int`, then the promotion of the `int` to a `float`.

The rules change when the operands are pointer types instead of built-in types. With one exception, pointer types need to match exactly. If they don't, you'll need to cast one of the pointers to the type of the other pointer.

The exception to this rule involves the `void` pointer (`void *`). The `void` pointer was designed to serve as a generic pointer type, pointing to a block of data whose type may not be known at compile time. In an expression where one of the two operands is a `void` pointer, no typecasting is necessary. This means that the following code will compile (even if it doesn't do very much):

```
void    *voidPtr;
short   *shortPtr;

voidPtr = shortPtr;
shortPtr = voidPtr;
```

When we get to the topic of automatic type conversion in C++ (see Chapter 4), you'll find that these rules change slightly.

Typecasting

Typecasting offers a more direct method for translating one variable data type to another. A typecast is a combination of types and * operators embedded in parentheses that determine the order of casting. The following code casts a `short` to a `long`:

```
(long)myShort
```

The next code casts a `short` pointer to a `long` pointer:

```
(long *)myShortPtr
```

The const Qualifier

When a variable is defined using the `const` qualifier, an initial value must be provided in the definition, and that value cannot be changed for the duration of the program. Here are two examples:

```
const float serialNumber = 523.5876;
const char  myName[] = "Dave Mark";
```

Storage-Class Specifiers

The storage-class specifiers `auto`, `extern`, `static`, `register`, and `volatile` define the mechanism used to create the associated variable. A variable marked as `auto` has the same properties as a local variable. This means that space for the variable is allocated when the defining block is entered and the same space is deallocated when the block is exited.

The `extern` specifier tells you that space for a variable is allocated outside the current scope. `static` variables retain their value even after the block they're defined in is exited. `register` variables are allocated using a register, if the current implementation allows for it.

Finally, `volatile` is a little used qualifier that marks a variable as modifiable from outside the program. `volatile` is implementation dependent. For more information on it, check the manual that comes with your development environment.

Pointers

A variable defined as a pointer is designed to hold the address of a variable of a specific type. The * operator combines with a normal variable definition to create a pointer variable, as in the following example:

```
long     myLong;
long     *myLongPtr;
```

These definitions create a `long` and a pointer to a variable of type `long`. To make the pointer point to a `long`, use the & operator. The & operator returns the address of its operand:

```
myLongPtr = &myLong;
```

To retrieve a value from a pointer, use the * operator. The * operator takes an address and returns the value at that address:

```
myLong = *myLongPtr;
```

As mentioned earlier, the -> operator can be used with a pointer to a struct to access one of the struct's fields. The * and . operators can be used in the same way. The code

```
myStructPtr->myField
```

has the same effect as the following code:

```
(*myStructPtr).myField
```

Pointers are frequently used to step through an array. To do this, you'll make use of the +, ++, -, and -- operators (described in the section on operators). The + and ++ operators increase the value of a pointer based on the size of the pointer's base type. The - and -- operators do the reverse. For example, + will increment a `char` pointer by 1 byte, a `short` pointer by 2 bytes, and a `long` pointer by 4 bytes. This is precisely the amount of memory you want to increment a pointer to move it from one element of an array to the next element.

   Pointer arithmetic comes in especially handy when you're working with character strings, which are traditionally implemented as an array of chars. For example, the following code copies one character string to another:

```
void  CopyString( char *source, char *dest )
{
  while ( *source != '\0' )
  {
    *dest = *source;
    dest++;
    source++;
  }
  *dest = '\0';
}
```

This example copies each byte of source to the corresponding byte in dest until source's terminating null byte is encountered. The ++ operator is used to bump the pointers along the character strings.

Here's a version of the preceding string-copying example that's preferred by many C programmers:

```
void CopyString( char *source, char *dest )
{
  while ( *dest++ = *source++ )
    ;
}
```

The key to this code is the combination of the =, *, and ++ operators inside the while clause. Take a few minutes to analyze this code. Though it looks confusing, this method of copying a zero-terminated string is so common (and elegant, in my opinion) that you may want to add it to your personal toolbox.

Operators   At the heart of C is an extensive set of operators that allow you to build complex expressions. Some of the operators work with a single operand. Others require two or more operands. Some operators are mathematical in nature. Some are comparative. This section lists the complete set of ANSI C operators.

Arithmetic Operators

The arithmetic operators are +, -, *, /, and %. Each of these operators is binary (takes two operands). +, -, and * perform addition, subtraction, and multiplication, respectively. / performs integer division, truncating its result to an integral value. % divides its first operand by its second and returns the remainder.

Assignment Operators

All of the assignment operators are binary. The = operator copies the value of its right side to the variable on its left side. All of the other assignment operators combine = with some other operator, as in this example:

```
leftSide += rightSide;
```

This expression is equivalent to the following statement:

```
leftSide = leftSide + rightSide;
```

The augmented assignment operators are +=, -=, *=, /=, %=, >>=, <<=, &=, |=, and ^=. Each of these operators follows the pattern just described. The operator portions of the augmented assignment operators are described individually throughout this section.

Bitwise Logical Operators

The bitwise logical operators are &, |, ^, <<, >>, and ~. ~ is a unary operator (takes a single operand). The remainder of the bitwise logical operators are binary. ~ produces a one's complement of its operand. & performs a bitwise AND, | a bitwise OR, and ^ a bitwise EXCLUSIVE OR on their two operands.

<< and >> perform a left and a right bit shift, respectively, on the left-hand argument. The right-hand argument determines the number of bit positions to shift.

The bitwise OR operator (|) is typically used to change the value of a specified bit to 1. For example, suppose you had a byte with a value, in binary, of 00001111, and you wanted to set its high bit to 1. Use the bitwise OR operator, along with the binary value 10000000:

```
unsigned char   highBitIsOne = 0x80;
   /* 10000000 */
unsigned char   myByte = 0x0F;
   /* 00001111 */

myByte |= highBitIsOne; /* Now myByte
   is 10001111 */
```

The bitwise AND operator (&) is typically used to test whether a bit is set to 1. Consider these two variables:

```
unsigned char   highBitIsOne = 0x80;
   /* 10000000 */
unsigned char   myByte = 0x0F;
   /* 00001111 */
```

To test whether the high bit of myByte is set, use the bitwise AND operator:

```
if ( (myByte & highBitIsOne) ==
   highBitIsOne )
```

This expression will evaluate to true only if the high bit of myByte is set to 1.

The Conditional Operator

The conditional operator (`? :`) is C's only ternary operator (requiring three operands). The operator takes the following form:

```
expression1 ? expression2 : expression3
```

The first expression is evaluated. If it evaluates to true, the second expression is evaluated and that result is the result of the entire `? :` operation. If, however, the first expression evaluates to false, the third expression is evaluated and that result is the result of the entire expression.

The conditional operator is more or less equivalent to an `if-else` statement. Many programmers (myself included) find the `if-else` much clearer and simpler to read and avoid `? :` altogether.

Increment and Decrement Operators

The increment and decrement operators offer a quick way to increment or decrement a variable. Both of these operators are unary. The increment operator (`++`) increments its operand by 1. The decrement operator (`--`) decrements its operand by 1. Applying either of these operators to an array pointer changes the value of the pointer to point to the next element (either up or down) in the array.

These two operators may be placed before the operand (prefix notation) or immediately after the operand (postfix notation). In prefix notation, the increment or decrement operation is performed before the enclosing expression is evaluated. In postfix notation, the increment or decrement operation is performed after the enclosing expression is evaluated.

Logical Operators

The three logical operators are &&, ||, and !. They manipulate their operands using Boolean logic according to the table in Figure 3.2. && and || are binary operators and perform logical AND and logical OR operations, respectively. ! is a unary operator and performs a logical NOT operation.

FIGURE 3.2
Logic table for the &&,
||, and ! operators.

A	B	!A	A&&B	A‖B
True	True	False	True	True
True	False	False	False	True
False	True	True	False	True
False	False	True	False	False

Relational Operators

The six relational operators are >, >=, <, <=, ==, and !=. All are binary operators and compare the first operand with the second. > returns true if the first operand is greater than the second. >= returns true if the first operand is greater than or equal to the second. < returns true if the first operand is less than the second. <= returns true if the first operand is less than or equal to the second. == returns true if the two operands are equal. != returns true if the two operands are not equal.

The Comma Operator

The comma operator (,) is used to fuse two expressions into a single expression. For example, the line of code

```
i++, j++;
```

increments the variables i and j. The expressions that surround the comma operator are evaluated from left to right. The result of the operation is the value of the rightmost expression.

The sizeof() Operator

Although it appears to be a function call, `sizeof()` is actually a C operator that takes a single parameter. `sizeof()` returns the size in bytes of the argument. If the argument is a variable, `sizeof()` returns the number of bytes allocated for that variable. If the parameter is a type, `sizeof()` returns the number of bytes necessary to allocate a variable of that type.

Operator Precedence

All of C's operators are ranked according to precedence. In this expression

```
6 + 3 * 5
```

the order in which the two operators are evaluated has a definite effect on the expression's value. If + has a higher precedence than *, the expression will evaluate to 45. If * has a higher precedence, the result will be 21 (the correct answer is 21, by the way).

Two factors determine the order in which an expression's operators are evaluated. If one operator has a higher precedence than another, that operator is evaluated first. If the operators have equal precedence, the operators are evaluated from either left to right or right to left, depending on the operators. The chart in Figure 3.3 ranks each of C's operators and, for each grouping of equal operators, tells whether that group is evaluated from left to right or right to left. To avoid confusion, use parentheses to specify the order of operator evaluation.

Operators (High to Low Precedence)	Order
->, .	Left to right
Typecast, *, &, unary + and -, !, ~, ++, --, sizeof	Right to left
Arithmetic *, /, %	Left to right
Arithmetic + and -	Left to right
<<, >>	Left to right
>, >=, <, <=,	Left to right
==, !=	Left to right
& (bitwise AND)	Left to right
^	Left to right
|	Left to right
&&	Left to right
||	Left to right
?:	Right to left
=, +=, -=, *=, /=, %=, >>=, <<=, &=, |=, ^=	Right to left
,	Left to right

Statements

C statements are terminated by a semicolon (;). They can be grouped into blocks by using a matching pair of curly braces (left { and right }). Figure 3.4 lists the keywords that can be used in the construction of ANSI C statements. You should be familiar with each of these keywords.

ANSI C Keywords				
auto	do	goto	short	typedef
break	double	if	signed	union
case	else	int	sizeof	unsigned
char	enum	long	static	void
const	extern	register	struct	volatile
continue	float	return	switch	while
default	for			

Functions C statements can be grouped into individually addressable functions. Every program contains at least one function, `main()`. `main()` is automatically called to start the program. When the program starts, `main()` takes two parameters, `argc` and `argv`. `argc` and `argv` are known as *command-line* arguments. `argc` specifies the number of parameters embedded in the second argument, `argv`. `argv` is an array of parameters.

Functions can take parameters, and those parameters may be passed by value or by reference. Each function can also return a value of a specified type. If you don't specify a return type, `int` is assumed by the compiler. The predefined type `void` indicates an absence of a return type or an absence of parameters. A function with no parameters and no return values might look like this:

```
void  GoodForNothing( void )
{
}
```

Typically, functions are declared at the top of the program file (or in a header file) by using function prototypes. Function prototypes allow references to functions that have not yet been encountered by the compiler.

The Ellipsis

Used at the end of a function's argument list, the ellipsis (...) indicates that a variable number of arguments may be passed to the function. For example, consider the following function declaration:

```
void  MyFunc( short atLeastOne, ... );
```

`MyFunc()` requires at least one parameter but may take more than one. The type of the first parameter is `short`. The type of any additional parameters is unspecified.

The classic example of ellipsis use is in the declaration of `printf()`:

```
int printf( char *format, ... );
```

The first parameter is a text string containing the format specification. The remaining arguments (if there are any) are determined by the format string.

In C, the ellipsis consists of three consecutive periods, like so:

...

Although many graphic character sets contain an ellipsis character, don't try to use one in your C program. Your compiler may react violently!

Preprocessor Directives

Traditional C compilers accomplish the task of compiling your program in two passes. The first of these two passes through your code is known as the *preprocessor pass*. There are a number of commands that you can place in your code to instruct the compiler to take a special action during this pass. These commands are known as *preprocessor directives* and always start with the pound sign (#).

The two most widely used preprocessor directives are #define and #include. #define takes two parameters and asks the preprocessor to substitute the second parameter for the first throughout the remainder of the code. Since this substitution happens during the first compiler pass, the substitutions are in place for the second pass.

#include includes the specified file in the source code, also in time for interpretation by the second pass of the compiler. Typically, the name of the included file ends in .h (instead of C's traditional .c). These files are known as *header files* and contain typedefs, #defines, function prototypes, and other useful nonexecutable statements.

Other preprocessor directives include #elif, #else, #endif, #error, #if, #ifdef, #ifndef, #line, #pragma, and #undef.

Modern style dictates that `const` variable definitions should be used in place of `#define`s in many situations where you are trying to establish a literal constant. `const` allows a constant with typechecking. `#define` doesn't allow for typechecking and can get you into trouble (parentheses nesting problems, for example).

Comments

The character combinations /* and */ have a special meaning in C. /* marks the beginning and */ marks the end of a source code comment. When the compiler encounters these characters in your code, it will ignore all characters in the comment, including /* and */.

C comments cannot be nested. This means that you can't put a comment block inside another comment block. Also, /* and */ lose their meaning when placed inside a string or character literal.

Summary

It is downright impossible to describe the entire C language in one chapter. However, if you understand the concepts presented here, you are definitely ready for C++. If you ran into trouble anywhere along the line, pick up a copy of *Learn C on the Macintosh* (by yours truly) or the second edition of *The C Programming Language* by Kernighan and Ritchie. Better yet, hook up with your local neighborhood C guru or ask your teacher for help. You'll get much more out of this book once you understand C.

When you're ready, turn the page. C++, here we come!

Chapter 4

Introducing C++

Welcome to the world of C++. This chapter covers all the basics, from operators and keywords to reference types and function name overloading.

This Chapter at a Glance

Getting C Code to Run under C++
Function Prototypes Are Required
Automatic Type Conversion
Scope Changes
New Features of C++
The // Comment Marker
Handling Input and Output
An iostream Output Example
An iostream Input Example
iostream and Objects
Default Argument Initializers
The Traditional Approach
A Default Argument Initializer Example
Reference Variables
The Reference Variable Alternative
A Reference Variable Example
Function Name Overloading
A Function Name Overloading Example
Matching Rules for Overloaded Functions
The new and delete Operators
What to Do When new Fails
A new Example
The Scope Operator
A Scope Operator Example
Inline Functions
An Inline Function Example
Summary

NOW THAT YOU'VE GOT A REVIEW OF C UNDER YOUR BELT, you're ready to tackle C++. C++ supports all the features of C, with a few twists and a lot more features thrown in.

This chapter starts with a comparison of C and C++, focusing on changes you'll need to make to compile your ANSI C code with an ANSI C++ compiler. It then moves on to some features unique to C++.

Getting C Code to Run under C++

Think of C++ as a superset of C. For the most part, every single feature you've come to know and love in C is available in C++ (albeit with a few changes). As in C, C++ programs start with a `main()` function. All of C's keywords and functions work just fine in C++. If you've ever written a C program that takes advantage of the command-line arguments `argc` and `argv`, you'll be glad to know that they're still around in C++.

In fact, with only a few tweaks here and there, your C programs should run quite well in the C++ world. Try not to get too wrapped up in this section. While it is important that you be aware of each of the issues discussed, some of this stuff is pretty subtle and you may never run into it in your own code. You may want to skim the rest of this section, then come back to it for a quick review once you start coding. Be sure you're back on full alert, however, when we get into new features of C++.

Function Prototypes Are Required

In C, function prototypes are optional. As long as there's no type conflict between a function call and the same function's declaration, your program will compile.

In C++, a function prototype is *required* for each of your program's functions. Your C++ program will not compile unless each and every function prototype is in place. As in C, you can declare a function without a return type. If no return type is present, the function is assumed to have a return type of `int`.

Automatic Type Conversion

If you haven't already, turn back to Chapter 3 and review the section that describe C's automatic type conversion. C++ uses the same rules as C for automatic type conversion, but with a slight twist.

Although a `void` pointer can be assigned the value of another pointer type without explicit typecasting, the reverse is not true. For example, although the following code compiles properly in C, it will *not* compile in C++:

```
void    *voidPtr;
short    *shortPtr;

voidPtr = shortPtr; /*  <-- This line is just
                            fine... */
shortPtr = voidPtr; /*  <-- This line is fine in C,
                            but WILL NOT compile in C++ */
shortPtr = (short *)voidPtr;  /*  <-- This works in
                                      C++ */
```

My philosophy on automatic type conversion is that if you're going to muck around with different data types, use explicit typecasting. It makes code easier to read, not only for you but also for whoever is going to maintain your code.

Scope Changes

There are several subtle differences between C and C++ involving **scope**. A variable's scope defines the availability of the variable throughout the rest of a program. For example, a global variable is available throughout a program, while a local variable is limited to the block in which it is declared. For the most part, C++ follows the same scope rules as C. There are a few differences you should be aware of, however.

For example, take a look at the following code. Try to guess the value of `size` at the bottom of `main( )`:

```c
char   dummy[ 32 ];

void   main( void )
{
  long   size;

    struct dummy
    {
      char   myArray[ 64 ];
    };

    size = sizeof( dummy );
}
```

In C, `size` ends up with a value of 32; the reference to dummy in the `sizeof()` statement matches the global variable declared at the top of the program. In C++, however, `size` ends up with a value of 64; the reference to dummy matches the `struct` tag inside `main()`.

The difference here is the scope of `struct` tags in C and C++. In C, the scope of a `struct` tag is limited to the `struct` declaration. In C++, `struct` tags have the same availability as a local variable. Thus, in our example, the `struct` tag obscures the global variable with the same name.

A second example involves the scope of an enumeration. Take a look at the following code:

```c
void   main( void )
{
  struct s
  {
    enum { good, bad, ugly } clint;
  };

    short good;
}
```

An ANSI C compiler will not compile this code, complaining that the identifier good was declared twice. The problem here is with the scope of the enumeration constant good. In C, an enumeration constant is granted the same scope as a local variable, even if it is embedded in a `struct` definition. When the compiler hits the `short` declaration, it complains that it already has a `good` identifier declared at that level.

In C++, this code compiles cleanly. Why? C++ enumeration constants embedded in a `struct` definition have the same scope as that `struct`'s fields. Thus, the enumeration constant `good` is hidden from the `short` declaration at the bottom of `main()`.

A third example involves multiple declarations of the same variable within the same scope. Consider the following code:

```
short    gMyGlobal;
short    gMyGlobal;  /* Cool in C, error in C++ */
```

The C compiler will resolve these two variable definitions to a single definition. The C++ compiler, on the other hand, will report an error if it hits two variable definitions with the same name. In C++, the rule of thumb is "declarations many, definitions once."

---

def'ə nish' ən

It's useful to be aware of the difference between a **definition** and a **declaration**.

For a variable, the definition is the statement that actually allocates memory. For example, the statement

```
short    myShort;
```

is a definition. However, an `extern` reference to the same variable, such as

```
extern short myShort;
```

is a declaration since this statement doesn't cause any memory to be allocated. Here's another example of a declaration:

```
typedef  MyType short;
```

For a function, the function prototype is a declaration, and the function implementation, complete with function code, is a definition.

New Features of C++

OK, here comes the good stuff! The remainder of this chapter will take you beyond C into the heart of C++. While we won't explore object programming in this chapter, we will cover just about every other C++ concept.

The // Comment Marker

C's comment block markers, /* and */, perform the same function in C++. In addition, C++ supports a single-line comment marker. When a C++ compiler encounters the characters //, it ignores the remainder of that line of code. Here's an example:

```
void  main( void )
{
    short numGuppies; // May increase suddenly!!
}
```

As you'd expect, the characters // are ignored inside a comment block. In the following example, // is included as part of the comment block:

```
void  main( void )
{
    /*    Just a comment...
    //    */
}
```

Conversely, the comment characters /* and */ have no special meaning inside a single-line comment. The start of the comment block in the following example is swallowed up by the single-line comment:

```
void  main( void )
{
    // Don't start a /* comment block
        inside a single-line comment...
        This code WILL NOT compile!!! */
}
```

The compiler will definitely complain about this example!

Handling Input and Output

In a standard C program, input and output are usually handled by Standard Library routines such as `scanf()` and `printf()`. While you can call `scanf()` and `printf()` from within your C++ program, there is an elegant alternative. The `iostream` facility allows you to send a sequence of variables and constants to an output stream, just as `printf()` does. Also, `iostream` makes it easy to convert data from an input stream into a sequence of variables, just as `scanf()` does.

Though the `iostream` features presented in this section may seem simplistic, don't be fooled. `iostream` is actually quite sophisticated. In fact, `iostream` is far more powerful than C's standard I/O facility. The material given here will allow you to perform the input and output you'll need to get through the next few chapters. Later in the book, we'll explore `iostream` in more depth.

`iostream` predefines three streams for input and output. `cin` is used for input, `cout` for normal output, and `cerr` for error output. The `<<` ("put to") operator is used to send data to a stream. The `>>` ("get from") operator is used to retrieve data from a stream.

def'ə nish' ən

The `<<` operator is also known as the **insertion operator** because it allows you to insert data into a stream. The `>>` operator is also known as the **extraction operator** because it allows you to extract data from a stream.

Here's an example of the `<<` operator:

```
#include <iostream.h>

void  main( void )
```

```
{
    cout << "Hello, world!";
}
```

This program sends the text string `"Hello, world!"` to the console, just as if you'd used `printf()`. The include file `<iostream.h>` contains all of the definitions needed to use `iostream`. Since `<<` is a binary operator, it requires two operands. In this case, the operands are `cout` and the string `"Hello, world!"`. The destination stream always appears on the left side of the `<<` operator.

> Just like the & and * operators, >> and << have more than one meaning (>> and << are also used as the right and left shift operators). Don't worry about confusion, however. The C++ compiler uses the operator's context to determine which meaning is appropriate.

As with any other operator, you can use more than one `<<` on a single line. Here's another example:

```
#include <iostream.h>

void  main( void )
{
    short   i = 20;

    cout << "The value of i is " << i;
}
```

This program produces the following output:

```
The value of i is 20
```

`iostream` knows all about C++'s built-in data types. This means that text strings are printed as text strings, `shorts` as `shorts`, and `floats` as `floats`, complete with decimal point. No special formatting is necessary.

An iostream Output Example

Here's an interesting example of `iostream` and output. Start up THIN C++ by double-clicking on a file named `THIN Project Manager`. You'll find the `THIN Project Manager` inside the `THIN C++ Development` folder, inside the `THIN C++ Folder`. THIN C++ will prompt you for a project file to open (Figure 4.1). Go into the folder called `THIN C++ Projects` (you'll have to move up one level to find it), then into the subfolder named `Chap 04.01 - cout`, and open the project file named `cout.π`.

FIGURE 4.1

THIN C++ prompts you for a project file to open.

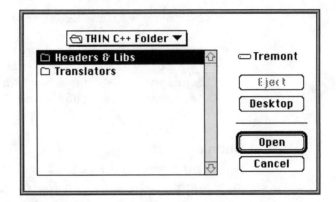

At this point, the `cout.π` project window will appear, as shown in Figure 4.2. Each of the four names in the project window represents a separate file. `cout.cp` is the file containing the C++ source code. The other three files are libraries containing various support routines. The `iostreams` library contains all the `iostream`

FIGURE 4.2

Project window for cout.π.

Name	obj size
cout.cp	0
CPlusLib	0
ANSI++	0
IOStreams	0

cout.π

functions, `CPlusLib` is a set of support routines for the C++ compiler, and `ANSI++` is the Standard Library from C with some modifications to support C++. You'll see these three libraries in all of your projects.

If you double-click on the name `cout.cp` in the project window, a new window will appear, containing the `cout` source code, as follows:

```
#include <iostream.h>

void  main( void )
{
  char  *name = "Dr. Crusher";

  cout << "char:     " << name[ 0 ] << '\n'
  << "short:    " << (short)(name[ 0 ]) << '\n'
  << "string:   " << name << '\n'
  << "address: " << (unsigned long)name;
}
```

Running cout.π

Select **Run** from the **Project** menu. THIN C++ will compile your source code, then run the compiled program. When the console window appears, compare your output with that shown in Figure 4.3. To exit the program, type a carriage return. Let's take a closer look at the code.

The cont Source Code

The program starts by initializing the `char` pointer `name`, pointing it to the text string `"Dr. Crusher"`. Next comes one giant statement featuring eleven different occurrences of the << operator. This statement produces four lines of output.

The following chunk of code

```
cout << "char:     " << name[ 0 ] << '\n'
```

produces this line of output:

```
char:     D
```

FIGURE 4.3
*THIN C++'s console
window, showing the
cout output.*

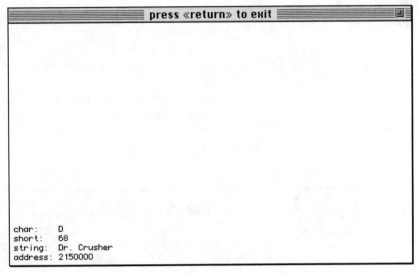

FIGURE 4.3
*THIN C++'s console
window, showing the
`cout` output.*

```
char:    D
short:   68
string:  Dr. Crusher
address: 2150000
```

As you'd expect, printing `name[ 0 ]` produces the first character
in `name`, an uppercase D.

The next chunk of code is

```
<< "short:    " << (short)(name[ 0 ]) << '\n'
```

The line of output associated with this chunk of code is as follows:

```
short:    68
```

This result was achieved by casting the character `'D'` to a `short`.
In general, `iostream` displays integral types (such as `short` and
`int`) as an integer. As you'd expect, a `float` is displayed in
floating-point format.

The next chunk of code

```
<< "string:    " << name << '\n'
```

produces this line of output:

```
string:  Dr. Crusher
```

When the `<<` operator encounters a `char` pointer, it assumes you
want to print a zero-terminated string.

The final chunk of code in our example shows another way to display the contents of a pointer:

```
<< "address: " << (unsigned long)name;
```

Again, `name` is printed, but this time is cast as an `unsigned long`. Here's the result:

```
address: 2150000
```

> Anytime you encounter an address, take it with a grain of salt. Since your computer and mine are probably quite different, your addresses will probably be different from those shown in the book.

As you can see, `cout` does what it thinks makes sense for each type it prints. Later in the book, you'll learn how to customize `cout` by using it to print data in a specified format or teaching it how to print your own data types.

An iostream Input Example

Our next example explores the flip side of `iostream` by reading data in as well as printing it out. Close `cout.π` by selecting **Close Project** from THIN C++'s **Project** menu. When prompted for a new project file to open, go back to the THIN C++ Projects folder, open the subfolder named Chap 04.02 – cin, and open the project file named `cin.π`.

Running cin.π

Select **Run** from the **Project** menu. First, you'll be prompted to type in your first name. Type in a single name (don't type in any spaces, tabs, or other white space characters) and hit return. Next, you'll be prompted for three numbers: a `short`, a `long`, and a `float`. Type all three numbers on the same line, separating each by a space, and then hit return. cin.π will then list your name, as well as each of the three numbers you typed in (Figure 4.4). Once you're done admiring your handiwork, type a carriage return to exit the program.

FIGURE 4.4
*THIN C++'s console
window, showing the
cin.π output.*

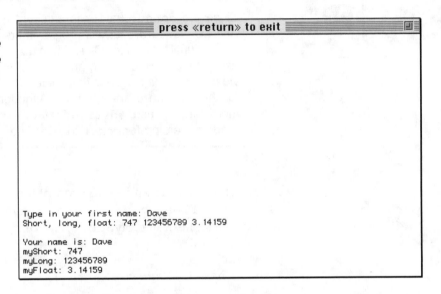

```
Type in your first name: Dave
Short, long, float: 747 123456789 3.14159

Your name is: Dave
myShort: 747
myLong:  123456789
myFloat: 3.14159
```

If things didn't go exactly as planned, try running the program again. This time, when prompted for your first name, be careful to type only a single word containing no white space characters. Next, be sure that the three numbers are in the proper order, a short, followed by a long, followed by a float. As you'll see, cin is pretty picky about the format of its input data.

The cin Source Code

As is always the case when you use iostream, the program starts by including the file <iostream.h>. Next, the constant kMaxNameLength is defined, providing a length for the char array name:

```
#include <iostream.h>
```

```
const short kMaxNameLength = 40;

void  main( void )
```

Since the `const` qualifier is a recent addition to the ANSI C standard, many C programmers don't find out about it until they tackle C++. When a variable is defined using the `const` qualifier, an initial value must be provided in the definition, and that value cannot be changed for the duration of the program. Although C programmers tend to use `#define` instead of `const`, C++ programmers prefer `const` to `#define`.

`cin.`π uses `cout` and `<<` to prompt for a text string, a `short`, a `long`, and a `float`. `cin` and `>>` are used to read the values into the four variables `name`, `myShort`, `myLong`, and `myFloat`:

```
{
  char  name[ kMaxNameLength ];
  short myShort;
  long  myLong;
  float myFloat;
```

The next line uses `<<` to send a text string to the console:

```
cout << "Type in your first name: ";
```

Next, `>>` is used to read in a text string:

```
cin >> name;
```

Type your first name and hit a carriage return. Be sure to type your first name only. When the `>>` operator reads a text string, it reads a character at a time until a white space character (like a space or a tab) is encountered.

Now, three more pieces of data are read using a single statement. First, display the prompt

```
cout << "Short, long, float: ";
```

Then, read in the data, separating the three receiving variables by consecutive >> operators:

```
cin >> myShort >> myLong >> myFloat;
```

> Be sure to separate each of the three numbers by a space (or some white space character). Also, make sure the numbers match the type of the corresponding variable. For example, it's probably not a good idea to enter 3.52 or 125000 as a short, although an integer like 47 works fine as a float.

Finally, display each of the variables we worked so hard to fill:

```
    cout << "\nYour name is: " << name;
    cout << "\nmyShort: " << myShort;
    cout << "\nmyLong: " << myLong;
    cout << "\nmyFloat: " << myFloat;
}
```

iostream and Objects

So far, iostream might seem primitive compared to the routines in C's Standard Library. After all, routines like scanf() and printf() give you precise control over your input and output. Routines like getchar() and putchar() allow you to process one character at a time, letting *you* decide how to handle white space.

Be patient. I promise you that iostream is awesome. The trouble is, to unleash iostream's true power, you must first come up to speed on object programming. The iostream concepts presented here are the bare minimum you'll need to get through the sample programs in the next few chapters. Later in the book, we'll examine iostream with an electron microscope. For now, basic input and output are all we need.

Default Argument Initializers

C++ allows you to assign default values (known as **default argument initializers**) to a function's arguments. For example, here's a routine designed to generate a tone at a specified frequency:

```
void  GenerateATone( short  frequency = 440 )
{
    // A frequency of 440 is equal to an A note
}
```

If you call this function with a parameter, the value you pass in is used. For example, the call

```
GenerateATone( 330 );
```

will generate a tone with a frequency of 330 beats per second, which, in musical notation, is equivalent to an E note. If you call the function without specifying a value, the default value is used. The call

```
GenerateATone();
```

will generate a tone with a frequency of 440, which represents an A note.

This technique works with multiple parameters as well, although the rules get a bit more complicated. You can specify a default value for a parameter only if you also specify a default for all the parameters that follow it. For example, this declaration is cool:

```
void  GotSomeDefaults( short manny, short moe=2,
char jack='x' );
```

Since the second parameter has a default, the third parameter *must* have a default. The next declaration *won't* compile, however, because the first parameter specifies a default and the parameter that follows does not:

```
void  WillNotCompile( long time=100L, short stack );
```

The Traditional Approach

By convention, all default parameter values are specified in the function prototype rather than in the function's implementation. For example, here's a function prototype, followed by the function itself:

```
void  MyFunc( short param1 = 27 );

void  MyFunc( short param1 )
{
  // Body of the function...
}
```

Many C++ programmers create a separate #include file for their function prototypes. Gathering all the function declarations, including parameters and default values, into a single list makes a handy reference tool. I keep my prototypes in alphabetical order and follow each one with a comment telling me where the actual code for that routine is. Here's an example:

```
void MyFunc( short param1 = 27 );
   // MySourceFile.cp
```

A Default Argument Initializer Example

Let's take default argument initializers out for a quick spin. Close cin.π, go back to the THIN C++ Projects folder, open the subfolder named Chap 04.03 - protoTester, and open the project file named protoTester.π. Next, run protoTester.π by selecting **Run** from the **Project** menu. Here's what you'll see:

```
MyFunc( 1, 0, 0 )
MyFunc( 1, 2, 0 )
MyFunc( 1, 2, 3 )
```

Hit a return to exit protoTester. Let's take a look at the code.

The protoTester Source Code

The key to `protoTester` lies in the function `MyFunc()` and its default-laden parameter list. After the obligatory `#include` of the file `<iostream.h>`, you'll find the prototype for `MyFunc()`:

```
#include <iostream.h>

void  MyFunc( short param1,
           short param2 = 0,
           short param3 = 0 );
```

Notice that defaults are provided for the second and third parameters only. Both of these parameters have a default value of 0.

`main()` calls `MyFunc()` using three different calling sequences. Since no default is provided for `MyFunc()`'s first parameter, all calls to `MyFunc()` *must* include at least one value. Calls like

```
MyFunc();
```

or

```
MyFunc( , 1 );
```

will cause the compiler to complain bitterly.

The first call of `MyFunc()` passes a single value, forcing `MyFunc()` to rely on its default values for the second and third parameters. The call

```
MyFunc( 1 );
```

produces this line of output:

```
MyFunc( 1, 0, 0 )
```

Notice that the default value of 0 is used for the second and third parameters.

Next, the code

```
MyFunc( 1, 2 );
```

produces this line of output:

```
MyFunc( 1, 2, 0 )
```

In this case, values are passed in for the first and second parameters, while the default value of 0 is used for the third parameter.
    Finally, the code

```
MyFunc( 1, 2, 3 );
```

produces this line of output:

```
MyFunc( 1, 2, 3 )
```

In this last case, the three values passed in override all of the parameter defaults.
    The function `MyFunc()` uses `iostream` to print the current values of `MyFunc()`'s three parameters:

```
void  MyFunc( short param1,
        short param2,
        short param3 )
{
  cout << "MyFunc( " << param1
    << ", " << param2
    << ", " << param3
    << " )\n";
}
```

Notice that the defaults are specified in the function prototype and not in the function title.

Interestingly, the C++ compiler will merge defaults specified in a function's prototype (declaration) and in the function's implementation (definition). For example, if the prototype is

```
void MyFunc( short param1 = 10,
        short param2 );
```

and the function's implementation is

```
void MyFunc( short param1,
    short param2 = 20 )
{
    .
    .
    .
}
```

the cumulative effect is to create a function with a default value for each of its parameters:

```
void MyFunc( short param1 = 10,
    short param2 = 20 );
```

While this effect may be interesting, don't try this in your own code (even if all your friends are doing it)! Keep your defaults in your function prototypes. You'll be glad you did.

Reference Variables

In C, all parameters are passed by value as opposed to being passed by reference. When you pass a parameter to a C function, the value of the parameter is passed on to the function. Any changes you make to this value are *not* carried back to the calling function.

Here's an example:

```
void  DoubleMyValue( short valueParam )
{
    valueParam *= 2;
}

void  main( void )
{
    short number = 10;

    DoubleMyValue( number );
}
```

main() sets number to 10, then passes it to the function DoubleMyValue(). Since number is passed by value, the call to `DoubleMyValue()` has no effect on `number`. When `DoubleMyValue()` returns, `number` still has a value of 10.

Here's an updated version of the program:

```
void  DoubleMyValue( short *numberPtr )
{
  *numberPtr *= 2;
}

void  main( void )
{
  short number = 10;

  DoubleMyValue( &number );
}
```

In this version, `number`'s address is passed to `DoubleMyValue()`. By dereferencing this pointer, `DoubleMyValue()` can reach out and change the value of `number`. When `DoubleMyValue()` returns, `number` will have a value of 20.

While this updated version works properly, there are a few problems to consider. Since a pointer is passed to `DoubleMyValue()`, you are forced to use pointer notation whenever you refer to the parameter. The line of code

```
number *= 2;
```

is easier to read than this one:

```
*numberPtr *= 2;
```

Although this inconvenience might seem minor, the clumsiness of pointer notation is magnified significantly when you start to deal with complex data structures.

The next issue is somewhat subtler and is far more dangerous. Take a look at the following code:

```
void  DoubleMyValue( short *numberPtr )
{
  *numberPtr *= 2;
}
```

```
void  main( void )
{
  short    *shortPtr;

  *shortPtr = 10;

  DoubleMyValue( shortPtr );
}
```

This code compiles cleanly, but it contains a scary error. No space is ever allocated for the `short` whose address is passed to `DoubleMyValue( )`. If you're going to work with pointers, you'll make this mistake periodically.

The Reference Variable Alternative

C++ offers a nice alternative to pointer-based parameters. **Reference variables** allow you to pass a parameter by reference, without using pointers.

Here's another version of the program, this time implemented with a reference variable:

```
void  DoubleMyValue( short &referenceParam )
{
  referenceParam *= 2;
}
```

```
void  main( void )
{
  short number = 10;

  DoubleMyValue( number );
}
```

Notice that this code looks just like the first version, with one small exception. `DoubleMyValue( )`'s parameter is defined using the & operator:

```
short &referenceParam
```

The & marks `referenceParam` as a reference variable and tells the compiler that `referenceParam` and its corresponding input parameter, `number`, are one and the same. Since both names refer to the same location in memory, changing the value of `referenceParam` is *exactly* the same as changing `number`.

A Reference Variable Example

Here's an example that should make things a little clearer. Close `protoTester.π`, go back to the THIN C++ Projects folder, open the subfolder named `Chap 04.04 - reference`, and open the project file named `reference.π`. Next, run `reference.π` by selecting **Run** from the **Project** menu. Here's what you'll see:

```
&number:      5306630
&longNumber:  5306632

&valueParam:  5306602
After ByValue: 12

&refParam:    5306630
After ByRef( short ): 24

&refParam:    5306628
After ByRef( long ): 12
```

The seven-digit numbers shown in this example are addresses. Unless you snuck in here and have been using my Mac, your addresses will probably be different.

Hit a carriage return to exit `reference`. Let's take a look at the code.

The reference Source Code

`reference` starts with a pair of function prototypes. Just like the routine `DoubleMyValue()` presented earlier, both of these routines take a single parameter and double its value:

```
#include <iostream.h>

void  CallByValue( short valueParam );
void  CallByReference( short &refParam );
```

Notice that `CallByValue()` takes a `short` as a parameter using the standard by-value parameter passing mechanism; while `CallByReference()` takes a reference variable as a parameter passed by reference.

  `main()` starts by defining two variables, a `short` and a `long`, initializing each to a value of 12:

```
void  main( void )
{
  short number = 12;
  long  longNumber = 12L;
```

Next, the address of both variables is printed in the console. When a parameter is successfully passed by reference, the calling and receiving parameters will have the same address:

```
cout << "&number:      " <<
    (unsigned long)&number << "\n";

cout << "&longNumber: " <<
    (unsigned long)&longNumber << "\n\n";
```

You may have noticed that `reference` prints its addresses in decimal, rather than hexadecimal, format. Later in the book, you'll learn how to customize `cout` to print data in any format you like. For the moment, we'll print out addresses by casting them to `unsigned longs`.

Next, `number` is passed by value to `CallByValue()`:

```
CallByValue( number );
```

`CallByValue()` prints the address of, and then doubles the value of, its parameter. `number`'s address, which we printed earlier, was `5306630`. The address of the value parameter is `5306602`. Clearly, this parameter was not passed by reference, which explains why `number`'s value is not changed by the call to `CallByValue()`. As proof, the value of `number` is printed again. As you can see by the output, the value stays at 12:

```
cout << "After ByValue: " << number << "\n\n";
```

Then, `number` is passed to `CallByReference()`:

```
CallByReference( number );
```

`CallByReference()` also prints the address of its parameter. When we compare this address with the address printed earlier, they match exactly. `number`'s address (printed earlier) was `5306630`. The address of `CallByReference()`'s parameter is also `5306630`. This call by reference was successful! As proof, when the value of `number` is printed for a third time, its value doubles to 24:

```
cout << "After ByRef( short ): " << number << "\n\n";
```

Finally, a `long` is passed to `CallByReference()`:

```
CallByReference( longNumber );
```

Since `CallByReference()` declares its parameter as a reference to a `short`, the compiler is faced with an interesting problem. Reference variables work only if the type of the variable being referenced agrees with the type of the reference variable. When this isn't the case, the compiler treats the call as a call by value.

In this case, the value of the `long` is passed on to `CallByReference()`. As proof, compare the address of `longNumber`, which is `5306632` with the parameter address printed out by `CallByReference()`, which is 5306628. As you can see, the addresses don't match, indicating that the call was by value and not by reference.

To add more proof to the pudding, when the value of `longNumber` is printed upon `CallByReference()`'s return, it remains at 12, unchanged from its original value:

```
cout << "After ByRef( long ): " << longNumber << "\n";
}
```

Reference variables are primarily used as call-by-reference parameters. However, they can also be used to establish a link between two variables in the same scope. Here's an example:

```
short     romulus;
short     &remus = romulus;
```

The first line of code defines a `short` with the name `romulus`. The second line of code declares a reference variable with the name `remus`, linking it to the variable `romulus`. Just as before, the `&` marks `remus` as a reference variable.

Now that `remus` and `romulus` are linked, they share the same location in memory. Changing the value of one is *exactly* the same as changing the value of the other.

It's important to note that a reference variable must be linked to a variable as soon as it is declared. The following code will not compile:

```
short     romulus;
short     &remus;  // Will not compile!!!

remus = romulus;
```

The reference variable must also be of the same type as the variable it references. The following code won't work:

```
short     romulus;
long      &remus = romulus; // Type mismatch!!!
```

In addition, once established, the link between a reference and a regular variable cannot be changed. In other words, once `remus` is linked to `romulus`, it cannot be set to reference a different variable.

Function Name Overloading

The next feature up for discussion, **function name overloading**, allows you to write several functions that share the same name.

Suppose you needed a function that would print the value of one of your variables, be it `long`, `short`, or a text string. You could write one function that takes four parameters:

```
Display( short  whichType,
         long   longParam,
         short  shortParam,
         char   *textParam );
```

The first parameter might act like a switch, determining which of the three types you were passing in for printing. The main code of the function might look like this:

```
if ( whichType == kIsLong )
  cout << "The long is:  " << longParam << "\n";
else if ( whichType == kIsShort )
  cout << "The short is: " << shortParam << "\n";
else if ( whichType == kIsText )
  cout << "The text is:  " << text << "\n";
```

Another solution is to write three separate functions, one for printing `short`s, one for `long`s, and one for text strings:

```
void  DisplayLong( long longParam );
void  DisplayShort( short shortParam );
void  DisplayText( char *text );
```

Each of these solutions has an advantage. The first solution groups all printing under a single umbrella, making the code somewhat easier to maintain. On the other hand, the second solution is more modular than the first. If you want to change the method you use to display `longs`, you modify only the routine that works with `longs`; you don't have to deal with the logic that displays other types.

As you might expect, there is a third solution that combines the benefits of the first two. Here's how it works.

As mentioned earlier, C++ allows several functions to share the same name by way of function name overloading. When an overloaded function is called, the compiler compares the parameters in the call with the parameter lists in each of the candidate functions. The candidate with the most closely matching parameter list is the one that gets called.

def'ə nish' ən

> A function's parameter list is also known as its **signature**. A function's name and signature combine to distinguish it from all other functions. Note that a function's return type is not part of its signature.

A Function Name Overloading Example

Earlier, we looked at two solutions to our multitype printing problem. As promised, here's a third solution that takes advantage of function name overloading. Close `reference.π`, navigate up a level, then down into the subfolder named `Chap 04.05 – overload` and open the project file named `overload.π`. Next, run `overload.π` by selecting **Run** from the **Project** menu. Here's what you'll see:

```
The short is: 3
The long is:  12345678
The text is:  Make it so...
```

Hit a carriage return to exit `overload`. Let's look at the code.

The overload Source Code

`overload` starts with three function prototypes, each of which shares the name `Display()`:

```
#include <stream.h>

void  Display( short shortParam );
void  Display( long longParam );
void  Display( char *text );
```

Notice that each version of `Display()` has a unique signature. This is important. You are *not* allowed to define two functions with the same name and the same signature.

`main()` starts by defining three variables: a `short`, a `long` and a text string.

```
void  main( void )
{
   short myShort = 3;
   long  myLong = 12345678L;
   char  *text = "Make it so...";
```

Next, `Display()` is called three times. First, a `short` is passed as a parameter. Since this call exactly matches one of the `Display()` routines, the compiler doesn't have a problem deciding which function to call:

```
   Display( myShort );
```

Similarly, the calls passing a `long` and a text string to `Display()` match perfectly with the `Display()` functions having `long` and text string signatures:

```
   Display( myLong );

   Display( text );
}
```

The signatures of these three versions of `Display()` feature a `short`, a `long`, and a text string, respectively:

```
void  Display( short shortParam )
{
   cout << "The short is: " << shortParam << "\n";
}
```

```
void  Display( long longParam )
{
  cout << "The long is:   " << longParam << "\n";
}

void  Display( char *text )
{
  cout << "The text is:   " << text << "\n";
}
```

Matching Rules for Overloaded Functions

The preceding example was fairly straightforward. The compiler had no difficulty deciding which version of `Display()` to call because each of the calls matched perfectly with one of the `Display()` functions. What do you think would happen if you passed a `float` to `Display()`?

```
Display( 1.0 );
```

When the compiler can't find an exact match for an overloaded function call, it turns to a set of rules that determine the best match for this call. After applying each of the rules, if no match is found, the compiler reports an error, labeling the call as ambiguous.

As you've already seen, the compiler starts the matching process by looking for an exact match between the name and signature of the function call and a declared function. If a match is not found, the compiler starts promoting the type of any integral parameters in the function call, following the rules for automatic type conversion described in Chapter 3. For example, a `char` or a `short` would be promoted to an `int` and a `float` would be promoted to a `double`.

If a match is still not found, the compiler starts promoting non-integral types. Finally, the ellipsis operator in a called function is taken into account, matching against zero or more parameters.

In answer to our earlier question, passing a `float` to `Display()` would result in an error, listing the function call as ambiguous. If we had written a version of `Display()` with a `float` or a `double` in its signature, the compiler would find the match.

STYLE

The function overload matching rules are fairly complex. In general, you should try to avoid nonobvious function overloading. The example program overload presented earlier was completely unambiguous. As you read through the code, there was no question which function matched which function call. In the interest of cleanly running code and readability, don't write code that depends on a specific type promotion sequence. As was the case with reference parameters, function overloading works best when the parameters match exactly.

The new and delete Operators

In C, memory allocation typically involves a call to malloc() paired with a call to free() when the memory is no longer needed. In C++, the same functionality is provided by the operators new and delete.

Call new when you want to allocate a block of memory. For example, the following code allocates a block of 1024 chars:

```
char    *buffer;

buffer = new char[ 1024 ];
```

new takes a type as an operand, allocates a block of memory the same size as the type, and returns a pointer to the block. To return the memory to the heap, use the delete operator. The next code frees up the memory just allocated:

```
delete buffer;
```

new can be used with any legal C++ type, including those you create yourself. Here are a few examples:

```
struct Wobble
{
  short    papaWobble;
  short    mamaWobble;
  long     littleBabyWobble;
} ;
```

```
short          *shortPtr;
long double    *longDoublePtr;
Wobble         *wobblePtr;

shortPtr = new short;
longDoublePtr = new long double;
wobblePtr = new Wobble;
```

Here's an example of a *bad* use of new, guaranteed to bring the compiler to its knees:

```
short *shortPtr;

shortPtr = new 1024;  // Will not compile!!!
```

Though you can pass a constant to `malloc()`, a constant is not a type and has no place in new.

What to Do When new Fails

Every program that allocates memory runs the risk that its request for memory will fall on deaf ears, most likely because there's no more memory left to allocate. If your program uses new to allocate memory, it had better detect, and handle, any failure on new's part.

Since new returns a value of NULL when it fails, the simplest approach just checks this return value, taking the appropriate action when new fails:

```
char  *bufPtr;

bufPtr = new char[ 1024 ];

if ( bufPtr == NULL )
  cout << "Not enough memory!!!";
else
  DoSomething( bufPtr );
```

This code uses new to allocate a 1024-byte buffer. If new fails, an error message is printed; otherwise, the program goes on its merry way.

This approach requires that you check the return value every time you call new. If your program performs a lot of memory allocation, this memory-checking code can really add up. As your programs get larger and more sophisticated, you might want to consider a second strategy.

C++ allows you to specify a single routine, known as a new handler, that gets called if and when new fails. Design your new handler for the general case so that it can respond to *any* failed attempt to allocate memory.

Whether or not you designate a new handler, new will still return NULL if it fails. This means you can design a two-tiered memory management strategy combining a new handler and code that runs if new returns NULL.

To specify a new handler, pass the handler's name to the function set_new_handler(). To use set_new_handler(), be sure to include the file <new.h>:

```
#include <new.h>

void  NewFailed( void );

void  main( void )
{
  set_new_handler( NewFailed );
      .
      .
      .
}
```

One common memory allocation strategy is to allocate a block of memory at the beginning of your program, storing a pointer to the block in a global variable. Then, when new fails, your program can free up the spare memory block, ensuring that it will have enough memory to perform any housekeeping chores that it requires in a memory emergency.

A new Example

Our next sample program repeatedly calls new until the program runs out of memory, keeps track of the number of memory requests, and then reports on the amount of memory allocated before failure. This program uses the spare memory scheme just described.

Close overload.π, navigate up a level, then down into the subfolder named Chap 04.06 – newTester, and open the project file named newTester.π. Next, run newTester.π by selecting **Run** from the **Project** menu. Here's what you'll see:

```
Installing NewHandler...
Number of blocks allocated: 25
```

The number of blocks you can allocate before you run out of memory depends on the amount of memory you make available to your program. Don't be too surprised if your number differs from the number of blocks shown in this example.

Hit a carriage return to exit newTester. Let's take a look at the code.

The newTester Source Code

newTester starts by including both `<iostream.h>` for access to the `iostream` library and `<new.h>` for access to the `set_new_handler()` function:

```
#include <iostream.h>
#include <new.h>
```

NewFailed() is the function we want called if new fails in its attempt to allocate memory:

```
void  NewFailed( void );
```

newTester makes use of two global variables. gDone acts as a flag, initially set to false, but set to true when we're ready to exit our memory allocation loop; gSpareBlockPtr is a pointer to the spare block of memory we allocate at the beginning of the program:

```
char   gDone = false;
char   *gSpareBlockPtr = NULL;
```

main() uses two local variables. myPtr acts as a pointer to the blocks of memory we allocate; numBlocks tracks the number of blocks we allocate before new finally fails:

```
void  main( void )
{
  char   *myPtr;
  long   numBlocks = 0;
```

Next, we'll send an appropriate message to the console. This message serves a subtle purpose. It causes iostream to allocate all the memory it needs for the console window before the program consumes all remaining free memory. This guarantees that our subsequent console output will appear.

```
  cout << "Installing NewHandler...\n";
```

set_new_handler() is called to set NewFailed() as the routine to be called if and when new fails:

```
set_new_handler( NewFailed );
```

Then, the spare block of memory (20 kilobytes) is allocated, and a pointer to the spare block is stored in gSpareBlockPtr:

```
gSpareBlockPtr = new char[20480];
```

> Your C++ environment most likely has a fixed limit on the size of a single block of memory. Many environments limit a single block to 32 kilobytes. If you need more memory than your environment allows, design a workaround using multiple blocks.

Next, we enter an endless loop, allocating a 1-kilobyte block and incrementing numBlocks:

```
while ( gDone == false )
{
  myPtr = new char[1024];
  numBlocks++;
}
```

> Notice that we don't squirrel away the pointers to these allocated blocks. Once we allocate a new block, we lose the pointer to the previously allocated block. That block can never be deleted and is lost forever. Not a particularly good memory management scheme, eh? Make sure you balance every use of new with a corresponding delete.

Once we've allocated all the available memory, new will fail and NewFailed() will be called. NewFailed() sets gDone to true, and the memory allocation loop exits. Once the loop exits, we print out the number of blocks we were able to allocate:

```
cout << "Number of blocks allocated: " <<
  numBlocks;
}
```

NewFailed() starts by checking to see whether gSpareBlockPtr actually points to a block of memory. After all, new might fail when we first try to allocate the spare block. If we were able to allocate the spare block, NewFailed() uses delete to return the block to the heap and gSpareBlockPtr is reset to NULL:

```
if ( gSpareBlockPtr != NULL )
{
  delete gSpareBlockPtr;
  gSpareBlockPtr = NULL;
}
```

Finally, gDone is set to true:

```
gDone = true;
}
```

The Scope Operator

The next feature we'll examine is C++'s **scope operator** (::). The scope operator precedes a variable, telling the compiler to look outside the current block for a variable of the same name.

Suppose you declare a global variable and a local variable with the same name:

```
short    number;

void  main( void )
{
  short    number;
```

```
    number = 5;      // local reference
    ::number = 10;   // global reference
}
```

Inside `main()`, the first assignment statement refers to the local definition of `number`. The second assignment statement uses the scope operator to refer to the global definition of `number`. This code leaves the local `number` with a value of 5 and the global `number` with a value of 10.

Many programmers start all their global variables with a lowercase g to differentiate them from local variables. If you use this convention, you'll never be in the situation where a local variable is obscuring a global variable.

This doesn't mean you should ignore the scope operator, however! Later in the book, as we get into object programming, you'll find that the scope operator is invaluable. For now, follow through the sample program, then file the scope operator away for future reference.

A Scope Operator Example

Our next sample program offers a quick demonstration of the scope operator. Close `newTester.π`, navigate up a level, then down into the subfolder named `Chap 04.07 - scopeTester`, and open the project file named `scopeTester.π`. Next, run `scopeTester.π` by selecting **Run** from the **Project** menu. Here's what you'll see:

```
yourValue: 5
yourValue: 10
yourValue: 5
```

Hit a carriage return to exit `scopeTester`. Let's look at the code.

The scopeTester Source Code

scopeTester defines a global variable with the name myValue, initializing it to a value of 5:

```
#include <iostream.h>

short myValue = 5;
```

main() defines a local variable named yourValue and assigns it the value in myValue:

```
void  main( void )
{
  short yourValue = myValue;
```

Then, yourValue is printed out, showing it with a value of 5, the same as the global myValue:

```
  cout << "yourValue: " << yourValue << "\n";
```

Next, a local with the name myValue is defined and initialized with a value of 10. When myValue is copied to yourValue, which variable is copied, the local or the global?

```
  short myValue = 10;
  yourValue = myValue;
```

As you can see from the output, the reference to myValue matches with the local declaration, showing yourValue with a value of 10:

```
  cout << "yourValue: " << yourValue << "\n";
```

Then, the scope operator is used to copy myValue to yourValue. When yourValue is printed again, it has a value of 5, showing that ::myValue refers to the global declaration of myValue:

```
  yourValue = ::myValue;
  cout << "yourValue: " << yourValue << "\n";
}
```

The scope operator can be applied only when a match is available. Applying the scope operator to a local variable without a corresponding global will generate a compile error. To see this for yourself, add the following code to the end of `main()` and try to compile it:

```
::yourValue = 20;
```

Since there is no global named `yourValue`, the code will not compile.

Inline Functions

OK. One final topic, then we'll move on to object programming. Traditionally, when a function is called, the CPU executes a set of instructions that move control from the calling function to the called function. At the very least, these instructions squirrel away a return address, jump to the beginning of the called function, execute the function's code, and then jump back to the return address.

Tiny as these instructions may be, they still take time. C++, however, provides **inline functions**, which allow you to bypass these instructions and save a bit of execution time. Here's how this feature works.

When you declare a function using the `inline` keyword, the compiler copies the body of the function into the calling function, making the copied instructions a part of the calling function as if it were written that way originally. The benefit to you is a slight improvement in performance. The cost is in memory usage. Why? If you call an inline function twenty times from within your program, twenty copies of the function will be grafted into your object code.

Since the performance benefit is so small compared to the memory cost, you'll probably want to use inline functions sparingly. On the other hand, if you've got a piece of code that you need to squeeze for every processor cycle you can get, inline functions may help.

An Inline Function Example

Our final sample program features a single inline function that returns the value achieved when its first argument is raised to its second argument's power. As an example, the following call will return the value $2^5 = 2*2*2*2*2 = 32$:

```
power( 2, 5 );
```

Close scopeTester.π, navigate up a level, then down into the subfolder named Chap 04.08 – inline, and open the project file named inline.π. Next, run inline.π by selecting **Run** from the **Project** menu. Here's what you'll see:

```
power( 2, 3 ): 8
power( 3, 6 ): 729
power( 5, 0 ): 1
power( -3, 4 ): 81
```

Hit a carriage return to exit inline. Let's take a look at the code.

The inline Source Code

inline starts with the standard include file, followed by a function prototype that features the keyword inline:

```
#include <iostream.h>

inline  long power( short base, short exponent );
```

main() calls power() four times and prints the result of each call:

```
void  main( void )
{
  cout << "power( 2, 3 ): " <<
      power( 2, 3 ) << "\n";

  cout << "power( 3, 6 ): " <<
      power( 3, 6 ) << "\n";
```

```
    cout << "power( 5, 0 ): " <<
        power( 5, 0 ) << "\n";

    cout << "power( -3, 4 ): " <<
        power( -3, 4 ) << "\n";
}
```

By preceding power( )'s declaration by the inline keyword, we've asked the compiler to replace each of the four function calls in main( ) with the code in power( ). Note that this replacement effects the object code and has no impact on the source code:

```
inline  long power( short base, short exponent )
{
  long  product = 1;
  short i;

  if ( exponent < 0 )
     return( 0 );

  for ( i=1; i<=exponent; i++ )
     product *= base;

  return( product );
}
```

Interestingly, there are no standards for producing inline code. Some compilers simply graft a copy of the inline function in place of each call. At the other end of the spectrum, some compilers perform a sophisticated analysis of the function, with optimal performance as its goal, and produce the fastest possible code that achieves the same result as the original function. Some compilers allow recursive inlines; some don't. Some compilers ignore inline completely. As you can see, inline code skates fairly close to the brink of nonportability. Use this feature with care.

Summary   Congratulations! You've reached the first summit in your quest for C++ mastery. You've moved well beyond the boundaries of C and covered most of the syntax you'll need to build your own C++ programs. Your next goal is to move on to Chapter 5 and explore the world of object programming.

Chapter 5

Object Programming Basics

This chapter introduces you to the basics of object programming, the heart and soul of C++. You'll learn all about objects and the C++ functions that allow you to create objects of your very own.

This Chapter at a Glance

The Organizational Power of the Struct
Bundling Data and Functions
Creating an Object
Accessing an Object's Data Members and Member Functions
    The Current Object
    The "this" Alternative
Deleting an Object
Writing Class Functions
    The Constructor Function
    Adding Parameters to Your Constructor
    The Destructor Function
Access Privileges
    Balancing Privacy with Accessibility
Bringing It All Together
    An Object Programming Example
The friends Mechanism
    Three Types of friends
    A Friendly Example
Summary

THIS CHAPTER INTRODUCES YOU TO THE POWER of object programming. Objects are like C structs on steroids. As you read through the chapter, focus on the sample programs. The concepts presented here form the basis of a whole new way of programming.

The Organizational Power of the Struct

One of the most valuable features shared by C and C++ is the **struct**. Without the struct, you have no way to group data that belongs together.

Suppose you want to implement an employee data base that tracks an employee's name, employee ID, and salary. You might design a struct that looks like this:

```
const short kMaxNameSize = 20;

struct Employee
{
  char    name[ kMaxNameSize ];
  long    id;
  float   salary;
};
```

The great advantage of this struct is that it lets you bundle several pieces of information together under a single name. For example, if you wrote a routine to print an employee's data, you could write:

```
struct Employee newHire;
  .
  .
  .
PrintEmployee( newHire.name, newHire.id,
  newHire.salary );
```

It would be so much more convenient, however, to pass the data in its bundled form like this:

```
PrintEmployee( &newHire );
```

Bundling allows you to represent complex information in a more natural, easily accessible form. In the C language, the struct is the most sophisticated bundling mechanism available. As you'll soon see, C++ takes bundling to a new level.

Bundling Data and Functions

While C limits you to pure data bundles, C++ supports bundles composed of both data and functions. These bundles are known as **classes**. Here's an example of a class declaration:

```
const short kMaxNameSize = 20;

class Employee
{
//      Data members...
    char        employeeName[ kMaxNameSize ];
    long        employeeID;
    float       employeeSalary;

//      Member functions...
    void        PrintEmployee( void );
};
```

A class declaration is similar in form to a struct declaration, except the `struct` keyword is replaced by the `class` keyword. The example just given declares a class with the name `Employee`. The `Employee` class bundles together three data fields as well as a function named `PrintEmployee()`. The data fields of a class are known as **data members** and the functions of a class are known as **member functions**.

Think of a class declaration as a specialized struct declaration. Just as you use a struct declaration to define an individual struct variable, you use a class declaration to create specialized variables known as **objects**.

When you define a struct variable, you allocate a block of memory large enough to hold all of the struct's fields. When you define an object, you allocate a block of memory large enough to hold the object's data members. In addition to the data members, the object also contains pointers to the member functions specified in the class declaration.

If you're feeling a little confused, hang on. The concept of classes and objects takes a while to get used to. Just keep reading. Later in the chapter, you'll come to a sample program that will make things much clearer.

Creating an Object

There are two ways to create a new object. The simplest method is to define the object directly, just as you would a regular variable. For example, the following definition

```
Employee  employee1;
```

creates an object named `employee1` belonging to the `Employee` class. Figure 5.1 shows this definition from a memory perspective. `employee1` consists of a block of memory large enough to accommodate each of the three `Employee` data members as well as a pointer to the single `Employee` function, `PrintEmployee()`.

FIGURE 5.1
An object created by definition.

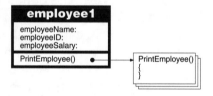

When you create an object by definition, as we just did, memory for the object is allocated automatically when the definition moves into scope. That same memory is freed up when the object drops out of scope. For example, you might define an object at the beginning of a function, as in the following code:

```
void  CreateEmployee( void )
{
  Employee  employee1;

    .
    .
    .

}
```

When the function is called, memory for the object is allocated right along with memory for the function's other local variables. When the function exits, the object's memory is deallocated.

def'ə nish' ən

Objects created by definition are known as **automatic objects** because memory for them is allocated and deallocated automatically.

Although automatic objects are simple to create, they do have a downside. Once they drop out of scope, they cease to exist. If you want your object to outlive its scope, take advantage of C++'s new operator (introduced in Chapter 4).

First, define an object pointer, then call new to allocate the memory for your object. new returns a pointer to the newly created object. Here's some code that creates an Employee object:

```
Employee  *employeePtr;

employeePtr = new Employee;
```

The first line of code defines a pointer designed to point to an Employee object. The second line uses new to create an Employee object. new returns a pointer to the newly created Employee.

Figure 5.2 shows what this looks like from a memory perspective. employeePtr is a pointer, pointing to an object of the Employee class. As was the case previously, the Employee object consists of a block of memory large enough to accommodate each of the three Employee data members as well as a pointer to the single Employee function, PrintEmployee().

FIGURE 5.2

An object pointer, pointing to an object, pointing to some code.

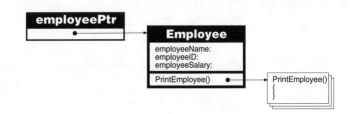

Suppose we create a second `Employee` object:

```
Employee  *employee1Ptr, *employee2Ptr;

employee1Ptr = new Employee;
employee2Ptr = new Employee;
```

Take a look at Figure 5.3. Notice that the second `Employee` object gets its own block of memory, with its very own copy of the `Employee` data members and its own function pointer. Notice that both objects point to the same copy of `PrintEmployee()` in memory. Every single `Employee` object gets its own copy of the `Employee` data members. At the same time, all `Employee` objects share a single copy of the `Employee` member functions.

FIGURE 5.3

A second `Employee`, *pointing to the same code.*

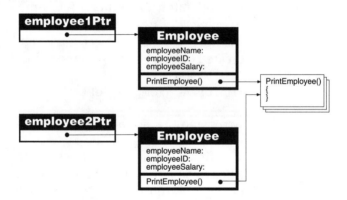

Accessing an Object's Data Members and Member Functions

Once you've created an object, you can call its functions and modify its data members. Remember, each object you create has its own copy of the data members defined by its class. You refer to an object's data members and member functions in much the same way as you refer to the fields of a struct. If you're defining the object directly, use the **.** operator:

```
Employee  employee1;

employee1.employeeSalary = 200.0;
```

If you're working with an object pointer, use the -> operator:

```
Employee  *employeePtr;

employeePtr = new Employee;

employeePtr->employeeSalary = 200.0;
```

To call a member function, use the same technique. If the object is created automatically, use the . operator:

```
Employee  employee1;

employee1.PrintEmployee();
```

If the object is created using new, use the -> operator:

```
Employee  *employeePtr;

employeePtr = new Employee;

employeePtr->PrintEmployee();
```

The Current Object

In the previous examples, each reference to a data member or member function started with an object or object pointer. Inside a member function, however, the object or object pointer isn't necessary. For example, inside the PrintEmployee() function, you can refer to the data member employeeSalary directly, without referring to an object or object pointer:

```
if ( employeeSalary <= 200 )
  cout << "Give this person a raise!!!";
```

This code is a bit puzzling. What object does employeeSalary belong to? After all, you're used to writing

```
myObject->employeeSalary
```

instead of just plain

```
employeeSalary
```

The key to this puzzle lies in knowing which object spawned the call of `PrintEmployee()` in the first place. Although this may not be obvious, a call to a member function *must* originate with a single object.

Suppose you called `PrintEmployee()` from a nonEmployee function such as `main()`. You *must* start this call with a reference to an object:

```
employeePtr->PrintEmployee();
```

Whenever a member function is called, C++ keeps track of the object used to call the function. This object is known as the **current object**.

In the call of `PrintEmployee()` just given, the object pointed to by `employeePtr` is the current object. Whenever this call of `PrintEmployee()` refers to an `Employee` data member or function *without* using an object reference, the current object (in this case, the object pointed to by `employeePtr`) is assumed.

Suppose `PrintEmployee()` then called another `Employee` function. The object pointed to by `employeePtr` is still considered the current object. A reference to `employeeSalary` will still modify the current object's copy of `employeeSalary`.

The point to remember is that a member function always starts with a single object in mind. This object, which we've called the current object, is always of the same class as the function.

The "this" Alternative

In the pursuit of legible code, C++ provides a generic object pointer, available inside any member function, that points to the current object. The generic pointer takes "`this`" for its name. For example, inside every `Employee` function, the line

```
this->employeeSalary = 400;
```

is equivalent to this line:

```
employeeSalary = 400;
```

You don't have to use `this`, but it does make the code a little easier to read. If you refer to a data member or function using `this`, it is quite clear that the data member or function is part of the class, and not a local or global variable.

> Another benefit of `this` occurs when you declare a local variable with the same name as that of a data member. For example, suppose `PrintEmployee()` declared a local variable (or had a parameter) named `employeeSalary`. When `employeeSalary` comes up in the code, does it refer to the local variable or the data member? As it turns out, the local variable (or parameter) wins out in case of a conflict, but you can avoid the conflict altogether either by using `this` or by naming your variables more carefully.

Deleting an Object

As mentioned earlier, objects created by definition are created and deleted automatically. For example, suppose the `Employee` function `PrintEmployee()` defined its own `Employee` object right at the beginning of the function:

```
Employee  localEmployee;
```

`localEmployee` is created automatically at the beginning of `PrintEmployee()` and is deleted as soon as `PrintEmployee()` exits.

Nonautomatic objects are another story altogether. If you create an object with `new`, you'll have to delete the object yourself by using the `delete` operator. Here's the syntax:

```
Employee  *employeePtr;

employeePtr = new Employee;

delete employeePtr;
```

As you'd expect, `delete` deletes the specified object, freeing up any memory allocated for the object. Note that this freed-up memory includes memory for the actual object only and does not include any extra memory you may have allocated. You'll have to free up that memory yourself.

Writing Class Functions

Once your class is defined, you're ready to write the member functions of the class. Member functions behave in much the same way as ordinary functions, with a few small differences. One difference, pointed out earlier, is that a member function automatically has access to the data members and functions of the object that called it.

Another difference lies in the function implementation's title line. Here's a sample:

```
void  Employee::PrintEmployee( void )
{
  cout << "Employee Name:   " << employeeName << "\n";
}
```

Notice that the function name is preceded by the class name and two colons (`::`). This notation is mandatory and tells the compiler that this function is a member of the specified class.

The Constructor Function

Typically, when you create an object, you'll want to perform some sort of initialization on the object. For instance, you might want to provide initial values for your object's data members. The **constructor function** is C++'s built-in initialization mechanism.

The constructor function (or just plain constructor) is a member function that has the same name as the class. For example, the constructor for the `Employee` class is named `Employee()`. When an object is created, the constructor for that class is called *automatically*.

Consider the following code:

```
Employee  *employeePtr;

employeePtr = new Employee;
```

In the second line, the new operator allocates a new Employee object, then immediately calls the object's constructor. Once the constructor returns, a pointer to the new object is assigned to employeePtr.

This same scenario holds true for an automatic object. In the following code,

```
Employee  employee1;
```

as soon as the object is created, its constructor is called.

Here's our Employee class declaration with the constructor declaration added in:

```
const short kMaxNameSize = 20;

class Employee
{
//      Data members...
    char       employeeName[ kMaxNameSize ];
    long       employeeID;
    float      employeeSalary;

//      Member functions...
               Employee( void );
    void       PrintEmployee( void );
};
```

Notice that the constructor is declared without a return value. Constructors *never* return a value. Thus, you won't want to call any functions that *do* return a value inside your constructor. As an example, it's not a good idea to allocate memory inside your constructor.

| def'ə nish' ən | In general, an object's constructor will initialize each of the object's data members. The constructor will *not* make any calls that return a status or that can fail. As your objects become more complex, you'll want to move to **two-stage construction**.
| | With two-stage construction, you create an additional member function that you call after the constructor returns. Typically, this second routine is named by an I followed by the class name. For example, the second-stage constructor for the Employee class would be named IEmployee(). |

> In general, an object's constructor will initialize each of the object's data members. The constructor will *not* make any calls that return a status or that can fail. As your objects become more complex, you'll want to move to **two-stage construction**.
>
> With two-stage construction, you create an additional member function that you call after the constructor returns. Typically, this second routine is named by an I followed by the class name. For example, the second-stage constructor for the Employee class would be named IEmployee().
>
> The following example creates an Employee object using two-stage construction:
>
> ```
> Employee *employeePtr;
> short    objectStatus;
>
> employeePtr = new Employee;
>
> objectStatus = employeePtr->IEmployee();
> ```
>
> Since IEmployee() can return a status, this is the perfect place to allocate memory or to perform any other initialization that has the potential of failing.

Here's a sample constructor:

```
Employee::Employee( void )
{
  employeeSalary = 200.0;
}
```

As mentioned earlier, the constructor is declared without a return value. This is proper form.

Constructors are optional. If you don't have any initialization to perform, don't define one. When an object is created, the constructor is called only if it is included in the class declaration.

Adding Parameters to Your Constructor

If you like, you can add parameters to your constructor. Constructor parameters are typically used to provide initial values for the object's data members.

Here's a new version of the `Employee()` constructor:

```
Employee::Employee( char *name, long id, float
  salary )
{
  strcpy( employeeName, name );
  employeeID = id;
  employeeSalary = salary;
}
```

The constructor copies the three parameter values into the corresponding data members. The object that was just created is always the constructor's current object. In other words, when the constructor refers to an `Employee` data member, such as `employeeName` or `employeeSalary`, it is referring to the copy of that data member in the newly created object.

Notice that this constructor uses different names for a parameter and its corresponding data member. Some programmers prefer to use the same name, using `this` to keep things straight, as in the following code:

```
Employee::Employee( char *employeeName, long
  employeeID, float employeeSalary )
{
  strcpy( this->employeeName, employeeName );
  this->employeeID = employeeID;
  this->employeeSalary = employeeSalary;
}
```

As you write your own code, choose a style you feel comfortable with and be consistent.

The following line of code supplies the new operator with a set of parameters to pass on to the constructor:

```
employeePtr = new Employee( "Dave Mark", 1000, 200.0 );
```

Notice that the parameter list is appended to the class name, making it look just like a function call. Don't be fooled! This line of code specifies the parameters to be passed to the new object's constructor function. It does not call the constructor directly. The constructor call happens behind the scenes, and no return value is generated. Just thought you'd like to know.

The next line of code creates an automatic object using parameters:

```
Employee  employee1( "Dave Mark", 1000, 200.0 );
```

As you'd expect, this code creates an object named employee1, then calls the Employee constructor, passing it the three specified parameters.

Just for completeness, here's the class declaration again, showing the new, parameterized constructor:

```
class Employee
{
//      Data members...
    char        employeeName[ kMaxNameSize ];
    long        employeeID;
    float       employeeSalary;

//      Member functions...
                Employee( char *name, long id, float
                    salary );
    void        PrintEmployee( void );
};
```

The Destructor Function

The **destructor function** is called automatically, just as the constructor is. Unlike the constructor, however, the destructor is called when an object in its class is deleted. Use the destructor to clean up after your object before it goes away. For instance, you might use the destructor to deallocate any additional memory your object may have allocated.

The destructor function is named by a tilde character (~) followed by the class name. For example, the destructor for the `Employee` class is named `~Employee()`. The destructor has *no* return value and *no* parameters.

Here's a sample destructor:

```
Employee::~Employee( void )
{
  cout << "Deleting employee #" << employeeID << "\n";
}
```

If your object is created using new, the destructor is called when you call `delete`:

```
Employee   *employeePtr;

employeePtr = new Employee;

delete employeePtr;
```

If your object is created automatically, the destructor is called just before the object is deleted. For example, if the object is declared at the beginning of a function, the destructor is called when the function exits.

If your object is defined as a global variable, its constructor is called at the beginning of the program and its destructor is called just before the program exits. Yes, global objects are automatic and have scope, just as local objects do.

Here's an updated `Employee` class declaration showing the constructor and destructor:

```
class Employee
{
//      Data members...
    char        employeeName[ kMaxNameSize ];
    long        employeeID;
    float       employeeSalary;

//      Member functions...
                Employee( char *name, long id, float
                    salary );
                ~Employee( void );
    void        PrintEmployee( void );
};
```

If you use two-stage initialization, check the return status of your extra initializer right away. If your request for additional memory fails, for example, you might want to `delete` the object you just created.

```
Employee *employeePtr;

employeePtr = new Employee();

if ( employeePtr->IEmployee() == false )
    delete employeePtr;
```

Whether you use two-stage initialization or not, it's a good idea to keep your constructor and destructor in sync. If you allocate extra memory, be sure your destructor has some way of knowing about it. For example, it's good practice to initialize your pointers to `NULL`. If your destructor encounters a non`NULL` pointer, it knows that additional memory has been allocated that must be deallocated.

Access Privileges

When you define a class, you need to decide which data members and functions you'd like to make available to the rest of the world. C++ gives you the power to hide the functions and data of a class from all of the other functions in your program or to allow access to a select few.

Suppose you define a `PayRaise()` function that increases the value of `employeeSalary` by 10% each time it is called. Do you want just anyone to be able to give an employee a raise? C++ allows you to assign an **access code** to any data member or member function of a class. The access code defines which of your program's functions have access to the specified data member or function. The access code must be one of `public`, `private`, or `protected`.

By default, every data member and function in a given class is marked as `private`. If a data member or function is marked as `private`, access to it is limited to member functions of the same class.

As you'll see later in the chapter, functions declared as "friends" of a class can access the `private` data members and functions of that class . For now, keep reading.

Because `private` is the default, a class declaration without any access codes is completely `private` and is pretty useless. Why useless?

Consider our `Employee` class declaration:

```
class Employee
{
//      Data members...
    char        employeeName[ kMaxNameSize ];
    long        employeeID;
    float       employeeSalary;
```

```
//        Member functions...
              Employee( char *name, long id, float
                 salary );
              ~Employee( void );
     void     PrintEmployee( void );
};
```

Since none of the data members and functions are marked otherwise, this class is completely `private`. Since `main()` is not part
of the `Employee` class, `main()` is not allowed to call any of the
`Employee` functions, including the `Employee` constructor. As a
result, `main()`, as well as all other non`Employee` functions,
cannot create an `Employee` object.

Luckily, there's a simple solution to this problem. The `public`
access code marks a data member or function as available to the
masses. A typical strategy is to mark all data members as `private`
and all member functions as `public`.

Here's a revised version of the `Employee` class declaration:

```
class Employee
{
//      Data members...
    char      employeeName[ kMaxNameSize ];
    long      employeeID;
    float     employeeSalary;

//        Member functions...
  public:
              Employee( char *name, long id, float
                 salary );
              ~Employee( void );
     void     PrintEmployee( void );
};
```

This definition marks all three `Employee` functions as `public`.
The three `Employee` data members are marked as `private` since
that is the default setting. When the compiler encounters an access code, all data members and functions that follow are marked
with that code, at least until another code is encountered. Be sure
to include the colon (`:`) after the access code.

The third C++ access code is `protected`. The `protected` access code offers the same protection as `private`, with one exception. A `protected` data member or function can also be accessed by a class *derived* from the current class. Since we won't get to derived classes until later in the book, we'll put off discussion of the `protected` access code until then.

Balancing Privacy with Accessibility

As mentioned earlier, a typical access strategy is to mark all data members as `private` and all member functions as `public`. Why would you want to mark anything as `private`? Isn't privacy just going to get in the way?

Actually, there are several good reasons for marking data members (and even functions) as `private`. The reason for the general strategy of marking data members as `private` is analogous to the metal casing around a computer hard drive: Both serve to keep prying eyes and poking fingers from mucking up the works.

Marking the data members of a class as `private` forces a user of that class to depend on the member functions and not the data members. For example, you might mark the `employeeSalary` data member as `private` and offer a `public` routine named `GetEmployeeSalary()` that returned `employeeSalary`'s value. If you wanted to, you could have `GetEmployeeSalary()` prompt the user for a password before the salary was returned. If the `employeeSalary` data member was `public`, you'd have no control over who could or couldn't access an employee's salary.

def'ə nish' ən

Functions designed specifically to provide access to a data member are known as **access functions**. In general, access functions are divided into two categories. Access functions that return the value of a data member are known as **getter functions**. Access functions that allow you to set the value of a data member are known as **setter functions**.

Privacy applies to functions as well. Earlier I mentioned a function named `PayRaise()` that increased the value of `employeeSalary` by 10% each time it was called. If we want to maintain any kind of control over an employee's salary, it's probably a good idea to mark this function as `private`.

Bringing It All Together

Later in the chapter, we'll take a closer look at this `PayRaise()` example. For now, here's a program that brings together all of the basic concepts presented in this chapter.

An Object Programming Example

If THIN C++ is already running, close the current project by selecting **Close Project** from the **Project** menu. If THIN C++ isn't running, launch it by doubling-clicking on the `THIN Project Manager` inside the `Development` folder, inside the `THIN C++ Folder`. Either way, when prompted for a project file to open, go into the `THIN C++ Projects` folder, open the subfolder named `Chap 05.01 - employee`, and open the project file named `employee.π`. Next, run `employee.π` by selecting **Run** from the **Project** menu. Here's what you'll see:

```
Creating employee #1
Creating employee #2
----
Name:   Dave Mark
ID:     1
Salary: 200
----
----
Name:   Steve Baker
ID:     2
Salary: 300
----
Deleting employee #2
Deleting employee #1
```

Hit a return to exit `employee`. Let's take a look at the source code.

The employee Source Code

As you look through the source code, you should see some familiar sights. This program takes the Employee class described throughout this chapter through its paces.

The first thing you'll notice is the additional include file <string.h>, which is needed for the call to strcpy() later in the program:

```
#include <iostream.h>
#include <string.h>
```

The constant kMaxNameSize and the Employee class declaration are identical to those presented earlier in the chapter:

```
const short kMaxNameSize = 20;

class Employee
{
//      Data members...
  private:
    char   employeeName[ kMaxNameSize ];
    long   employeeID;
    float  employeeSalary;

//      Member functions...
  public:
          Employee( char *name, long id, float
            salary );
          ~Employee( void );
    void  PrintEmployee( void );
};
```

Notice that the data members are all marked as private (unnecessary, but it does make the code easier to read) while the member functions are marked as public.

The Employee class has three member functions: a constructor, a destructor, and a utility routine named PrintEmployee(). The constructor, Employee(), uses its three parameters to initialize each of the Employee data members:

```
Employee::Employee( char *name, long id, float
  salary )
```

this is used to access each of the `Employee` data members. As pointed out earlier, `this` represents the current object, which in this case is the object whose creation caused this constructor to be called:

```
{
    strcpy( this->employeeName, name );
    this->employeeID = id;
    this->employeeSalary = salary;
```

Notice that we used `this`, even though we didn't have to. Personally, I think `this` makes the code easier to read.

Once the data members are initialized, the constructor sends a message to the console, that tells us which `Employee` object was just created:

```
    cout << "Creating employee #" << employeeID << "\n";
}
```

Since no extra memory was allocated, there's not a whole lot for the destructor to do. Just like the constructor, the destructor sends a message to the console, that tells us which `Employee` object was just deleted:

```
Employee::~Employee( void )
{
    cout << "Deleting employee #" << employeeID << "\n";
}
```

`PrintEmployee()` displays the contents of the three data members of the current object:

```
void  Employee::PrintEmployee( void )
{
    cout << "----\n";
    cout << "Name:    " << employeeName << "\n";
    cout << "ID:      " << employeeID << "\n";
    cout << "Salary: " << employeeSalary << "\n";
    cout << "----\n";
}
```

Notice that `PrintEmployee()` doesn't use `this`. Do you see where `this` could have been used? If not, go back and check out the constructor.

    `main()` is the control center where all the action is. First, we define an automatic `Employee` object, passing three parameters that will be passed on to the constructor:

```
void  main( void )
{
  Employee  employee1( "Dave Mark", 1, 200.0 );
```

As the `Employee` object is created, its constructor is called, displaying the following line on the console:

```
Creating employee #1
```

Next, an `Employee` object pointer is defined, and, this time, `new` is used to create a second `Employee` object:

```
  Employee  *employee2;

  employee2 = new Employee( "Steve Baker", 2, 300.0 );
```

Once again, the `Employee` constructor is called, sending another line to the console, as follows:

```
Creating employee #2
```

    Now, both objects are used to call the `PrintEmployee()` member function. `employee1` is an object and uses the `.` operator to access its member function; `employee2` is a pointer and uses the `->` operator to access the `PrintEmployee()` function:

```
  employee1.PrintEmployee();
  employee2->PrintEmployee();
```

These two calls result in the following output:

```
----
Name:    Dave Mark
ID:      1
```

```
Salary: 200
----

----
Name:    Steve Baker
ID:      2
Salary: 300
----
```

Then, the object pointed to by `employee2` is deleted:

```
  delete employee2;
}
```

This causes `employee2`'s destructor to be called, resulting in the following line of output:

```
Deleting employee #2
```

Finally, `main()` exits and all of `main()`'s local variables, including `employee1`, are deleted. As soon as `employee1` is deleted, its destructor is called, sending a final line of output to the console:

```
Deleting employee #1
```

Notice that `employee1`'s destructor isn't called until `main()` has exited.

Before you move on to the next section, take another look at your program's output. If you like, run the program again. Notice that every single line of output was produced by an object's member function. Although you did call `PrintEmployee()` directly, the constructor and destructor functions were called for you when you created and deleted an object.

Consider the following line of code used to delete an `Employee` object:

```
delete employee1;
```

This line of code does not contain a function call. It does not contain code that prints information to the console. Even so, a function call *was* made (the destructor function, called for you). A line of output *was* sent to the console.

The point here is that there's action going on behind the scenes. Stuff happens automatically. You delete an object, and the destructor is called for you. This might seem like a minor point, but it gives you your first peek at the power of object programming.

The friends Mechanism

In the preceding program, the Employee class shared its member functions with the rest of the program by declaring them all as public. Sometimes, this strategy doesn't make sense. Consider the PayRaise() function discussed earlier in the chapter. PayRaise() raises the salary of the specified Employee by 10%. If you mark PayRaise() as public, any function in the program can give any Employee a raise. Not much control there.

On the other hand, if you mark PayRaise() as private, only Employees will be able to give Employees raises. Suppose you create a Supervisor class whose job it is to give out Employee raises. You'll need a way to give Supervisors access to the PayRaise() function without opening the function up to the rest of the world.

The solution to this problem is provided by C++'s friend mechanism. C++ allows you to designate a class or a single member function as a friend to a specific class. For example, you could define a Supervisor class and designate it as a friend to the Employee class:

```
class Supervisor
{
//      Data members...
  private:
    char   supervisorName[ kMaxNameSize ];
    long   supervisorID;
    float  supervisorSalary;
```

```
//      Member functions...
  public:
        Supervisor( char *name, long id, float
          salary );
        ~Supervisor( void );
};

class Employee
{
  friend class Supervisor;

//      Data members...
  private:
    char  employeeName[ kMaxNameSize ];
    long  employeeID;
    float employeeSalary;

//      Member functions...
    void  PayRaise( void ); // This one's private!!
  public:
        Employee( char *name, long id, float
          salary );
        ~Employee( void );
    void  PrintEmployee( void );
};
```

The `friend` statement (see the first line of the `Employee` class declaration) is always placed in the class whose data members and functions are being shared. In this case, the `Employee` class is willing to share its `private` data members and functions with its new `friend`, the `Supervisor` class. Once the `Supervisor` class has `friend` access to the `Employee` class, it can access `private` data members and functions such as `employeeSalary` and `PayRaise()`.

If you wanted to, you could write a `Supervisor` function that called an `Employee` object's `PayRaise()` function. If you marked the `Supervisor`'s `PayRaise()`-calling function as `public`, you'd be taking advantage of the `friend` access to give the world access to a `private` `Employee` function. While this may be interesting, it's probably not a very good design approach.

Three Types of friends

There are three ways to designate a `friend`. First, as you've already seen, you can designate an entire class as a `friend` to a second class.

Second, you can designate a specific class function as a `friend` to a class. For example, suppose the `PayRaise()` function were included in the `Supervisor` class instead of the `Employee` class. You could designate this function as a `friend` of the `Employee` class. Here's the code:

```
class Supervisor
{
//      Data members...
  private:
    char  supervisorName[ kMaxNameSize ];
    long  supervisorID;
    float supervisorSalary;

//      Member functions...
  public:
          Supervisor( char *name, long id, float
            salary );
          ~Supervisor( void );
    void  PayRaise( Employee *employeePtr );
};

class Employee
{
  friend void Supervisor::PayRaise( Employee
    *employeePtr );

//      Data members...
  private:
    char  employeeName[ kMaxNameSize ];
```

```
        long  employeeID;
        float employeeSalary;

//        Member functions...
  public:
            Employee( char *name, long id, float
              salary );
            ~Employee( void );
      void  PrintEmployee( void );
};
```

In this code, the `friend` definition specifies a specific `Supervisor` function instead of an entire class. Since the definition refers to a member function of another class, the full name of the function (including the class name and the two colons) is included.

> The eagle-eyed among you may have noticed the addition of a parameter to the `PayRaise()` function. When `PayRaise()` belonged to the `Employee` class, there was no need to specify the `Employee` receiving the raise. The object used to call `PayRaise()` was the `Employee` whose salary was increased. But, when `PayRaise()` was moved to the `Supervisor` class, there was no longer an implicit reference to an `Employee`. Thus, it was necessary to designate the `Employee` object by passing a pointer to it as a parameter.

Third, you can designate a nonmember function as a `friend`. For example, you could designate `main()` as a `friend` to the `Employee` class. Here's the code:

```
class Employee
{
  friend void main( void );

//        Data members...
  private:
    char  employeeName[ kMaxNameSize ];
```

```
        long   employeeID;
        float employeeSalary;

//       Member functions...
    public:
            Employee( char *name, long id, float
              salary );
            ~Employee( void );
      void  PrintEmployee( void );
};
```

This arrangement gives `main()` access to all `Employee` data members and functions, even those marked as `private`. Just because `main()` is a `friend` doesn't give any special privileges to any other functions, however. Choose your `friends` carefully!

A Friendly Example

Our next example combines the `Employee` class created earlier with the `Supervisor` class described in this section. Close `employee.π` by selecting **Close Project** from the **Project** menu. When prompted for a project file to open, go back up to the `THIN C++ Projects` folder, open the subfolder named `Chap 05.02 - friends`, and open the project file named `friends.π`. Next, run `friends.π` by selecting **Run** from the **Project** menu. Here's what you'll see:

```
Creating employee #1000
Creating supervisor #1002
----
Name:   Dave Mark
ID:     1000
Salary: 200
----
----
Name:   Dave Mark
ID:     1000
Salary: 220
----
Deleting employee #1000
Deleting supervisor #1002
```

Hit a return to exit `friends`. Let's take a look at the source code.

The friends Source Code

`friends.cp` starts out just like `employee.cp`, with the same two `#include`s and the same `const` definition:

```
#include <iostream.h>
#include <string.h>

const short kMaxNameSize = 20;
```

Since the `Supervisor` class declaration refers to the `Employee` class, and the `Employee` class refers to the `Supervisor` class, we need a forward declaration of one of the two classes. In this case, we start with a forward declaration of the `Employee` class. The proper declaration will appear following the `Supervisor` class declaration:

```
class Employee;
```

The `Supervisor` data members are similar to the `Employee` data members. All three are marked as `private`:

```
class Supervisor
{
//      Data members...
  private:
    char  supervisorName[ kMaxNameSize ];
    long  supervisorID;
    float supervisorSalary;
```

The `Supervisor` member functions include a constructor, a destructor, and a `PayRaise()` function. Notice that `PayRaise()` takes a pointer to an `Employee` object as a parameter:

```
//      Member functions...
  public:
          Supervisor( char *name, long id, float
            salary );
```

```
          ~Supervisor( void );
     void  PayRaise( Employee *luckyPerson );
};
```

The Employee class declaration starts with a friend statement, giving the Supervisor class access to all the Employee class data members and functions:

```
class Employee
{
  friend class Supervisor;
```

The Employee data members and functions should look familiar:

```
//      Data members...
  private:
    char  employeeName[ kMaxNameSize ];
    long  employeeID;
    float employeeSalary;

//      Member functions...
  public:
        Employee( char *name, long id, float
          salary );
        ~Employee( void );
    void  PrintEmployee( void );
};
```

The Employee constructor hasn't changed:

```
Employee::Employee( char *name, long id, float
  salary )
{
  strcpy( this->employeeName, name );
  this->employeeID = id;
  this->employeeSalary = salary;

  cout << "Creating employee #" << employeeID << "\n";
}
```

Neither has the `Employee` destructor or the `PrintEmployee()` member function:

```
Employee::~Employee( void )
{
  cout << "Deleting employee #" << employeeID << "\n";
}

void  Employee::PrintEmployee( void )
{
  cout << "----\n";
  cout << "Name:    " << employeeName << "\n";
  cout << "ID:     " << employeeID << "\n";
  cout << "Salary: " << employeeSalary << "\n";
  cout << "----\n";
}
```

The `Supervisor` constructor operates much like the `Employee` constructor. It uses the three parameters to initialize its data members and then sends an appropriate message to the console:

```
Supervisor::Supervisor( char *name, long id, float
  salary )
{
  strcpy( this->supervisorName, name );
  this->supervisorID = id;
  this->supervisorSalary = salary;

  cout << "Creating supervisor #" << supervisorID <<
     "\n";
}
```

The `Supervisor` destructor also sends a message to the console that describes the object just deleted:

```
Supervisor::~Supervisor( void )
{
  cout << "Deleting supervisor #" << supervisorID <<
     "\n";
}
```

The `PayRaise()` function gives the lucky `Employee` a 10% raise in salary (since the `Employee` data member `employeeSalary` is marked as `private`, this function couldn't work if it weren't a `friend` of the `Employee` class):

```
void  Supervisor::PayRaise( Employee *luckyPerson )
{
  luckyPerson->employeeSalary *= 1.10;
}
```

Once again, `main()` is where the action is. We start by defining a couple of pointers, one to an `Employee` object and one to a `Supervisor` object:

```
void  main( void )
{
  Employee    *employeePtr;
  Supervisor  *supervisorPtr;
```

Next, we create a new `Employee` object and a new `Supervisor` object:

```
  employeePtr = new Employee( "Dave Mark", 1000,
    200.0 );
  supervisorPtr = new Supervisor( "Carlos Derr",
    1002, 600.0 );
```

These two lines of code produce the following two lines of output:

```
Creating employee #1000
Creating supervisor #1002
```

Notice that the `Employee` constructor produced the first line while the `Supervisor` constructor produced the second line.

Now, the `Employee`'s `PrintEmployee()` function is called:

```
  employeePtr->PrintEmployee();
```

Take a look at the current salary, as displayed by `PrintEmployee()`:

```
----
Name:   Dave Mark
ID:     1000
Salary: 200
----
```

Then, `employeePtr` is passed to the `Supervisor`'s `PayRaise()` function, and `PrintEmployee()` is called again:

```
supervisorPtr->PayRaise( employeePtr );
employeePtr->PrintEmployee();
```

Here's the output from this second call to `PrintEmployee()`. Notice the new salary?

```
----
Name:   Dave Mark
ID:     1000
Salary: 220
----
```

Finally, the `Employee` and `Supervisor` objects are deleted:

```
    delete employeePtr;
    delete supervisorPtr;
}
```

As each object is deleted, its respective destructor is called, producing the following two lines of output:

```
Deleting employee #1000
Deleting supervisor #1002
```

Summary

So far, you've gotten a taste of object programming. You've learned how to create a class and how to define objects of that class either automatically or by using new. You've also learned about constructors and destructors, and you've seen how these routines are called automatically when an object is created or deleted. Moreover, you've discovered the difference between `private` and `public` data members and functions, and you've learned how to establish a `friend` relationship between a class and another class or function.

Perhaps most important of all, you've started down a new programming path. You're now well on your way to becoming an object programmer. In Chapter 6, you'll move further down that path, exploring some of the fundamental techniques you'll want to develop as your C++ programs become more and more sophisticated.

Chapter 6

Derived Classes

C++ allows you to create classes that are based on other classes. These derived classes retain access to all the data members and member functions of their base class. This feature, known as inheritance, plays a critical role in object programming.

This Chapter at a Glance

Inheritance
  The Protected Access Code
  A Class Derivation Example
Derivation, Constructors, and Destructors
  The Derivation Chain
  A Derivation Chain Example
**Base Classes and Constructors with
    Parameters**
  Another Classy Example
Overriding Member Functions
  Creating an Overriding Function
  An Overriding Example
Summary

C++ ALLOWS YOU TO USE ONE CLASS declaration, known as a **base class**, as the basis for the declaration of a second class, known as a **derived class**. For example, you might declare an `Employee` class that describes your company's employees. Next, you might declare a `Sales` class, based on the `Employee` class, that describes employees in the sales department.

This chapter is filled with examples that emphasize the advantages of classes derived from other classes. As you read through the chapter, focus on the syntax and techniques demonstrated by each example. The mechanics and philosophy presented here form the body and soul of that part of object programming known as **class derivation**.

Inheritance One of the most important features of class derivation is **inheritance**. Just like the cherished heirlooms you hope to inherit from your granduncle Morty, a derived class inherits all of the *nonprivate* data members and member functions from its base class.

As an example, consider the following class declaration:

```
class Base
{
  public:
    short    baseMember;

    void     Base::SetBaseMember( short baseValue );
};
```

This class, `Base`, has two members, a data member named `baseMember` and a member function named `SetBaseMember()`. Both of these members are `public` and will be inherited by any classes derived from this class. Figure 6.1 shows how an object of the `Base` class might look from a memory perspective.

FIGURE 6.1
An object of the Base
class.

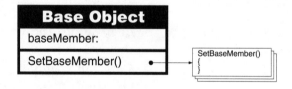

Here's another class declaration:

```
class Derived : Base
{
  public:
    short    derivedMember;

    void     Derived::SetDerivedMember( short
                derivedValue );
}
```

This class is a derived class named, appropriately enough, `Derived`. The ": `Base`" at the end of the title tells you that this class is derived from the class named `Base`. Figure 6.2 shows what a `Derived` object might look like from a memory perspective. As you'd expect, this object has its own copy of the data member `derivedMember` as well as a pointer to the member function `SetDerivedMember()`.

FIGURE 6.2
An object of the `Derived` *class.*

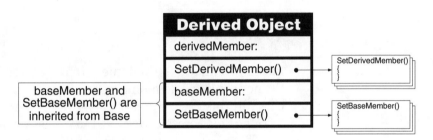

What you might not have expected are the members *inherited* by this object, that is, the `Base` class data member `baseMember` as well as a pointer to the `Base` class member function `SetBaseMember()`. The memory allocated for `baseMember` and the pointer to `SetBaseMember()` belongs to this object, just like the memory allocated for `derivedMember` and the pointer to `SetDerivedMember()`.

Here's some code that allocates a `Derived` object, then accesses various data members and functions:

```
Derived *derivedPtr;

derivedPtr = new Derived;

derivedPtr->SetDerivedMember( 20 );

cout << "derivedMember = " << derivedPtr->derivedMember;

derivedPtr->SetBaseMember( 20 );

cout << "\nbaseMember = " << derivedPtr->baseMember;
```

Notice that the object pointer `derivedPtr` is used to access its own data members and functions as well as its inherited data members and functions. Notice also that the example does not create a `Base` object. This is important. When an object inherits data members and functions from its base class, the compiler allocates the extra memory needed for all inherited members right along with memory for the object's own members. Inheritance is automatic.

The Protected Access Code

Earlier, we made the statement that a derived class inherits all of the nonprivate data members and member functions from its base class. In this case, the term *nonprivate* refers to the `public` and `protected` access codes used in a class declaration.

The `public` access code should be pretty familiar to you by now. A `public` data member or member function is available to any and all of your program's functions. A `protected` data member or function can be accessed only by member functions or friends of its class or by member functions or friends of any classes derived from its class.

In Chapter 5, we adopted the strategy of declaring our data members as `private` and our member functions as `public`. This approach works well for classes with no derived classes. If you plan on using a class as the basis for other classes, declare your data members as `protected` and your member functions as `public`. While this strategy will not work all the time, it is a good starting point.

A Class Derivation Example

So far in this chapter, you've learned how to derive one class from another and you've been introduced to the `protected` access code. Our first sample program brings these lessons to life.

If THIN C++ is already running, close the current project by selecting **Close Project** from the **Project** menu. If THIN C++ isn't running, launch it by double-clicking on the THIN Project

Manager inside the Development folder, inside the THIN C++ folder. Either way, when prompted for a project file to open, go into the THIN C++ Projects folder, open the subfolder named Chap 06.01 - derived, and open the project file named derived.π. Next, run derived.π by selecting **Run** from the **Project** menu. Here's what you'll see:

```
baseMember was set to 10
derivedMember was set to 20
```

Hit a return to exit derived. Let's take a look at the source code.

The derived Source Code

As usual, derived.cp starts by including <iostream.h>:

```
#include <iostream.h>
```

Next, we declare a class named Base, which we'll use later as the basis for a second class named Derived:

```
//------------------------------------- Base

class Base
{
```

Base has a single data member, a short named baseMember, which is declared as protected. Because baseMember is declared as protected and not private, it will be inherited by any classes derived from Base:

```
//      Data members...
  protected:
    short baseMember;
```

Base also includes a member function named SetBaseMember(), which is declared as public:

```
//      Member functions...
  public:
    void  Base::SetBaseMember( short baseValue );
};
```

`SetBaseMember()`, a perfect example of a setter function, sets `baseMember` to the value passed as a parameter:

```
void  Base::SetBaseMember( short baseValue )
{
  baseMember = baseValue;
}
```

Our second class, `Derived`, is derived from `Base`:

```
//-------------------------------------
Base:Derived

class Derived : public Base
{
```

The `public` keyword following the colon in the class title line specifies the access code you'd like assigned to data members and functions inherited from the base class. Here's how this works.

If you attach the `public` keyword to a base class name, all inherited members retain their original access codes. That is, inherited `public` members remain `public` and inherited `protected` members remain `protected`. As mentioned earlier, `private` members are not inherited.

If you attach the `private` keyword to a base class name, or if you don't specify an access code, all inherited members become `private` in the derived class. Take a look at the following two title lines:

```
class Derived : Base
class Derived : private Base
```

These two lines have exactly the same effect. All members inherited by a class marked this way will become `private`. You'd use this technique if you wanted to end the inheritance chain with this class. Why? If a derived class is declared using the `private` keyword, all inherited members will be marked as `private` and are no longer eligible for inheritance by a class using this as a base class.

As a general rule, you should always declare your derived classes using `public` inheritance:

```
class Derived : public Base
```

It's rare that you'd want to reduce the amount of information inherited by a derived class. Most of the time, a derived class is created to *extend* the reach of the base class by adding new data members and functions. As you go through the examples in this and later chapters, the idea of derived classes as extenders will appear again and again.

`Derived` has a single data member, a `short` named `derivedMember`, which, unlike `baseMember`, is declared as `private`:

```
//      Data members...
  private:
    short derivedMember;
```

If we ever used `Derived` as a base class, the new derived class would inherit `baseMember` but it wouldn't inherit `derivedMember`. If we were planning for the future, we might change the `private` to `protected` so that a future class derivation would inherit all possible members.

`Derived` also sports a pair of member functions, `SetDerivedMember()` and `PrintDataMembers()`:

```
//      Member functions...
  public:
    void  Derived::SetDerivedMember( short
            derivedValue );
    void  Derived::PrintDataMembers( void );
};
```

`SetDerivedMember()` is another setter function and sets `derivedMember` to the value passed as a parameter:

```
void  Derived::SetDerivedMember( short derivedValue )
{
  derivedMember = derivedValue;
}
```

`PrintDataMembers( )` prints the value of both `baseMember` and `derivedMember`:

```
void  Derived::PrintDataMembers( void )
{
  cout << "baseMember was set to "
    << baseMember << '\n';

  cout << "derivedMember was set to "
    << derivedMember << '\n';
}
```

What's interesting here is that `baseMember` is inherited, yet it is treated just as if it were one of `Derived`'s data members. When space for a `Derived` object is allocated, space for its inherited members is allocated as well. In this case, 2 bytes is allocated for the object's copy of `baseMember`, and 4 bytes is allocated for the object's pointer to `SetBaseMember( )`. This space is in addition to the space allocated for the data members and functions declared as part of the `Derived` class.

`main( )` starts by declaring a `Derived` pointer and then using `new` to create a new `Derived` object (since we didn't include a constructor for either of our classes, nothing exciting has happened yet):

```
//------------------------------------  main()

void  main( void )
{
  Derived    *derivedPtr;

  derivedPtr = new Derived;
```

Now, things start to get interesting. First, we use the `Derived` object pointer to call the two setter functions (remember, `SetBaseMember( )` is inherited):

```
derivedPtr->SetBaseMember( 10 );
derivedPtr->SetDerivedMember( 20 );
```

Next, we call the `Derived` member function `PrintDataMembers()`:

```
  derivedPtr->PrintDataMembers();
}
```

As you saw when you ran the program, the values of the two data members are successfully set:

```
baseMember was set to 10
derivedMember was set to 20
```

Just as the `Derived` object pointer is able to take advantage of inheritance to call `SetBaseMember()`, `PrintDataMembers()` is able to print the value of the inherited data member `baseMember`.

For the moment, don't worry too much about the advantages of inheritance. Instead, concentrate on the mechanics and syntax of inheritance. Once you master the *how*, the *why* will come naturally.

Derivation, Constructors, and Destructors

When an object is created, its constructor is called to initialize the object's data members. When the object is deleted, its destructor is called to perform any necessary cleanup.

Suppose the object belongs to a derived class, and suppose it inherits a few data members from its base class. How do these inherited data members get initialized? When the object is deleted, who does the cleanup for the inherited data members?

As it turns out, C++ solves this tricky issue for you. Before the compiler calls an object's constructor, it first checks to see whether the object belongs to a derived class. If so, the constructor belonging to the base class is called and then the object's own constructor is called. The base class constructor initializes the object's inherited members, while the object's own constructor initializes the members belonging to the object's class (Figure 6.3).

The *reverse* holds true for the destructor. When a derived object is deleted, the object's destructor is called and then the inherited destructor is called.

FIGURE 6.3

The base class constructor is called before the derived class constructor.

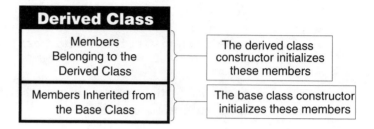

The Derivation Chain

There will frequently be times when you derive a class from a base class that is, itself, derived from some other class. Each of these classes acts like a link in a **derivation chain**. The constructor/destructor calling sequence just described still holds, no matter how long the derivation chain.

Suppose you declare three classes, A, B, and C, where class B is derived from A and C is derived from B. Take a look at Figure 6.4.

FIGURE 6.4

Three classes in a single derivation chain where class B is derived from A and C is derived from B.

Class A	Class B : public A	Class C : public B
Data Members and Member Functions	Data Members and Member Functions	Data Members and Member Functions
	Inherited Members from Class A	Inherited Members from Class B
		Inherited Members from Class A

When you create an object of class B, it will inherit the nonprivate members from class A. When you create an object of class C, it will inherit the nonprivate members from class B, which may include some previously inherited members from class A.

When an object from class C is created, the compiler follows the derivation chain from C to B to A and discovers that A is the ultimate base class in this chain. The compiler calls the class A constructor, then the class B constructor, and finally the class C constructor.

When the object is deleted, the class C destructor is called first, followed by the class B destructor and, finally, by the class A destructor.

A Derivation Chain Example

Our second sample program demonstrates the order of constructor and destructor calls in a three-class derivation chain. Close the current project by selecting **Close Project** from the **Project** menu. When prompted for a project file to open, go up to the THIN C++ Projects folder, open the subfolder named Chap 06.02 - gramps, and open the project file named gramps.π. Next, run gramps.π by selecting **Run** from the **Project** menu. Here's what you'll see:

```
Gramps' constructor was called!
Pops' constructor was called!
Junior's constructor was called!
----
Junior's destructor was called!
Pops' destructor was called!
Gramps' destructor was called!
```

Hit a return to exit gramps. As you can see by the output, each class constructor was called once, then each class destructor was called once in reverse order. Let's take a look at the source code.

The gramps Source Code

gramps.cp starts with the usual #include:

```
#include <iostream.h>
```

Next, the Gramps class is declared:

```
//----------------------------------- Gramps

class Gramps
{
//      Data members...
```

Notice that none of the classes in this program have any data members. For the moment, we're interested only in the order of constructor and destructor calls.

Both the constructor and the destructor are declared `public`, so that they'll be inherited by any class derived from `Gramps`:

```
//      Member functions...
  public:
        Gramps( void );
        ~Gramps( void );
};
```

The `Gramps` constructor and destructor are pretty simple; each prints an appropriate message to the console:

```
Gramps::Gramps( void )
{
  cout << "Gramps' constructor was called!\n";
}

Gramps::~Gramps( void )
{
  cout << "Gramps' destructor was called!\n";
}
```

Our next class is derived from the `Gramps` class:

```
//-------------------------------- Pops:Gramps

class Pops : public Gramps
{
//      Data members...
```

Notice that we use the `public` keyword in the class title line. This ensures that the constructor and the destructor inherited from `Gramps` are marked as `public` inside the `Pops` class. If the `public` keyword were missing from the title line, any class derived from `Pops` would not inherit the `Gramps` constructor and destructor.

Once again, this class has no data members. Both the constructor and the destructor are marked as `public` so that they'll be inherited by any class derived from `Pops`:

```
//       Member functions...
  public:
        Pops( void );
        ~Pops( void );
};
```

> Do you see how easy it is to break the derivation chain? In general, it's a good idea to make things `public` unless you have a reason not to.
>
> One reason to mark something as `private` or `protected` is to hide a piece of data. Just be sure you don't hide your data so well that the rest of your program can't see it!

Just like those of `Gramps`, the `Pops` constructor and destructor are simple and to the point; each sends an appropriate message to the console:

```
Pops::Pops( void )
{
  cout << "Pops' constructor was called!\n";
}

Pops::~Pops( void )
{
  cout << "Pops' destructor was called!\n";
}
```

`Junior` is to `Pops` what `Pops` is to `Gramps`. `Junior` inherits not only the `Pops` members but the `Gramps` members as well (as you'll see in a minute, when you create and then delete a `Junior` object, both the `Gramps` and the `Pops` constructor and destructor will be called):

```
//------------------------------- Junior:Pops

class Junior : public Pops
{
//      Data members...

//      Member functions...
  public:
        Junior( void );
        ~Junior( void );
};
```

The `Junior` constructor and destructor are just like those of `Gramps` and `Pops`; each sends an appropriate message to the console:

```
Junior::Junior( void )
{
  cout << "Junior's constructor was called!\n";
}

Junior::~Junior( void )
{
  cout << "Junior's destructor was called!\n";
}
```

`main()`'s job is to create and delete a single `Junior` object. Watch what happens:

```
//------------------------------------ main()

void  main( void )
{
  Junior    *juniorPtr;
```

When the `Junior` object is created, the derivation chain is followed backward until the ultimate base class, `Gramps`, is reached:

```
  juniorPtr = new Junior;
```

The `Gramps` constructor is called, giving the `Gramps` class a chance to initialize its data members. Next, the `Pops` constructor is called, and, finally, the `Junior` constructor is called:

```
Gramps' constructor was called!
Pops' constructor was called!
Junior's constructor was called!
```

Then, a dividing line is printed, just for looks:

```
    cout << "----\n";
```

Next, the `Junior` object is deleted, and, this time, the derivation chain is followed in the reverse order. The `Junior` destructor is called, then the `Pops` destructor, and, finally, the `Gramps` destructor:

```
    delete juniorPtr;
}
```

Here's the output produced by these destructor calls:

```
Junior's destructor was called!
Pops' destructor was called!
Gramps' destructor was called!
```

Base Classes and Constructors with Parameters

Our first program in this chapter, `derived`, declared two classes, `Base` and `Derived`. Neither of these classes included a constructor. Our second program, `gramps`, featured three classes. Though all three classes declared a constructor, none of the constructors declared any parameters.

Our next example enters uncharted waters by declaring classes whose constructors contain parameters. What's the big deal about constructor parameters? In a world without class derivation, not much. When you add derived classes into the picture, however, things get a bit more complex. Here's why.

Imagine a base class whose constructor sports a single parameter:

```
class Base
{
  Base( short baseParam );
};
```

Now, add a derived class, based on this base class:

```
class Derived : public Base
{
  Derived( void );
};
```

Notice that the derived class constructor is declared without a parameter. When a `Derived` object is created, the `Base` constructor is called. What parameter is passed to this constructor?

The secret lies in the definition of the derived class constructor. When a base class constructor has parameters, you have to provide some extra information in the derived class constructor's title line. This information tells the compiler how to map data from the derived class constructor to the base class constructor's parameter list.

For example, we might define the derived class constructor this way:

```
Derived::Derived( void ) : Base( 20 )
{
  cout << "Inside the Derived constructor";
}
```

Notice the ": Base(20)" at the end of the title line. This code tells the compiler to pass the number 20 as a parameter when the `Base` constructor is called.

This technique is really useful when your derived class constructor also has parameters. Check out the following piece of code:

```
Derived::Derived( short derivedParam ) : Base(
  derivedParam )
{
}
```

This constructor takes a single parameter, `derivedParam`, and maps it to the single parameter in its base class constructor. When a `Derived` object is created, as follows,

```
Derived *derivedPtr;

derivedPtr = new Derived( 20 );
```

the parameter is passed to the `Base` constructor. Once the `Base` constructor returns, the same parameter is passed to the `Derived` constructor.

In the preceding example, the `Derived` constructor does nothing but pass along a parameter to the `Base` constructor. Though it may take some getting used to, this technique is quite legitimate. It is perfectly fine to define an empty function whose sole purpose is to map a parameter to a base class constructor.

Another Classy Example

Our next example combines the class derivation techniques from our first two programs with the constructor parameter-mapping mechanism described in the previous section. Close the current project by selecting **Close Project** from the **Project** menu. When prompted for a project file to open, go into the THIN C++ Projects folder, open the subfolder named Chap 06.03 - square, and open the project file named square.π. Next, run square.π by selecting **Run** from the **Project** menu. Here's what you'll see:

```
Area is: 100
Area is: 150
```

Hit a return to exit `square`. Let's take a look at the source code.

The square Source Code

`square.cp` starts in the usual way, by including `<iostream.h>`:

```
#include <iostream.h>
```

Next, the first of two classes is declared. `Rectangle` will act as a base class:

```
//-------------------------------------- Rectangle

class Rectangle
{
```

As was done in the past, the data members of our base class are declared as `protected`; the member functions, `public`. `height` and `width` hold the height and width of a `Rectangle` object:

```
//      Data members...
  protected:
    short height;
    short width;
```

The `Rectangle()` constructor takes two parameters, `heightParam` and `widthParam`, that are used to initialize the `Rectangle` data members. The member function `DisplayArea()` displays the area of the current object:

```
//      Member functions...
  public:
        Rectangle( short heightParam, short
          widthParam );
    void  DisplayArea( void );
};
```

`Rectangle()` uses its two parameters to initialize the `Rectangle` data members:

```
Rectangle::Rectangle( short heightParam, short
  widthParam )
{
```

```
    height = heightParam;
    width = widthParam;
}

void  Rectangle::DisplayArea( void )
{
  cout << "Area is: " <<
    height * width << '\n';
}
```

The `Square` class is derived from the `Rectangle` class. Just as a square is a specialized form of rectangle (a rectangle whose sides are all equal), a `Square` object is a specialized `Rectangle` object. The `Square` class has no data members, just a single member function, the `Square()` constructor:

```
//-------------------------------------
Rectangle:Square

class Square : public Rectangle
{
//       Data members...
```

The `Square()` constructor takes a single parameter, a `short` named `side`:

```
//       Member functions...
  public:
        Square( short side );
};
```

The `Square()` constructor has one purpose in life. It maps the single `Square()` parameter to the two parameters required by the `Rectangle()` constructor. A square whose side has a length of `side` is equivalent to a rectangle with a height of `side` and a width of `side`:

```
Square::Square( short side ) : Rectangle( side, side )
{
}
```

main() starts by declaring a Square pointer and a Rectangle pointer:

```
//------------------------------------ main()

void  main( void )
{
  Square    *mySquare;
  Rectangle *myRectangle;
```

The Square pointer is used to create a new Square object with a side of 10:

```
  mySquare = new Square( 10 );
```

As specified by the Square() constructor's title line, the compiler calls Rectangle(), passing 10 as both heightParam and widthParam. The Rectangle() constructor initializes the Square object's inherited data members height and width to 10, just as if you'd created a Rectangle with a height of 10 and a width of 10.

Next, the Square object's inherited member function, DisplayArea(), is called:

```
  mySquare->DisplayArea();
```

DisplayArea() uses the inherited data members height and width to calculate the area of the Square:

```
Area is: 100
```

As far as DisplayArea() is concerned, the object whose area it just calculated was a Rectangle. It had no idea it was working with data members *inherited* from a Rectangle. That's part of the power of object programming.

Finally, the `Rectangle` pointer is used to create a new `Rectangle` object with a height of 10 and a width of 15:

```
myRectangle = new Rectangle( 10, 15 );
myRectangle->DisplayArea();
}
```

When we call `DisplayArea()`, it displays the appropriate area:

```
Area is: 150
```

An Important Lesson

This program demonstrates a very important point. With just a few lines of code, we can add a new dimension to an existing class *without modifying the existing class.*

The `Square` class takes advantage of what's already in place, building on the data members and member functions of its base class. Essentially, `Square` added a shortcut to the `Rectangle` class, a quicker way to create a `Rectangle` when the height and width are the same.

This may not seem like a significant gain to you, but there's an important lesson behind this example. C++ makes it easy to build upon existing models, to add functionality to your software by deriving from existing classes.

As you gain experience in object programming, you'll build up a library of classes that you'll use again and again. Sometimes, you'll use the classes "as is." At other times, you'll extend an existing class by deriving a new class from it. With standard, procedural programming, the only way to extend existing code is to rewrite it. By deriving new classes from existing classes, you get the best of both worlds. Code that depends on the base classes will continue to work quite well without modification. Code that takes advantage of the new, derived classes will work just as well, allowing these classes to live in harmony with their base class siblings.

In my mind, this is what object programming is all about.

**Overriding
Member
Functions**

In the preceding example, the derived class, `Square`, inherited the member function, `DisplayArea()`, from its base class, `Rectangle`. Sometimes, it's useful to override a member function from the base class with a more appropriate function in the derived class. For example, you could have provided `Square` with its own version of `DisplayArea()` that based its area calculation on the fact that the height and width of a square are equal.

Here's another example. Suppose you create a base class named `Shape` and a series of derived classes such as `Rectangle`, `Circle`, and `Triangle`. You can create a `DisplayArea()` function for the `Shape` class, then override `DisplayArea()` in each of the derived classes.

Suppose you want to create a linked list of `Shapes`. To simplify matters for the software that manages the linked list, you can treat the derived objects as `Shapes`, no matter what their actual type. Then, when you call the `Shape`'s `DisplayArea()` function, their true identity will emerge. A `Triangle` will override the `Shape` `DisplayArea()` function with a `Triangle` `DisplayArea()` function. The `Rectangle` and `Circle` will have their own versions as well. The point here is that C++ will call the overriding function, if there is one.

Creating an Overriding Function

Creating an overriding function is easy. For starters, make sure the function to be overridden is part of the base class. Next, add the function to your derived class. Finally, add the `virtual` keyword to the function's declaration *in the base class*.

The `virtual` keyword tells the compiler that although this function exists, any calls to it may be overridden. The compiler then builds a table of functions that override this function. Then, when the function is called, instead of jumping to the function's code, the table is used to select the appropriate overriding function.

An Overriding Example

Our final program in this chapter provides a simple example of function overriding by using a base class named Shape and two derived classes, Rectangle and Triangle. Close the current project by selecting **Close Project** from the **Project** menu. When prompted for a project file to open, go into the THIN C++ Projects folder, open the subfolder named Chap 06.04 – whatAmI, and open the project file named whatAmI.π. Next, run whatAmI.π by selecting **Run** from the **Project** menu. Here's what you'll see:

```
I'm a rectangle!
I'm a triangle!
I don't know what kind of shape I am!
```

Hit a return to exit whatAmI. Let's take a look at the source code.

The whatAmI Source Code

whatAmI.cp starts in the usual way, by including <iostream.h>:

```
#include <iostream.h>
```

Next, the base class Shape is declared. Shape contains a single member function, WhatAmI(). When it is called, WhatAmI() tells you what kind of shape it belongs to. Notice that it is declared using the virtual keyword, which tells the compiler that you'd like any overriding function to be called, if one exists:

```
//------------------------------------ Shape

class Shape
{
//      Data members...

//      Member functions...
  public:
    virtual void  WhatAmI( void );
};
```

Here's the definition of `Shape::WhatAmI()`:

```
void  Shape::WhatAmI( void )
{
  cout << "I don't know what kind of shape I am!\n";
}
```

Notice that the `virtual` keyword isn't used here. The `virtual` keyword is only allowed in the function declaration inside the class declaration.

Our next class, `Rectangle`, is derived from the `Shape` class. `Rectangle` also has a single member function named `WhatAmI()`:

```
//-------------------------------------
Shape:Rectangle

class Rectangle : public Shape
{
//       Data members...

//       Member functions...
  public:
    void  WhatAmI( void );
};
```

`Rectangle`'s version of `WhatAmI()` is called when the object doing the calling is a `Rectangle`:

```
void  Rectangle::WhatAmI( void )
{
  cout << "I'm a rectangle!\n";
}
```

Our next class, `Triangle`, is also derived from `Shape`:

```
//-------------------------------------
Shape:Triangle

class Triangle : public Shape
{
//       Data members...
```

```
//       Member functions...
  public:
    void  WhatAmI( void );
};
```

Once again, `Triangle` has its own version of `WhatAmI()`:

```
void  Triangle::WhatAmI( void )
{
  cout << "I'm a triangle!\n";
}
```

Now comes the fun part. `main()` declares three `Shape` pointers, `s1`, `s2`, and `s3`:

```
//----------------------------------- main()

void  main( void )
{
  Shape *s1, *s2, *s3;
```

Each of these pointers is used to create a new object, a `Rectangle`, a `Triangle`, and a `Shape`:

```
  s1 = new Rectangle;
  s2 = new Triangle;
  s3 = new Shape;
```

You may be wondering why the three pointers are all declared as `Shape`s while the objects assigned to the pointers are of three different types. This is intentional. In general, when you pass a derived object around, you refer to it by using its base class type.

For example, if you're building a linked list of shapes, you can store each object in the list as a `Shape` rather than as a `Rectangle` or `Triangle`. In this way, your list management software doesn't have to know what type of shape it is dealing with. If you want to call `WhatAmI()` (or some other, more useful function) for each object in the list, you just step through the list, one object at a time, treating each object as if it were a `Shape`. If the object belongs to a derived class that overrides the function, C++ will make sure the correct function is called.

Once our three objects are created, we try using each object to call `WhatAmI()`:

```
s1->WhatAmI();
s2->WhatAmI();
s3->WhatAmI();
}
```

When the `Rectangle` object is used to call `WhatAmI()`, we get this result:

```
I'm a rectangle!
```

When the `Triangle` object is used to call `WhatAmI()`, we get this result:

```
I'm a triangle!
```

Finally, when the `Shape` object is used to call `WhatAmI()`, we get this result:

```
I don't know what kind of shape I am!
```

In this example, the `Shape` class exists just so that we can create useful, derived classes from it. Creating a `Shape` object is not particularly useful.

def'ə nish' ən

A base class whose sole purpose is to provide a basis for derived classes is known as an **abstract class**. In general, you'll never create an object belonging to an abstract class. Instead, you'll create objects by using classes derived from the abstract class.

Summary   Congratulations! You've made it through the hardest part of object programming with C++. You've mastered most of the skills you'll need to write your own object-oriented programs.

The remainder of this book is dedicated to filling in the gaps. Though there's still a major topic or two to cover, you'll find that most of the toughest aspects of C++ are behind you. Once again, congratulations, and welcome to the world of object programming!

Chapter 7

Operator Overloading

C++ allows you to overload its built-in operators, customizing them to work with objects you define. This chapter provides examples that show you how to take full advantage of this powerful and creative technique.

This Chapter at a Glance

The Operator Overloading Alternative
Calling an Operator Overloading Function
Operator Overloading Using a
   Member Function
Multiple Overloading Functions
An Operator Overloading Example
A Few Restrictions
Covering All the Bases
Overloading an Overloading Function
How Many Versions Are Needed?
An Overloader Overloading Example
Special Cases
Overloading new and delete
An operator new Example
Overloading ()
An operator() Example
Overloading []
An operator[] Example
Overloading ->
An operator-> Example
Overloading =
An operator= Example
Summary

THE C++ FEATURE UP FOR DISCUSSION IN THIS CHAPTER is **operator overloading**. In C++, you can overload any of the built-in operators, such as + or *, giving each one your own personal twist.

For instance, imagine that you're running a restaurant and you want to write some software to handle your billing, print your menus, and so on. Your program might create a `MenuItem` class that looks something like this:

```
class MenuItem
{
  private:
    float    price;
    char     name[ 40 ];

  public:
             MenuItem::MenuItem( float itemPrice,
                char *itemName );
    float    MenuItem::GetPrice( void );
};
```

Your software would define a `MenuItem` object for each item on the menu. When someone orders, you'd calculate the bill by adding together the `price` of each `MenuItem`. Here's an example:

```
MenuItem chicken( 8.99, "Chicken Kiev with salad" );
MenuItem houseWine( 2.99, "Riesling by the glass" );
float    total;

total = chicken->GetPrice()
      + houseWine->GetPrice();
```

This particular diner had the chicken and a glass of the house wine. The total is calculated using the member function `GetPrice()`. Nothing new here.

The Operator Overloading Alternative

Operator overloading provides an alternative way of figuring up the bill. If things are set up properly, the compiler will interpret the statement

```
total = chicken + houseWine;
```

by adding the `price` of `chicken` to the `price` of `houseWine`. Ordinarily, the compiler would complain if you tried to use a nonintegral type with the + operator. You can get around this limitation by giving the + operator a new meaning.

To do this, create a function to overload the + operator:

```
float operator+( MenuItem item1, MenuItem item2 )
{
  return( item1.GetPrice() + item2.GetPrice() );
}
```

Notice the name of this new function. Any function whose name follows the form

```
operator<C++ operator>
```

is said to *overload the specified operator*. When you overload an operator, you're asking the compiler to call your function instead of interpreting the operator as it normally would.

Calling an Operator Overloading Function

When the compiler calls an overloading function, it maps the operator's operands to the function's parameters. For example, suppose the function

```
float operator+( MenuItem item1, MenuItem item2 )
{
  return( item1.GetPrice() + item2.GetPrice() );
}
```

is used to overload the + operator. When the compiler encounters the expression

```
chicken + houseWine
```

it calls `operator+( )`, passing `chicken` as the first parameter and `houseWine` as the second parameter. `operator+( )`'s return value is used as the result of the expression.

The number of operands taken by an operator determines the number of parameters passed to its overloading function. For example, a function designed to overload a unary operator takes a single parameter; a function designed to overload a trinary operator takes three parameters.

Operator Overloading Using a Member Function

You can also use a member function to overload an operator. For example, the function

```
float MenuItem::operator+( MenuItem item )
{
  return( this->GetPrice() + item.GetPrice() );
}
```

overloads the + operator and performs pretty much the same function as the earlier example. The difference lies in the way a member function is called by the compiler.

When the compiler calls an overloading member function, it uses the first operand to call the function and passes the remainder of the operands as parameters. So with the function just given in place, the compiler handles the expression

```
chicken + houseWine
```

by calling `chicken.operator+()`, passing `houseWine` as a parameter, as if you had made the following call:

```
chicken.operator+( houseWine )
```

Again, the value returned by the function is used as the result of the expression.

Multiple Overloading Functions

The previous example brings up an interesting point. What will the compiler do when it encounters several functions that overload the same operator? For example, both of the following functions overload the + operator:

```
float operator+( MenuItem item1, MenuItem item2 )

float MenuItem::operator+( MenuItem item )
```

If both are present, which one is called?

The answer to this question is, neither! The compiler will not allow you to create an ambiguous overloading situation. You *can* create several functions that overload the same operator, however. You might create one version of `operator+()` that handles `MenuItems` and another that allows you to add two arrays together. The compiler chooses the proper overloading function based on the types of the operands.

An Operator Overloading Example

Here's an example that brings some of these concepts to life. First, we'll declare a `Time` class and use it to store a length of time specified in hours, minutes, and seconds. Then, we'll overload the + and *= operators and use them to add two times together and to multiply a time by a specified value.

If THIN C++ is already running, close the current project by selecting **Close Project** from the **Project** menu. If THIN C++ isn't running, launch it by double-clicking on the THIN Project

`Manager`. Either way, when prompted for a project file to open, go into the `THIN C++ Projects` folder, open the subfolder named `Chap 07.01-time`, and open the project file named `time.π`. Next, run `time.π` by selecting **Run** from the **Project** menu. Here's what you'll see:

```
(1:10:50)
(2:24:20)
--------
(3:35:10)
*       2
--------
(7:10:20)
```

Hit a return to exit `time`. Let's take a look at the source code.

The time Source Code

As usual, `time.cp` starts by including `<iostream.h>`:

```
#include <iostream.h>
```

Next, we declare the `Time` class, which is used to store time in `hours`, `minutes`, and `seconds`:

```
class Time
{
//      Data members...
  private:
    short hours;
    short minutes;
    short seconds;
```

The constructor, `Time()`, initializes the three data members according to the values specified by the three parameters. `NormalizeTime()` converts any overflow in the `seconds` and `minutes` data members; for example, 70 seconds is converted to 1 minute and 10 seconds:

```
//      Member functions...
  public:
        Time( short h, short m, short s );
    void  NormalizeTime( void );
```

Display() displays the time stored in the current object.
operator+() overloads the + operator, and operator*=()
overloads the *= operator:

```
    void  Display( void );
    Time  *operator+( Time aTime );
    void  operator*=( short num );
};
```

After the constructor initializes its data members, it calls
NormalizeTime() to fix any overflow:

```
Time::Time( short h, short m, short s )
{
  seconds = s;
  minutes = m;
  hours = h;

  NormalizeTime();
}
```

NormalizeTime() starts by adding the seconds overflow
to minutes, and then it adds the minutes overflow to hours:

```
void  Time::NormalizeTime( void )
{
  hours += ((minutes + (seconds/60)) / 60);
```

Next, the same calculation is performed to calculate a new value
for minutes and then for seconds:

```
  minutes = (minutes + (seconds/60)) % 60;

  seconds %= 60;
}
```

Display() is self-explanatory:

```
void  Time::Display( void )
{
  cout << "(" << hours << ":" << minutes
       << ":" << seconds << ")\n";
}
```

`operator+()` is called when the + operator is used to add two `Time` objects together. The first operand is used as the current object, and the second operand corresponds to the parameter `aTime`:

```
Time   *Time::operator+( Time aTime )
{
   short h;
   short m;
   short s;
   Time   *tempTimePtr;
```

Next, the `hours`, `minutes`, and `seconds` data members of the two objects are added together and stored in the local variables h, m, and s:

```
   h = hours + aTime.hours;
   m = minutes + aTime.minutes;
   s = seconds + aTime.seconds;
```

These local variables are used to create a new `Time` object. Note that the `Time()` constructor automatically normalizes its data members (we don't have to do that here):

```
   tempTimePtr = new Time( h, m, s );
```

Finally, a pointer to our new `Time` object is returned:

```
   return( tempTimePtr );
}
```

`operator*=()` is called when the *= operator is used to multiply a `Time` object by a constant. Notice that `operator*=()` does not return a value because the multiplication is performed inside the `Time` object that appears as the first operand:

```
void  Time::operator*=( short num )
{
```

Each of the `Time` object's data members is multiplied by the specified `short`:

```
hours *= num;
minutes *= num;
seconds *= num;
```

Since we won't be creating a new `Time` object, we call `NormalizeTime()` to fix any overflow problems that may have just been caused:

```
NormalizeTime();
}
```

In general, your overloading functions return a value if it makes sense for the operator being overloaded. If the operator includes an =, chances are you'll make your changes in place and won't return a value, as we did with `operator*=()`. If the operator doesn't include an =, you'll most likely return a value, as we did with `operator+()`.

Before you make the decision, build a few expressions using the operator under consideration. Do the expressions resolve to a single value? If so, then you want your overloading function to return a value.

`main()` starts by defining two `Time` objects (the values in parentheses represent the `hours`, `minutes`, and `seconds`, respectively):

```
void  main( void )
{
  Time   firstTime( 1, 10, 50 );
  Time   secondTime( 2, 24, 20 );
```

`sumTimePtr`, which is a pointer to a `Time` object, is used to receive the result of the + operation:

```
Time   *sumTimePtr;
```

`Display()` is called to display the data members of the two `Time` objects, and then a line is drawn under the two `Time`s:

```
firstTime.Display();
secondTime.Display();

cout << "--------\n";
```

Here are the results:

```
(1:10:50)
(2:24:20)
--------
```

Next, the + operator is used to add the two `Time`s together, and the resulting object is displayed:

```
sumTimePtr = firstTime + secondTime;
sumTimePtr->Display();
```

Here's what this result looks like:

```
(3:35:10)
```

Now, two more lines are sent to the console:

```
cout << "*        2\n";
cout << "--------\n";
```

Here's what they look like:

```
*        2
--------
```

These lines indicate that we'll be multiplying our previous result by 2.

We accomplish this multiplication by using the `*=` operator and then display the results:

```
(*sumTimePtr) *= 2;
sumTimePtr->Display();
}
```

Here's the final time:

```
(7:10:20)
```

If you like, try substituting your own numbers and run the program again.

A Few Restrictions Now that you've mastered the basics of operator overloading, you need to be aware of a few restrictions. First, you can only overload C++'s built-in operators (see Figure 7.1). This means that you can't create any new operators. You can't suddenly assign a new meaning to the letter *z*, for example.

FIGURE 7.1
You can overload these operators.

Overloadable Operators				
+	-	*	/	%
^	&	|	~	!
,	=	<	>	<=
>=	++	--	<<	>>
==	!=	&&	||	+=
-=	/=	%=	^=	&=
|=	*=	<<=	>>=	[]
()	->	->*	new	delete

Second, it may not be obvious from Figure 7.1, but there are a few built-in operators that you can't overload (see Figure 7.2).

FIGURE 7.2
You can't overload these operators.

Nonoverloadable Operators				
.	.*	::	?:	sizeof()

Third, you can't change the way an operator works with a predefined type. For example, you can't write your own `operator()` function to add two `int`s together.

Here's a rule of thumb for you. If you want the compiler to even consider calling your overloading function, either make the function a class member function, or else make one of its parameters an object. Remember, the compiler will complain if you write an `operator()` function designed to work solely with C++'s built-in types.

Fourth, when you overload the `++` and `--` operators, the compiler will not pass the operator's context on to the overloading function. In other words, your overloading function has no way of knowing whether `++` or `--` appeared using prefix or postfix notation. If you overload `++` or `--`, make sure your usage doesn't depend on the positioning of the operator.

Fifth, you can't change an operator's precedence by overloading it. If you want to force an expression to be evaluated in a specific order, use parentheses.

Sixth, overloading functions cannot specify default parameters. This restriction makes sense since a function with default parameters can be called with a variable number of arguments. For example, you could call the function

```
MyFunc( short a=0, short b=0, short c=0 )
```

using anywhere from zero to three arguments. If an `operator()` function allowed default parameters, you'd be able to use an operator without any operands! If you did that, how would the compiler know which overloading function to call? You get the idea.

Covering All the Bases

Earlier in the chapter, we looked at a function that overloaded the `+` operator and was designed to add the `price` of two `MenuItems` together:

```
float operator+( MenuItem item1, MenuItem item2 )
{
  return( item1.GetPrice() + item2.GetPrice() );
}
```

When the compiler encountered an expression like

```
chicken + houseWine
```

where both `chicken` and `houseWine` were declared as `MenuItems`, it called `operator+()`, which passed the two operands as parameters. The `float` produced by adding both `prices` together was returned as the result of the expression.

What happens when the compiler evaluates an expression like

```
chicken + houseWine + applePie
```

This expression seems innocent enough, but look at it from the compiler's viewpoint. First, the subexpression

```
chicken + houseWine
```

is evaluated, resolving to a `float`. Next, this `float` is combined with `applePie` in the expression

```
<float> + applePie
```

Hmmm...what does the compiler do with this expression? We designed an overloading function that handles the + operator when its operands are both `MenuItems`, but we don't have one that handles a `float` as the first operand and a `MenuItem` as the second operand.

Now take a look at the following expression:

```
chicken + (houseWine + applePie)
```

First, the compiler evaluates the subexpression

```
(houseWine + applePie)
```

resolving it to a `float`. That leaves us with the expression

```
chicken + <float>
```

Once again, we designed an `operator+()` function that handles + and two `MenuItems`, but we don't have one that handles a `MenuItem` as the first operand and a `float` as the second operand.

Overloading an Overloading Function

As you can see, you frequently need more than one version of the same `operator()` function. To accomplish this task, you use a technique introduced back in Chapter 4, function overloading. Just as with any other function, you can overload an `operator()` function by providing more than one version, each with its own unique signature.

Remember, a function's signature is based on its parameter list and not on its return value.

How Many Versions Are Needed?

Figuring out how many versions of an `operator()` function to provide is actually pretty straightforward. Start by making a list of the number of possible types you want to allow for each of the operator's operands. Don't forget to include the type returned by your `operator()` function.

In the previous example, we wanted `operator+()` to handle a `float` or a `MenuItem` as either operand, which yields the possibilities shown in Figure 7.3. The left column shows the possibilities for the left operand; the right column shows the possibilities for the right operand. Your list will have `left * right` entries in it, where `left` is the number of types allowed for the left operand and `right` is the number of types allowed for the `right` operand.

FIGURE 7.3

Possible operands for the + operator, given that each operand can be either a float or a MenuItem.

Left	+	Right
float		float
float		MenuItem
MenuItem		float
MenuItem		MenuItem

Figure 7.3 lists four possible operand combinations. The first case involves an expression of the form

```
<float> + <float>
```

As pointed out earlier, you can't create an `operator()` function based solely on built-in types. Fortunately, the compiler does a perfectly fine job of adding two `float`s together.

With this first case taken care of by the compiler, we're left to construct the remaining three `operator+()` functions. Our next program, `menu`, uses function overloading to do just that.

An Overloader Overloading Example

Close the current project by selecting **Close Project** from the **Project** menu. When prompted for a project file to open, go up to the `THIN C++ Projects` folder, open the subfolder named `Chap 07.02 – menu`, and open the project file named `menu.π`. Next, run `menu.π` by selecting **Run** from the **Project** menu. Here's what you'll see:

```
MenuItem::operator+( MenuItem item )
operator+( float subtotal, MenuItem item )

Total: 15.97

MenuItem::operator+( MenuItem item )
MenuItem::operator+( float subtotal )

Total: 15.97
```

Hit a return to exit menu. Let's take a look at the source code.

The menu Source Code

menu starts with two include files and a single constant:

```
#include <iostream.h>
#include <string.h>

const short kMaxNameLength = 40;
```

Next, the `MenuItem` class is declared. The `MenuItem` class contains two data members. `price` lists the price of the item while `name` contains the item's name as it might appear on a menu:

```
//------------------------------------------- MenuItem

class MenuItem
{
   private:
      float    price;
      char     name[ kMaxNameLength ];
```

Notice that both data members are marked as `private`, which shouldn't be a problem since we won't be deriving any new classes from `MenuItem`.

The `MenuItem` class features four member functions. The constructor, `MenuItem()`, initializes the `MenuItem` data members; the `GetPrice()` function serves as a getter function for the `price` data member:

```
   public:
              MenuItem( float itemPrice,
                 char *itemName );
      float   GetPrice( void );
```

The two `operator+()` functions handle the cases where a `MenuItem` object appears as the first operand to the + operator. If the second operand is also a `MenuItem`, the first of the two functions is called; if the second operand is a `float`, the second function is called:

```
      float   operator+( MenuItem item );
      float   operator+( float subtotal );
};
```

The `MenuItem()` constructor copies its first parameter into the `price` data member, and then it uses `strcpy()` to copy the second parameter into the `name` data member:

```
MenuItem::MenuItem( float itemPrice, char *itemName )
{
```

```
    price = itemPrice;
    strcpy( name, itemName );
}
```

GetPrice() returns the value stored in the data member price. Note that this->price is used instead of price (use whichever form you feel more comfortable with):

```
float MenuItem::GetPrice( void )
{
    return( this->price );
}
```

The first version of operator+() handles expressions of the form

```
<MenuItem> + <MenuItem>
```

First, it prints out a message showing which operator+() function is called:

```
float MenuItem::operator+( MenuItem item )
{
    cout << "MenuItem::operator+( MenuItem item )\n";
```

Next, it adds together the two versions of price representing the left and the right operands. this->GetPrice() retrieves the price of the left operand (the MenuItem acting as the current object), and item.GetPrice() retrieves the price of the right operand (the MenuItem passed as a parameter). The sum of these two prices is returned as a float:

```
    return( this->GetPrice() + item.GetPrice() );
}
```

The second version of operator+() handles expressions of the form

```
<MenuItem> + <float>
```

First, it prints out a message showing which `operator+()` function is called:

```
float MenuItem::operator+( float subtotal )
{
    cout << "MenuItem::operator+( float subtotal )\n";
```

Next, it adds together the `price` of the current object, retrieved by calling `GetPrice()`, and the `float` passed as a parameter. The sum is returned as a `float`:

```
    return( this->GetPrice() + subtotal );
}
```

The third version of `operator+()` is, by necessity, not a member function of any class. To understand why this is so, take a look at the expressions this version of `operator+()` is designed to handle:

```
<float> + <MenuItem>
```

As mentioned earlier, the compiler uses the first operand to determine how the overloading `operator()` function is called. If the first parameter is an object, that object is used to call the `operator()` function and all other operands are passed to the function as parameters. If the first parameter is not an object, the compiler's list of candidate overloading functions is reduced to the program's nonclass `operator()` functions. Once a matching function is located, the compiler calls it, passing *all* of the operands as parameters.

Some C++ programmers use the term *object* to designate any structure that occupies memory. Under this model, an int and a `struct` are both objects. Personally, I find that confusing. To me, an object is a variable declared as a member of a class. When you see the word *object* in this book, think *class*.

Just like its compatriots, the third version of `operator+()` starts by printing a message showing which `operator+()` function is called:

```
//------------------------------------ operator+()

float operator+( float subtotal, MenuItem item )
{
  cout << "operator+( float subtotal,
    MenuItem item )\n";
```

Next, the `float` and the `MenuItem`'s `price`, retrieved by calling `GetPrice()`, are added together and returned as a `float`:

```
  return( subtotal + item.GetPrice() );
}
```

OK, here comes the good stuff! `main()` declares three `MenuItem` objects, initializing each with a `price` and a `name`:

```
//------------------------------------ main()

void  main( void )
{
  MenuItem   chicken( 8.99, "Chicken Kiev with salad" );
  MenuItem   houseWine( 2.99, "Riesling by the glass" );
  MenuItem   applePie( 3.99, "Apple Pie a la Mode" );
```

Next, three MenuItems are added together, and a total is printed:

```
  cout << "\nTotal: " <<
    chicken + houseWine + applePie
    << "\n\n";
```

When the compiler encounters the expression

```
chicken + houseWine + applePie
```

it first processes the subexpression

```
chicken + houseWine
```

Since we're adding two `MenuItems` together, the compiler calls the first of our three `operator+()` functions, as shown by the first line of output:

```
MenuItem::operator+( MenuItem item )
```

Next, this subtotal is used to process the remainder of the expression:

```
<subtotal> + applePie
```

Since we're now adding a `float` to a `MenuItem`, the compiler calls the third `operator+()` function, as shown by the next line of output:

```
operator+( float subtotal, MenuItem item )
```

Once the calculations are complete, the total is printed:

```
Total: 15.97
```

Then, the same operators and operands are used, but with a slight wrinkle—the addition of parentheses wrapped around the last two operands:

```
  cout << "\nTotal: " <<
    chicken + (houseWine + applePie);
}
```

These parentheses force the compiler to start by evaluating the subexpression

```
(houseWine + applePie)
```

Once again, we're adding two `MenuItems` together, as shown by the next line of output:

```
MenuItem::operator+( MenuItem item )
```

Next, this subtotal is used to process the remainder of the expression:

```
chicken + <subtotal>
```

Since we're now adding a `MenuItem` to a `float`, the compiler calls the second `operator+()` function, as shown by the following line of output:

```
MenuItem::operator+( float subtotal )
```

Finally, the total is printed and, as expected, matches the earlier total:

```
Total: 15.97
```

Special Cases The remainder of this chapter is dedicated to a few special cases. Specifically, we'll focus on writing `operator()` functions that overload the `new`, `delete`, `()`, `[ ]`, `->`, and `=` operators.

> One characteristic shared by each of these operators is that they can only be overloaded by a class member function. Basically, this means that you won't be using the non-class `operator()` function strategy from our previous example for any of the operators in this section.

Overloading new and delete

In most cases, you won't have any need to overload `new` and `delete`. One exception comes about when you design your own memory management scheme. For instance, you might allocate a large block of memory at the beginning of your program and then use customized versions of `new` and `delete` to parcel out and free up sections of the larger block from within your program.

An operator new Example

Here's a small example you can use as the basis for your own `new` and `delete` `operator()` functions. Close the current project by selecting **Close Project** from the **Project** menu. When prompted for a project file to open, go up to the THIN C++ Projects folder, open the subfolder named Chap 07.03 – new, and open the project file named new.π. Next, run new.π by selecting **Run** from the **Project** menu. Here's what you'll see:

```
new: 2 bytes.
delete: 2 bytes.
```

Hit a return to exit new. Let's take a look at the source code.

The new Source Code

new starts with a couple of #includes, including one we haven't used before, <stddef.h>. The <stddef.h> file contains the definition for size_t (a type that may be familiar to you from the C world):

```
#include <iostream.h>
#include <stddef.h>
```

new defines a class named Blob, which doesn't do much, but it does contain overloading functions for new and delete:

```
//-------------------------------------- Blob

class Blob
{
  public:
    void  *operator new( size_t blobSize );
    void  operator delete( void *blobPtr,
          size_t blobSize );
};
```

There are lots of details worth noting in the new and delete operator() functions. First, notice the space between the words operator and new and between operator and delete. Without the space, the compiler might think you were creating a function called operatornew(), a perfectly legal C++ function name.

Next, note that operator new() returns a void *. This is required. In general, your version of new will return a pointer to the newly allocated object or block of memory. If your memory management scheme calls for relocatable blocks, you might want to return a handle (pointer to a pointer) instead. The choice is yours.

```
void  *Blob::operator new( size_t blobSize )
{
  cout << "new: " << blobSize << " bytes.\n";
  return NULL;
}
```

The `operator new` function must take at least one parameter of type `size_t`. The value for this parameter is provided automatically by the compiler and specifies the size of the object to be allocated. Any parameters passed to `new` will follow the `size_t` in the parameter list.

The `operator delete` function never returns a value and *must* be declared to return a `void`. `delete` always takes at least one parameter, a pointer to the block to be deleted. The second parameter, a `size_t`, is optional. If you provide it, it will be filled with the size, in bytes, of the block pointed to by the first parameter.

```
void  Blob::operator delete( void *blobPtr, size_t
blobSize )
{
  cout << "delete: " << blobSize << " bytes.\n";
}
```

You need this second parameter if you plan on deriving new classes from your original class. Why? Well, even if you know the size of your base class, you have no way of knowing in advance whether this call of `new` is from the base class or a derived class. Basing your allocation on the `size_t` parameter is a bulletproof strategy. Use it in good health!

`main()` creates a new `Blob` and then deletes it:

```
//------------------------------------ main()

void  main( void )
{
  Blob  *blobPtr;

  blobPtr = new Blob;
  delete blobPtr;
}
```

When the `Blob` is created, the overriding `new` is called, and the following line of output appears:

```
new: 2 bytes.
```

Where did the value 2 come from? This value is actually compiler dependent. THIN C++ allocates a minimum of 2 bytes for an object, regardless of whether the object has any data members or not. Pointers to the member functions of a class are stored in a separate table and are not included in the space allocated for an object.

When the object is deleted, the overriding version of `delete` is called, and the next line of output is generated:

```
delete: 2 bytes.
```

It's worth noting that your `operator new` function can itself call `new`, albeit with a different type. For example, you might use the following line of code to allocate a block of 1024 bytes:

```
myBlock = new char[ 1024 ];
```

Overloading ( )

The next special case is the function that overrides the `( )` operator, also known as the *call operator*. One reason to overload the call operator is to provide a shorthand notation for accessing an object's critical data members. As mentioned earlier, ( ) can only be overloaded by a class member function. Here's an example.

An operator( ) Example

Close the current project by selecting **Close Project** from the **Project** menu. When prompted for a project file to open, go up to the THIN C++ Projects folder, open the subfolder named Chap 07.04 – call, and open the project file named call.π. Next, run call.π by selecting **Run** from the **Project** menu. Here's what you'll see:

```
Price of Stimpy doll: $36.990002
Price with 4.5% tax:  $38.654552
```

Hit a return to exit call. Let's take a look at the source code.

The call Source Code
call starts with the standard #include:

```
#include <iostream.h>
```

Next, call defines an Item class. An Item object represents an item for sale at Uncle Ren's Toy-o-rama. For the purpose of this example, I've kept things pretty simple. Item features a single data member, price, and two member functions, the Item() constructor and a function designed to overload the call operator:

```
//----------------------------------- Item

class Item
{
  private:
    float    price;

  public:
        Item( float itemPrice );
    float operator()( float taxRate );
};
```

The `Item( )` constructor copies its parameter into the `price` data member:

```
Item::Item( float itemPrice )
{
  price = itemPrice;
}
```

The `operator( )( )` function may look odd, but the syntax using two pairs of parentheses is correct:

```
float Item::operator()( float taxRate = 0 )
{
```

The first pair of parentheses designates the operator being overloaded; the second pair surrounds any parameters being passed to the function. In this case, one parameter, `taxRate`, is specified. Notice that `taxRate` has a default value of 0. You'll see why in a minute.

The `operator( )( )` function takes the specified `taxRate` and applies it to the `Item`'s `price`, returning the `Item`'s total price:

```
    return( ((taxRate * .01) + 1) * price );
}
```

Since the call operator can only be overloaded by a class member function, the previous reference to `price` refers to the data member of the object used in combination with the call operator.

main( ) starts by creating an `Item` object. The Stimpy doll was Uncle Ren's biggest seller last year (although Log came in a close second):

```
//------------------------------------- main()

void  main( void )
{
  Item  stimpyDoll( 36.99 );
```

Here's where the call overload comes into play:

```
cout << "Price of Stimpy doll: $" << stimpyDoll();
```

By taking advantage of the default parameter, the function call

```
stimpyDoll()
```

returns `stimpyDoll`'s price. We could have accomplished the same thing by coding

```
stimpyDoll.price
```

or

```
stimpyDoll( 0 )
```

but the simpler form is somewhat more elegant and easier on the eye, to boot.

Next, we use the same function to calculate the cost of the doll with 4.5% tax included:

```
cout << "\nPrice with 4.5% tax:  $"
     << stimpyDoll( 4.5 );
}
```

Once again, we take advantage of the overloaded call operator. This time, we provide a parameter. Notice that the same overloading function is used for two different (though closely related) purposes.

You may have noticed that the Stimpy doll's price (including tax) printed as

```
Price with 4.5% tax:  $38.654552
```

Wouldn't it be nice if you could trim the price to `$38.65` (who needs those extra digits, anyway)? Well, stick around until Chapter 8, where you'll learn how to customize `iostream` in all sorts of ways.

The key to properly overloading the call operator is to use it to provide access to a key data member. If your object represents a character string, you might overload ( ) to provide access to a substring, using a pair of parameters to provide the starting position and length of the substring.

Another strategy uses ( ) as an iterator function for accessing data kept in a sequence or list. Each call to ( ) bumps a master pointer to the next element in the list and returns the new data element. No question about it, the call operator is a useful operator to overload.

Overloading [ ]

Another useful operator to overload is [ ], also known as the *subscript operator*. Although it can be used for other things, [ ] is generally overloaded to provide range checking for arrays. You'll see how to do this in a moment.

The subscript overloading syntax is similar to that of the call operator. In the statement

```
myChar = myObject[ 10 ];
```

the [ ] overloading belonging to the same class as myObject is called with a single parameter, 10. The value returned by the function is assigned to the variable myChar.

On the flip side of the coin, the [ ] overloading function *must* support a [ ] expression on the left side of the assignment statement, like so:

```
myObject[ 10 ] = myChar;
```

The next example shows you how to properly overload [ ].

An operator[ ] Example

Close the current project by selecting **Close Project** from the **Project** menu. When prompted for a project file to open, go up to the THIN C++ Projects folder, open the subfolder named

Chap 07.05 – `subscript`, and open the project file named
`subscript.π`. Next, run `subscript.π` by selecting **Run** from
the **Project** menu. Here's what you'll see:

```
B. X. Clinton
index out of bounds!!!
Z. X. Clinton
```

Hit a return to exit `subscript`. Let's take a look at the source
code.

The subscript Source Code

`subscript` starts with some familiar `#includes` and a constant
that is used to declare a string data member:

```
#include <iostream.h>
#include <string.h>

const short kMaxNameLength = 40;
```

The `Name` class is fairly simple. It is designed to hold a NULL-
terminated string containing a person's name as well as a `short`
containing the length of the string:

```
//------------------------------------ Name

class Name
{
  private:
    char      nameString[ kMaxNameLength ];
    short     nameLength;
```

The member functions include a constructor as well as two
operator overloading functions. One function overloads `[ ]`; the
other overloads `( )`:

```
  public:
            Name( char *name );
    void    operator()( void );
    char    &operator[]( short index );
};
```

The constructor copies the provided string to the `nameString` data member and places the length of the string in the `nameLength` data member:

```
Name::Name( char *name )
{
  strcpy( nameString, name );
  nameLength = strlen( name );
}
```

The ( ) operator overloading function simply prints the character string in `nameString`:

```
void  Name::operator()( void )
{
  cout << nameString << "\n";
}
```

The [ ] operator overloading function takes a single parameter, an index into the character string. Notice the unusual return type. By specifying a `char` reference as a return type, the function ensures that the [ ] operator can appear on either side of an assignment statement. Essentially, an expression such as

```
myObject[ 0 ]
```

is turned into a `char` variable containing the character returned by the [ ] overloading function:

```
char& Name::operator[]( short index )
{
```

Here's the real advantage to overloading the [ ] operator. Before you access the specified character, you can first do some bounds checking, making sure the character is actually *in* the character string! If the specified `index` is out-of-bounds, we print a message and point to the first character in the string. In real life, you'd probably want to jump to some error-handling code, but I've decided to keep things simple here:

```
  if ( ( index < 0 ) || ( index >= nameLength ) )
  {
```

```
      cout << "index out of bounds!!!\n";
      return( nameString[ 0 ] );
   }
```

If the `index` is in bounds, the specified character is returned:

```
   else
      return( nameString[ index ] );
}
```

    `main()` contains the proof of the pudding. First, a `Name` object is created, bearing a presidential tag:

```
//------------------------------------ main()

void  main( void )
{
   Name  pres( "B. J. Clinton" );
```

Next, the fourth character in the string is replaced by the character 'X':

```
   pres[ 3 ] = 'X';
   pres();
```

When `pres()` is called, the modified string is displayed:

```
B. X. Clinton
```

Then, the character 'Z' is placed well out-of-bounds and the string is displayed again:

```
   pres[ 25 ] = 'Z';
   pres();
}
```

The `[ ]` overloading function lets you know that the specified index is out-of-bounds and the assignment is performed on the first character of the string instead:

```
index out of bounds!!!
Z. X. Clinton
```

Overloading ->

Next on the special cases list is the -> operator, also known as the *arrow* or *member selection operator*. Like the other operators presented in this section, overloading -> provides a shorthand notation that can save you code and add an elegant twist to your program.

When the compiler encounters the -> operator, it checks the type of the left-hand operand. If the operand is a pointer, -> is evaluated normally. If the operand is an object or object reference, the compiler checks to see whether the object's class provides an -> overloading function.

If no -> overloading function is provided, the compiler reports an error, since the -> operator requires a pointer, not an object. If the -> overloading function *is* present, the left operand is used to call the overloading function. When the overloading function returns, its return value is substituted for the original left operand, and the evaluation process is repeated. When used this way, the -> operator is known as a **smart pointer**.

If these rules sound confusing, hold on. The next example should make them loud and clear.

An operator-> Example

Close the current project by selecting **Close Project** from the **Project** menu. When prompted for a project file to open, go up to the THIN C++ Projects folder, open the subfolder named Chap 07.06 - smartPtr, and open the project file named smartPtr.π. Next, run smartPtr.π by selecting **Run** from the **Project** menu. Here's what you'll see:

```
Name: Bill Clinton
```

Hit a return to exit smartPtr. Let's take a look at the source code.

The smartPtr Source Code

smartPtr starts with some #includes and a constant that you know and love:

```
#include <iostream.h>
#include <string.h>

const short kMaxNameLength = 40;
```

smartPtr defines two classes. The Name class holds two zero-terminated strings containing a person's first and last names. The member function DisplayName() displays the name in the console window:

```
//------------------------------------- Name

class Name
{
  private:
    char    first[ kMaxNameLength ];
    char    last[ kMaxNameLength ];

  public:
          Name( char *lastName, char *firstName );
    void  DisplayName( void );
};

Name::Name( char *lastName, char *firstName )
{
  strcpy( last, lastName );
  strcpy( first, firstName );
}

void  Name::DisplayName( void )
{
  cout << "Name: " << first << " " << last;
}
```

The Politician class represents a politician. To keep things simple, the info is limited to the politician's age and a pointer to a Name object containing the politician's name:

```
//-------------------------------------- Politician

class Politician
{
  private:
    Name     *namePtr;
    short    age;

  public:
            Politician( Name *namePtr, short age );
```

The Politician class also contains a member function designed to overload the -> operator. The function returns a pointer to the politician's Name object (the fact that it returns a pointer is key, as you'll see):

```
    Name     *operator->( void );
};

Politician::Politician( Name *namePtr, short age )
{
  this->namePtr = namePtr;
  this->age = age;
}

Name   *Politician::operator->( void )
{
  return( namePtr );
}
```

main() embeds a last and first name into a Name object and then uses that object to create a new Politician object (so far, no big deal):

```
//-------------------------------------- main()

void  main( void )
{
  Name          myName( "Clinton", "Bill" );
  Politician  billClinton( &myName, 46 );
```

Next, the `Politician` object is combined with the smart pointer to call `DisplayName()`:

```
    billClinton->DisplayName();
}
```

There are several problems here. First, `billClinton` is an object and not a pointer, yet it is used with the `->` operator. Second, the member function `DisplayName()` is not a member of the `Politician` class. How can it be called directly from a `Politician` object?

Basically, the `->` overloading function is doing its thing as a smart pointer by bridging the gap between a `Politician` object and a `Name` member function. When the compiler encounters the `->` operator, it checks the type of the left operand. Since `billClinton` is not a pointer, the compiler checks for an `->` overloading function in the `Politician` class. When the overloading function is found, it is called, using `billClinton` as the current object. The function returns a pointer to a `Name` object. The compiler substitutes this return value for the original, yielding

```
namePtr->DisplayName();
```

The compiler again checks the type of the left operand. This time, the operand is a pointer and the `->` operator is evaluated normally. The `namePtr` is used to call the `Name` function `DisplayName()`, resulting in the following line of output:

```
Name: Bill Clinton
```

As you can see, overloading the `->` operator provides a shortcut that allows you to run a direct line between two different classes.

You can take this model one step further by supposing that the -> overloading function returns a Name object rather than a pointer to a Name object. The compiler then substitutes the Name object in the original expression and reevaluates:

```
myName->DisplayName( );
```

Once again, since the left operand is an object and not a pointer, the left operand's class is examined in search of another -> overloading function. This substitution and call of -> overloading functions is repeated until a pointer is returned (the end of the chain is reached). Only then is the -> operator evaluated in its traditional form.

You can use this technique to walk along a chain of objects. Each -> overloading function evaluates some criteria, returning an object if the search should continue or a pointer if the end condition has been met. C++ is cool, eh?

Overloading =

And now, finally, we've reached the last of the special cases, the operator=( ) function. Why overload the = operator? To best understand why, take a look at what happens when you assign one object to another.

Suppose you define a String class, like this:

```
class String
{
  private:
    char    *s;
    short   stringLength;

  public:
          String( char *theString );
};
```

The data member s points to a NULL-terminated string. The data member **stringLength** contains the length of the string. The constructor **String()** initializes both data members. Notice that no memory has been allocated for s. This is done inside the constructor.

Now suppose you create a pair of **Strings**, like this:

```
String   source( "from" );
String   destination( "to" );
```

And then, you assign one of the **String** objects to the other, like this:

```
destination = source;
```

What happens?

As it turns out, the = operator copies one object to another by a process called **memberwise assignment**. Basically, this means that each data member within one object is copied, one at a time, to the corresponding data member in the receiving object.

The trouble with memberwise assignment is in the way it deals with allocated memory, such as you'd find with a NULL-terminated character string. When one (char *) is copied to another, the address stored in the (char *) is copied, not the data pointed to by the address. Once the statement

```
destination = source;
```

executes, both **Strings** point to the same NULL-terminated string in memory. The default = operator isn't smart enough to allocate the appropriate amount of new memory and then use **strcpy()** to make a copy of the string. That's where **operator=()** comes in.

If you want the ability to assign the contents of one object another, and the objects contain allocated memory, you should write a smart = overloading function that knows how to do it right. Here's an example.

An operator= Example

Close the current project by selecting **Close Project** from the **Project** menu. When prompted for a project file to open, go up to the THIN C++ Projects folder, open the subfolder named Chap 07.07 - equals, and open the project file named equals.π. Next, run equals.π by selecting **Run** from the **Project** menu. Here's what you'll see:

```
String address: 3259462
String address: 3259472
----
String address: 3259462
String address: 3261024
```

Hit a return to exit equals. Let's take a look at the source code.

The equals Source Code

equals starts with the same old #includes:

```
#include <iostream.h>
#include <string.h>
```

The String class described earlier is defined next, with a few additions:

```
//-------------------------------------- String

class String
{
  private:
    char    *s;
    short   stringLength;
```

The constructor still allocates the memory for the specified string, but now two operator overloading functions are added:

```
  public:
          String( char *theString );
    void  operator()( void );
```

```
String  &String::operator=( const String&
    fromString );
};
```

The constructor starts by calculating the length of the specified string, storing the result in `stringLength`. Next, `new` is used to allocate the proper amount of memory (the extra byte is for the `NULL` at the end of the string). Finally, `strcpy()` is called to copy the source string to the data member `s`:

```
String::String( char *theString )
{
  stringLength = strlen( theString );
  s = new char[ stringLength + 1 ];

  strcpy( s, theString );
}
```

If `s` is declared as an array of fixed size, instead of as a dynamic string pointer, memberwise initialization works just fine since the memory for the array is part of the object itself. Since `s` points to a block of memory outside the object, memberwise initialization passes it by.

We again take advantage of the `()` operator to give us a shorthand way of displaying the address of a string:

```
void  String::operator()( void )
{
  cout << "String address: " << (unsigned long)s <<
        "\n";
}
```

Here's the = overloading function. Just like `operator[]()`, this function must return an l-value. In this case, we return a reference to a `String` object. We also take a `String` reference as a parameter. Use the following sample code as a template for all your `operator=()` functions:

```
String   &String::operator=( const String& fromString )
{
```

> Since you can only assign an object to another object of the same class, the type of the return value will always agree with the type of the parameter. `const` in the parameter declaration just marks the parameter as read-only.

`operator=()` starts by freeing up the memory occupied by the old string. Next, the new value for the data member `stringLength` is copied from the source `String`. After that, `new` is used to allocate a block for the new string, and `strcpy` is used to copy the source string into `s`:

```
delete this->s;

this->stringLength = fromString.stringLength;

s = new char[ this->stringLength + 1 ];

strcpy( this->s, fromString.s );
```

Since `this` is a pointer to the current object, `*this` is the object itself. We return `*this` to satisfy our need to return an l-value.

```
return( *this );
}
```

`main()` puts everthing to the test. First, two `String` objects are created and initialized:

```
//------------------------------------ main()

void  main( void )
```

```
{
   String    captain( "Picard" );
   String    doctor( "Crusher" );
```

Next, the address of each `String`'s string is displayed, using the overloaded ( ) operator:

```
captain( );
doctor( );
```

The result is the following two lines of output:

```
String address: 3259462
String address: 3259472
```

Notice that the addresses of the two strings are different.
    Now, a separator line is printed:

```
cout << "----\n";
```

Here's the result:

```
----
```

Then, the object `captain` is assigned to the object `doctor`, and the addresses of the two text strings are again displayed:

```
doctor = captain;

captain( );
doctor( );
}
```

Again, notice that the addresses are different:

```
String address: 3259462
String address: 3261024
```

If the = operator is not overloaded, the address of the `captain` string simply copies into the `doctor` object's s data member and both addresses are the same. Want to prove this? Easy. Comment out the `operator=()` function (every single line, not just the insides) as well as its declaration inside the `String` class declaration, and run the program again.

> To open a source code file, either select **Open** from the **File** menu or double-click on the file name in the project window. Once you make your changes, run the program again by selecting **Run** from the **Project** menu.

Summary

Congratulations are definitely in order here! Personally, I think that operator overloading is the most difficult part of C++ to understand but provides the most fun in experimentation.

Well, the fun isn't over yet. In Chapter 8, You're going to dive into `iostream`. You'll find out how to overload the `<<` and `>>` operators, giving you more control over your output, and you'll learn the difference between file handling in C and file handling in C++. Let's go!

Chapter 8

Inside
iostream

Every sample program in this book has taken advantage of C++'s iostream library. This chapter takes a closer look at iostream's rich feature set.

This Chapter at a Glance

The Character-Based Interface
The iostream Classes
istream and ostream
Working with istream and ostream
Some Useful Utilities
Working with Files
Reading Data from a File
A File-Reading Example
The iostream State Bits
The Coolness of good()
A good() Example
More File Info
Writing Data to a File
Customizing iostream
An >> and << Overloading Example
Formatting Your Output
The Formatting Flags
A Formatting Example
More Flags and Methods
Using Manipulators
The Manipulators
istrstream and ostrstream
A strstream Example
Summary

THROUGHOUT THIS BOOK, WE'VE DEPENDED ON `iostream`'s insertion operator (<<) for all of our output and `iostream`'s extraction operator (>>) for all of our input. While these operators serve us well, there's much more to `iostream` than has been demonstrated so far.

For example, you can easily customize `iostream` so that the >> and << operators recognize your own personally designed data structures and classes. You can also use `iostream` to write to and read from files or even character arrays. As you'll see, `iostream` is a powerful extension of the C++ language.

The Character-Based Interface

`iostream`'s basic unit of currency is the character. Before a number is written to a file, it is converted to a series of `char`s. When a number is read from the console, it is read as a series of `char`s and then, if necessary, converted to the appropriate numerical form and stored in a variable.

`iostream` was designed to support a character-based user interface. As characters are typed on the user's keyboard, they appear on the console. When your program has something to say to the user, it uses `iostream` to send a stream of characters to the console.

If you plan to write programs for environments such as the Macintosh, Windows, or perhaps even a graphical version of Unix (Motif, X-windows, whatever), you'll probably do all your user-interface development using class libraries that come with your development environment. `iostream` doesn't know a thing about drop-down menus, windows, or even a mouse, but as you'll see, it's more than a library of user-interface routines.

Even if your user interface isn't character-based, `iostream` still has a lot to offer. You can use the same mechanisms you'd use to manage your console I/O to manage your program's file I/O. The same methods you'd use to write a stream of characters to a file can be used to write those same characters to an array in memory. What links these disparate techniques is their common ancestry.

The iostream Classes

The `iostream` library is built upon a set of powerful classes. The `iostream` base class is named `ios`. While you might not work directly with an `ios` object, you'll definitely work with `ios'` members as well as with classes derived from `ios`.

istream and ostream

You've already started to work with two classes derived from ios. The istream class is designed to handle input from the keyboard. cin is an istream object that C++ automatically creates for you. The ostream class is designed to handle output to the console. cout, cerr, and clog are ostream objects that are also automatically created for you. As you've already seen, cout is used for standard output. cerr and clog are used in the same way as cout. They provide a mechanism for directing error messages.

Usually cerr is tied to the console, although some operating systems (such as Unix) allow you to redirect cerr, perhaps sending the error output to a file or to another console. cerr is *unbuffered* which means that output sent to cerr appears immediately on the cerr device. clog is a *buffered* version of cerr and is not supported by all C++ development environments. To decide which error output vehicle to use (clog or cerr), consult your operating system manual.

Working with istream and ostream

Up to this point, your experience with iostream has centered on the extraction (>>) and insertion (<<) operators. For example, the following code reads in a number, stores it in a variable, and then prints out the value of the number:

```
short    myNum;

cout << "Type a number: ";

cin >> myNum;

cout << "Your number was: " << myNum;
```

There are a couple of things worth noting in this example. First, the `iostream` input and output are buffered. Just as in C, all input and all output are accumulated in buffers until either the buffers are filled or the buffers are flushed. On the input side, the buffer is traditionally flushed when a carriage return is entered. On the output side, the buffer is usually flushed either when input is requested or when the program ends. Later in the chapter, you'll learn how to flush your own buffers (how exciting!).

The second feature worth noting is that `>>` eats up white space. In other words, `>>` ignores spaces and tabs in the input stream. To `>>`, the line

```
123
```

is the same as this line:

```
123
```

If you're reading in a series of numbers, this works out pretty well. But if you're trying to read in a stream of text, you might want to preserve the white space interspersed throughout your input. Fortunately, `istream` offers some member functions that are white-space savvy.

get( )

The `istream` member function `get()` reads a single character from the input stream. `get()` comes in three different flavors.

The first version of `get()` takes a `char` reference as a parameter and returns a reference to an `istream` object:

```
istream &get(char &destination);
```

Since `get()` is an `istream` member function, you can use `cin` to call it (after all, `cin` is just an `istream` object):

```
char   c;

cin.get( c );
```

This version of `get()` reads a single character from the input stream, writes the `char` into its `char` parameter (`c`), and then returns the input stream reference (`cin`). Since `get()` returns the input stream, it can be used in a sequence, as in the following example:

```
char  c;
short myShort;

cout << "Type a char and a short: ";

cin.get( c ) >> myShort;
```

This code grabs the first character from the input stream and stores it in `c`. Next, the input stream is parsed for a `short`, and the `short` is placed in `myShort`. If the input to this example were

```
123
```

then `c` would end up with the character 1, while `myShort` would end up with the value 23.

The second version of `get()` is declared as follows:

```
istream &get(char *buffer, int length, char
           delimiter = '\n');
```

This version of `get()` extracts up to `length` characters and stores them in the memory pointed to by `buffer`. If the `char` `delimiter` is encountered in the input stream, the `char` is pushed back into the stream and the extraction stops. For example, the code

```
char  buffer[ 10 ];

cin.get( buffer, 10, '*' );
```

starts to read characters from the input stream. If a `*` is encountered, the extraction stops, the `*` is pushed back into the stream, and a `NULL` is placed at the end of the string just read into `buffer`.

If no * is encountered, nine characters are read into `buffer`, and, again, `buffer` is NULL-terminated. Notice that `get()` reads only *n* – 1 characters, where *n* is specified as the second parameter; `get()` is smart enough to save one byte for the NULL terminator.

If the third parameter is left out, this version of `get()` uses `'\n'` as the terminating character. This allows you to use `get()` to extract a full line of characters without overflowing your input buffer. For example, the code

```
char   buffer[ 50 ];

cin.get( buffer, 50 );
```

reads up to 49 characters or one line from the input stream, whichever is shorter. Either way, the string stored in `buffer` gets NULL-terminated.

The third version of `get()` is declared as follows:

```
int get();
```

This version of `get()` reads a single character from the input stream and returns the character, cast as an `int`, as in the following example:

```
int   c;

while ( (c = cin.get()) != 'q' )
   cout << (char)c;
```

This code reads the input stream, one character at a time, until a q is read. Each character is echoed to the console as it is read.

The third version of `get()` returns an `int` and not a `char` to allow it to return the end-of-file character. Typically, EOF has a value of –1. By returning an `int`, `get()` allows for 256 possible `char` values as well as for the end-of-file character. Although EOF isn't particularly useful when reading from the console, we'll use this version of `get()` later in the chapter to read the contents of a file.

getline( )

Another `istream` member function that you might find useful is `getline()`:

```
istream &getline(char *buffer, int length, char
delimiter = '\n');
```

`getline()` behaves just like the second version of `get()`, but it returns the delimiter character instead of pushing it back into the input stream.

ignore( )

`ignore()` is used to discard characters from the input stream:

```
istream &ignore(int length = 1, int delimiter = EOF);
```

`ignore()` follows the same basic algorithm as `getline()`. It reads up to `length` characters from the input stream and discards them. This extraction stops if the specified `delimiter` is encountered. Notice that each of these parameters has a default value, which allows you to call `ignore()` without parameters.

Here's an example:

```
char  buffer[ 100 ];

cin.ignore( 3 ).getline( buffer, 100 );

cout << buffer;
```

This code drops the first three characters from the input stream and then reads the remainder of the first line of input into `buffer`. Next, the string stored in `buffer` is sent to the console. Notice that the value returned by `ignore()` is used to call `getline()`. This is equivalent to the following sequence of code:

```
cin.ignore( 3 );
cin.getline( buffer, 100 );
```

Once again, pick a style you're comfortable with and stick with it.

peek( )

peek( ) allows you to sneak a peek at the next character in the input stream without removing the character from the stream:

```
int peek();
```

Just like the third version of get( ), peek( ) returns an int rather than a char. This allows peek( ) to return the end-of-file character, if appropriate, which makes peek( ) perfect for peeking at the next byte in a file.

putback( )

putback( ) puts the specified char back into the input stream, making it the next character to be returned by the next input operation:

```
istream &putback(char c);
```

Note that c must be the last character extracted from the stream. Since putback( ) returns an istream reference, it can be used in a sequence, similar to the example combining ignore( ) and getline( ) shown earlier.

put( )

The ostream member function put( ) provides an alternative to the << operator for writing data to the output stream:

```
ostream &put(char c);
```

put( ) writes the specified character to the output stream. It then returns a reference to the stream, so put( ) can be used in a sequence. Here's an example:

```
cout.put( 'H' ).put( 'i' ).put( '!' );
```

As you might have guessed, the preceding line of code produces this friendly message:

```
Hi!
```

seekg( ) and seekp( )

The `istream` member function `seekg()` gives you random access to an input stream:

```
istream&   seekg(streampos p);
```

Call `seekg()` to position a stream's `get` pointer exactly where you want it. A second version of `seekg()` allows you to position the `get` pointer relative to the beginning or end of a stream or relative to the current `get` position:

```
istream&   seekg( streamoff offset, relative_to
  direction );
```

In this second version of `seekg()`, the second parameter is one of `ios::beg`, `ios::cur`, or `ios::end`.

The `ostream` member function `seekp()` gives you random access to an output stream:

```
ostream&   seekp(streampos p);
```

Just like `seekg()`, `seekp()` allows you to position a stream's put pointer exactly where you want it. `seekp()` also comes in a second flavor:

```
ostream&   seekp( streamoff offset, relative_to
  direction );
```

For more detail on `seekg()`, `seekp()`, and their miscellaneous support routines, browse through `<iostream.h>`.

Some Useful Utilities

To aid you with your stream input and output operations, C++ provides a set of standard utilities that you may find useful (plain old ANSI C also provides these routines). To use any of the utilities described in this section, you must include the header file `<ctype.h>`.

Each of the thirteen functions takes an `int` as a parameter. The `int` represents an ASCII character. Two of the functions, `tolower()` and `toupper()`, map this character either to its lowercase or its uppercase ASCII equivalent. For example, `tolower( 'A' )` would return `'a'`, while `toupper( 'x' )` would return `'X'`.

The remaining eleven functions return either `true` or `false`, depending on the nature of the character passed in. The function `isalpha()` returns `true` if its argument is a character in the range `'a'` through `'z'` or in the range `'A'` through `'Z'`. The function `isdigit()` returns `true` if its argument is a character in the range `'0'` through `'9'`. The function `isalnum()` returns `true` if its argument causes either `isalpha()` or `isdigit()` to return `true`.

The function `ispunct()` returns `true` if the character is a punctuation character. The punctuation characters are ASCII characters in the ranges 33–47, 58–64, 91–96, and 123–126 (consult your nearest ASCII chart). The function `isgraph()` returns `true` if its argument causes `isalpha()`, `isdigit()`, or `ispunct()` to return `true`.

`islower()` returns `true` if the character is in the range `'a'` through `'z'`. `isupper()` returns `true` if the character is in the range `'A'` through `'Z'`. `isprint()` returns `true` if the character is a printable ASCII character. `iscntrl()` returns `true` if the character is a control character. `isspace()` returns `true` if the character has an ASCII value in the range 9–13 or if it has a value of 32 (space). Finally, `isxdigit()` returns `true` if the character is a legal hex digit (0–9, a–f, or A–F).

The thirteen functions just described are summarized in the table in Figure 8.1.

Working with Files

`iostream` contains two classes created especially for working with files. The `ifstream` class is derived from `istream` and is designed to read data from a file. Since `ifstream` inherits `istream`'s member functions, you can use an `ifstream` object to take advantage of `istream` functions like `get()`.

FIGURE 8.1
*Some useful utilities.
Don't forget to include
the file <ctype.h>.*

Some Useful Utilities	
int isalnum(int);	True if char isalpha() or isdigit().
int isalpha(int);	Is char in range a–z or A–Z?
int iscntrl(int);	Is char control character?
int isdigit(int);	Is char in range 0–9?
int isgraph(int);	True if char isalpha() or isdigit() or ispunct().
int islower(int);	Is char in range a–z?
int isprint(int);	Is char printable ASCII character?
int ispunct(int);	Is char in ASCII range 33–47, 58–64, 91–96, 123–126?
int isspace(int);	Is char in ASCII range 9–13 or 32?
int isupper(int);	Is char in range A to Z?
int isxdigit(int);	Is char in ASCII range 0–9, a–f, A–F?
int tolower(int);	Maps upper case to lower case.
int toupper(int);	Maps lower case to upper case.

The `ofstream` class is derived from `ostream` and is designed to write data to a file. Since `ofstream` inherits `ostream`'s member functions, you can use an `ofstream` object to take advantage of `ostream` functions like `put()`.

Reading Data from a File

The `ifstream` constructor comes in several varieties. The most widely used of these takes two parameters:

```
ifstream(const char* name, int mode=ios::in );
```

The first parameter is a `NULL`-terminated string containing the name of a file to be opened. The second describes the mode used to open the file. The legal modes are described in the table in Figure 8.2. They are declared as part of the `ios` class (check out `<iostream.h>`). The default mode is `ios::in`, which opens the file for reading.

FIGURE 8.2

These file-opening modes are declared as part of the ios class.

File-Opening Modes	
ios::in	Input allowed
ios::out	Output allowed
ios::ate	Seek to EOF at open
ios::app	Output allowed, append only
ios::trunc	Output allowed, discard existing contents
ios::nocreate	Open fails if file *doesn't* exist
ios::noreplace	Open fails if file *does* exist

Some operating systems (such as Unix) support a third, optional parameter for `ifstream` (and for `ofstream` as well). The third parameter specifies the protection level used to open the file. In general, the protection parameter is used only with multiple-user operating systems where more than one person has access to the same set of files. Read your development environment manual to see whether this extra parameter is supported.

Since you'll most likely want to use the default mode of `ios::in` when you open a file for reading, you can leave off the last parameter when you create an `ifstream` object:

```
ifstream    readMe( "My File" );
```

This definition creates an `ifstream` object named `readMe`. Next, it opens a file named `My File` for reading, attaching the open file to `readMe`.

`ifstream` objects have data members that track whether a file is attached to the stream and, if so, whether the file is open for reading. If a file is attached and open for reading, a `get` pointer is maintained that marks how far you've read into the file. Normally, the `get` pointer starts life at the very beginning of the file.

Once your file is opened for reading, you can use all of the `iostream` input functions described earlier to read data from the file. For example, the following code opens a file and then reads a single character from it:

```
char        c;
ifstream    readMe( "My File" );

readMe.get( c );
```

A File-Reading Example

Our first sample program uses this technique to read a file and display the contents in the console window. If THIN C++ is already running, close the current project by selecting **Close Project** from the **Project** menu. If THIN C++ isn't running, launch it by double-clicking on the THIN Project Manager. Either way, when prompted for a project file to open, go into the THIN C++ Projects folder, open the subfolder named Chap 08.01 – readMe, and open the project file named readMe.π. Next, run readMe.π by selecting **Run** from the **Project** menu. Here's what you'll see:

```
The Darlan-Ferengi wars raged on
for centuries before the final battle,
known as the "Dawn of Arcturus", was fought.
```

Hit a return to exit readMe. Let's take a look at the source code.

The readMe Source Code

As usual, readMe.cp starts by including <iostream.h>. Next, you'll encounter a new include file, <fstream.h>, which contains the declarations of the ifstream and ofstream classes (take some time and look through this include file; you'll learn a lot about the nooks and crannies of iostream file management):

```
#include <iostream.h>
#include <fstream.h>
```

main( ) starts by defining an `ifstream` object named `readMe`, asking the constructor to open the file named `My File` with the default mode of `ios::in`:

```
void  main( void )
{
  ifstream  readMe( "My File" );
```

We're now ready to read the contents of the file.

The variable `c` is used to hold each character read from the file:

```
char    c;
```

Next comes a `while` loop that reads the contents from the file associated with `readMe`, one character at a time. Each time a character is successfully read, it is written out to the console. Notice that the `ifstream` object `readMe` is used just like the `istream` object `cin` when it comes to calling `get()`, which is true for all of the other `istream` member functions as well:

```
while ( readMe.get( c ) )
  cout << c;
}
```

You may be wondering how this loop ever terminates. Since `get()` returns an `istream` reference, how will `readMe.get( c )` ever evaluate to false? The answer to this question lies in understanding the `iostream` state bits.

The iostream State Bits

Every stream, whether an `istream` or an `ostream`, has a series of four **state bits** associated with it:

```
enum io_state
{
  goodbit=0,
  eofbit=1,
  failbit=2,
  badbit=4
};
```

iostream uses these bits to indicate the relative health of their associated stream. You can poke and prod these bits yourself, but there are four functions that reflect each bit's setting.

For example, the function

```
int good();
```

returns nonzero if the stream used to call it is ready for I/O. Basically, if good() returns true, you can assume that all is right with your stream and expect that your next I/O operation will succeed.

The function

```
int eof();
```

returns true if the last I/O operation puts you at end-of-file.

The function

```
int fail();
```

returns true if the last operation fails for some reason. As an example, an input operation might fail if you try to read a short but encounter a text string instead.

The function

```
int bad();
```

returns true if the last operation fails *and* the stream appears to be corrupted. When bad() returns true, you're in deep guacamole.

Finally, the function

```
void    clear( int newState=0 );
```

is used to reset the state bits to the state specified as a parameter. In general, you should call clear() without specifying a parameter. clear()'s default parameter sets the state bits back to the pristine, good setting. If you don't clear the state bits after a failure, you won't be able to continue reading data from the stream. (You'll see an example of this in a moment.)

For the most part, you should focus on the value returned by `good()`. As long as `good()` returns `true`, there's no need to check any of the other functions. Once `good()` returns `false`, you can find out why by querying the other three state functions.

The Coolness of good( )

Now comes the cool part. In the program `readMe.cp`, we encountered a `while` loop that used an `iostream` function as its conditional expression:

```
while ( readMe.get( c ) )
    cout << c;
```

What caused this `while` loop to exit? `readMe.get( c )` returns a reference to `readMe`, correct? Actually, this is where the C++ compiler displays a little sleight of hand. When the compiler detects an `iostream` I/O function used as a conditional expression, it checks to see whether the function returns a stream reference. If so, the compiler uses the current value of `good()` as the return value for the function. The previous `while` loop exits when `readMe.get( c )` either fails or hits an end-of-file.

A good( ) Example

Our second sample program demonstrates the basics of working with the `iostream` state bits and state bit functions. Close the current project by selecting **Close Project** from the **Project** menu. When prompted for a project file to open, go up to the `THIN C++ Projects` folder, open the subfolder named `Chap 08.02 - stateBits`, and open the project file named `stateBits.π`. Next, run `stateBits.π` by selecting **Run** from the **Project** menu. Here's what you'll see:

```
Type a number:
```

Type a number small enough to fit inside a `short`, like 256:

```
Type a number: 256
```

When you hit a return, `stateBits` will tell you what your number is and then ask you to type another:

```
Your number is: 256

Type a number:
```

This time, type the letter *x* and hit a return. `stateBits` will tell you that the *x* is not a number and then ask you for another number:

```
Type a number: x
x is not a number...Type 0 to exit

Type a number:
```

Now type the number 0, which tells `stateBits` to drop out of its main loop:

```
Type a number: 0
Goodbye...
```

Hit a return to exit `stateBits`. Let's take a look at the source code.

The stateBits Source Code

`stateBits.cp` starts with the usual `#include` (since we won't be doing any file I/O, there's no need to include `<fstream.h>`):

```
#include <iostream.h>
```

`stateBits` creates a loop that reads in a number and then prints the number in the console window. If the number entered is 0, the program exits. Things start to get interesting when a letter is entered instead of a number.

```
void  main( void )
{
  char  done = false;
  char  c;
  short number;
```

Note that done acts as a Boolean logic operator. When it is set to true, the loop exits. c and number are used to hold data read from the console.

> Some C++ environments declare true and false; others don't. Since true and false aren't technically part of the ANSI C++ standard, be prepared to add them to your header files. THIN C++ takes care of this for you.

We enter the main loop, are prompted for a number and then use >> to read the number from the console:

```
while ( ! done )
{
  cout << "Type a number: ";
  cin >> number;
```

If a number appropriate for a short is typed at the prompt, cin.good() returns true:

```
  if ( cin.good() )
```

If the number typed is 0, we say goodbye and drop out of the loop; otherwise, we display the number and start all over again:

```
  {
    if ( number == 0 )
    {
      cout << "Goodbye...";
      done = true;
    }
    else
      cout << "Your number is: " << number
              << "\n\n";
  }
```

If the input is of the wrong type (the letter *x* or 1.34, for instance) or is a number that is too large (99999) or too small (–72999), the input operation fails and `cin.fail()` returns `true`:

```
else if ( cin.fail() )
```

The first thing we must do is call `clear()` to reset the state bits (if we don't clear the state bits back to their supple, healthy state, we won't be able to continue reading data from the stream):

```
{
  cin.clear();
```

Once the state bits are reset, we read the character that caused the the stream to choke. Since we're not trying to interpret this character as a number, this read won't fail. Having read in the offending character, we display it, along with an appropriate message on the console:

```
cin.get( c );
cout << c << " is not a number...";
cout << "Type 0 to exit\n\n";
}
```

This example implements a pretty simple-minded recovery algorithm. If you typed in something like *xxzzy*, the loop would fail five times since you knock out only a single character with each recovery. You might want to try your hand at a more sophisticated approach. For example, you might use `cin.ignore()` to suck in all the characters up to and including a carriage return. Better yet, you might use `cin.get()` to read in the remainder of the offending characters and then package them in an appropriate error message.

The final possibility lies with a call to bad(). Since the bad bit will likely never be set, you'll probably never see this message. No sense taking chances, though:

```
else if ( cin.bad() )
{
  cout << "\nYikes!!! Gotta go...";
  done = true;
}
}
}
```

More File Info

Earlier, the ifstream constructor was used to open a file for reading:

```
ifstream  readMe( "My File" );
```

In the same way, the ofstream constructor can be used to open a file for writing:

```
ofstream writeMe( "My File" );
```

Writing Data to a File

The ofstream constructor takes two parameters, with ios::out used as the default mode parameter. Note that you can pass more than one mode flag at a time. To open a file for writing if the file *doesn't* already exist, try something like this:

```
ofstream writeMe( "My File", ios::out |
ios::nocreate );
```

Refer back to the table in Figure 8.2 for the rest of the mode flags.

There is a way to open a file for both reading and writing. The heck you say? It's true! Use the `fstream` class and pass both the `ios::in` and `ios::out` mode flags, like this:

```
fstream  inAndOut( "Read and Write", ios::in
  | ios::out );
```

The `fstream` class is set up with two file position indicators, one for reading and one for writing. You really should read through the file `<fstream.h>`. You'll find all kinds of cool stuff in there. While you're at it, read through `<iostream.h>` as well. If you see a file named `<stream.h>`, beware! `<stream.h>` was written to support a library known as `streams`, a predecessor to `iostream`. `<stream.h>` is obsolete.

Once your file is open, you can close it by calling the `close()` member function:

```
writeMe.close();
```

In general, this call isn't really necessary since the `ifstream` and `ofstream` destructors automatically close the file attached to their associated stream.

You can also create an `ifstream` or `ofstream` without associating it with a file. Why would you want to do this? If you planned on opening a series of files, one at a time, you might want to do this by using a single stream, not by declaring one stream for each file. Using a single stream is more economical. Here's an example:

```
ifstream    readMe;

readMe.open( "File 1" );
// Read contents - be sure to include error
checking!
readMe.close();
```

```
readMe.open( "File 2" );
// Read contents - be sure to include error
checking!
readMe.close();

// Repeat this as necessary...
```

read( ), write( ), and Others

There are some `istream` member functions that are particularly useful when dealing with files. The member function `read( )` reads a block of `size` bytes and stores the bytes in the buffer pointed to by `data`:

```
istream &read(void *data, int size);
```

As you'd expect, if an end-of-file is reached before the requested bytes are read, the `fail` bit is set. The member function `istream::gcount( )` returns the number of bytes successfully read:

```
size_t gcount( );
```

The member function `write( )` inserts a block of `size` bytes from the buffer pointed to by `data`:

```
ostream &write(const void *data, size_t size);
```

The member function `ostream::pcount( )` returns the number of bytes inserted by the preceding `write( )` call:

```
size_t pcount( );
```

Customizing iostream

There are times when the standard operators and member functions of `iostream` just don't cut it. For example, remember the `MenuItem` class we declared in Chapter 7:

```
class MenuItem
{
  private:
    float    price;
    char     name[ 40 ];
```

```
    public:
            MenuItem::MenuItem( float itemPrice,
              char *itemName );
    float   MenuItem::GetPrice( void );
};
```

Suppose you want to display the contents of a `MenuItem` using `iostream`. You can write a `DisplayMenuItem()` member function that takes advantage of `iostream`, but that is somewhat awkward. If you want to display a `MenuItem` in the middle of a `cout` sequence, you have to break the sequence up, sandwiching a call to `DisplayMenuItem()` in the middle:

```
cout << "Today's special is: ";
myItem.DisplayMenuItem();
cout << "...\n";
```

Wouldn't it be nice if `iostream` knew about `MenuItems` so that you could do something more convenient, like this:

```
cout << "Today's special is: " << myItem << "...\n";
```

Why, there *is* a way to do this, after all! Using the techniques covered in Chapter 7, you create an `operator<<()` function that knows exactly how you want your `MenuItem` displayed. (You'll see an example of this in a moment.)

What's more, you can overload the `>>` operator, providing an `operator>>()` function that knows how to read in a `MenuItem`. The only restriction on both of these cases is that your `>>` and `<<` overloading functions must return the appropriate stream reference so that you can use the `>>` and `<<` operators in a sequence.

An >> and << Overloading Example

Our next sample program extends the `ostream` and `istream` classes by adding functions that overload both `>>` and `<<`. Close the current project by selecting **Close Project** from the **Project** menu. When prompted for a project file to open, go into the THIN C++ Projects folder, open the subfolder named Chap 08.03 – overload, and open the project file named overload.π. Next, run overload.π by selecting **Run** from the **Project** menu. Here's what you'll see:

```
Spring Rolls ($2.99)
Hot and Sour Soup ($3.99)
Hunan Chicken ($8.99)
General Tso's Shrimp ($9.99)
```

Hit a return to exit overload. Let's take a look at the source code.

The overload Source Code

overload.cp starts with some familiar #includes and a const definition from Chapter 7's menu program:

```
#include <iostream.h>
#include <fstream.h>
#include <string.h>

const short kMaxNameLength = 40;
```

The MenuItem class is a slightly modified version of the one in Chapter 7. For one thing, the constructor is left out. Instead of initializing the data members when a MenuItem is created, iostream is used to read in a series of MenuItems from a file and initialize each data member using the newly added SetName() and SetPrice() member functions:

```
//------------------------------------ MenuItem

class MenuItem
{
  private:
    float    price;
    char     name[ kMaxNameLength ];

  public:
    void     SetName( char *itemName );
    char     *GetName( void );
    void     SetPrice( float itemPrice );
    float    GetPrice( void );
};
```

SetName() is used to set the value of the name data member:

```
void  MenuItem::SetName( char *itemName )
{
  strcpy( name, itemName );
}
```

GetName() returns a pointer to the name data member. By giving the caller of this public function direct access to name, we're sort of defeating the purpose of marking name as private. A more appropriate approach might be to have GetName() return a copy of name. For the purposes of discussion, the version of GetName() shown next will do:

```
char  *MenuItem::GetName( void )
{
  return( this->name );
}
```

SetPrice() is used to set the value of the price data member:

```
void  MenuItem::SetPrice( float itemPrice )
{
  price = itemPrice;
}
```

GetPrice() returns the value of the price data member:

```
float MenuItem::GetPrice( void )
{
  return( this->price );
}
```

The operator>>() function is called by the compiler whenever the >> operator is encountered having an istream as its left operand and a MenuItem as its right operand. Since all >> sequences are resolved to istream references, the left operand is always an istream object. To make this a little clearer, imagine an >> sequence with several objects in it:

```
cin >> a >> b;
```

`iostream` starts by evaluating this expression from the left, as if it were written like this:

```
(cin >> a) >> b;
```

Since the >> operator resolves to an `istream` object, the expression `cin >> a` resolves to `cin`, leaving this:

```
cin >> b;
```

The same logic holds true for the << operator:

```
cout << a << b;
```

As the compiler evaluates this expression from left to right, the left operand of the << operator is always an `ostream` object.

The point is, whether `istream` or `ostream`, all an `operator()` function needs to do to support sequences is to return the stream reference passed in as the first parameter:

```
//------------------------  iostream operators


istream &operator>>( istream &is, MenuItem &item )
{
  float itemPrice;
  char  itemName[ kMaxNameLength ];
```

`operator>>()` reads a single `MenuItem` object from the specified input stream. First, `getline()` is used to read the item's name. Notice that the second parameter to `getline()` is used to limit the number of characters read in, ensuring that `itemName` doesn't exceed its bounds. `SetName()` is used to copy the entered name into the `name` data member:

```
  is.getline( itemName, kMaxNameLength );
  item.SetName( itemName );
```

Then, >> is used to read the item's price into itemPrice, and SetPrice() is used to copy itemPrice into the price data member:

```
is >> itemPrice;
item.SetPrice( itemPrice );
```

When the extraction operator reads the price from the input stream, it leaves the carriage return following the number unread. ignore() is used to grab the carriage return, leaving the stream set up to read the next MenuItem:

```
is.ignore( 1, '\n' );
```

Finally, the stream passed in to the operator>>() function is returned, preserving the integrity of the sequence:

```
    return( is );
}
```

operator<<() is somewhat simpler. It uses << to output the name and price data members:

```
ostream &operator<<( ostream &os, MenuItem &item )
{
  os << item.GetName() << " ($"
     << item.GetPrice() << ") ";
```

Once again, the stream passed in as the first parameter is returned:

```
    return( os );
}
```

main() declares an ifstream object and ties it to the file named Menu Items. This file contains a list of MenuItems with the name and price of each item appearing on its own line:

```
//----------------------------------- main()

void  main( void )
{
  ifstream  readMe( "Menu Items" );
```

`main()` also declares a `MenuItem` object named `item`. Notice that no parameters are passed because there's no constructor to do anything with the parameters:

```
MenuItem   item;
```

Next, a `while` loop is used to read in all the `MenuItems` that can be read from the input stream (which is, in this case, a file named `Menu Items`). The overloaded version of `>>` is used to read in a `MenuItem`, and the overloaded version of `<<` is used to display the `MenuItem` in the console window:

```
while ( readMe >> item )
    cout << item << "\n";
}
```

Here's what appears on the console:

```
Spring Rolls ($2.99)
Hot and Sour Soup ($3.99)
Hunan Chicken ($8.99)
General Tso's Shrimp ($9.99)
```

It's important to note that `operator>>()` and `operator<<()` are designed to work with any input and output stream. In this case, the `MenuItems` are read from a file and displayed in the console window. By making a few changes to `main()`—and *not* changing the two `operator()` functions—you can easily change the program to read from standard input (you'd probably want to add in a prompt or two) and send the output to a file. That's the real beauty of `iostream`!

Formatting Your Output

In the preceding program, we overloaded the `<<` operator so that we could display a `MenuItem` precisely the way we wanted it to appear. Unfortunately, there's no way to overload the `<<` operator to customize the appearance of built-in data types such as `short` or `float`. Fortunately, `iostream` provides several mechanisms that allow you to customize your I/O operations.

In general, `iostream` follows some fairly simple rules when it comes to formatting output. If you insert a single `char` in a stream, exactly one character position is used. When some form of integral data is inserted, the insertion is exactly as wide as the number inserted, including space for a sign, if applicable. No padding characters are used.

When a `float` is inserted, room is made for up to six places of precision to the right of the decimal place. Trailing zeros are dropped. If the number is either very large or very small (how big or how small depends on the implementation), exponential notation is used. Again, room is made for a sign, if applicable. For example, the number 1.234000 takes up five character positions in the stream since the trailing zeros are dropped:

```
1.234
```

When a string is inserted, each character, not including any NULL terminator, takes up one character position.

The Formatting Flags

The `ios` class maintains a set of flags that control various formatting features. You can use the `ios` member functions `setf()` and `unsetf()` to turn these formatting features on and off. Each feature corresponds to a bit in a bit field maintained by the `ios` class.

Some features are independent, while others are grouped together. For example, the flag `ios::skipws` determines whether white space is skipped during extraction operations. This feature is not linked to any other features, so it may be turned on and off without impacting any of the other formatting flags.

To turn an independent flag on and off, you use the `setf()` and `unsetf()` member functions as follows:

```
cin.setf( ios::skipws ); // Skip whitespace on input
cin.unsetf( ios::skipws ); // Don't skip whitespace
                          // on input
```

Alternatively, you can use the `flag()` member function to retrieve the current flag settings as a group, OR the new flag into the group, and then use `flag()` again to reset the flag settings with the newly modified bit field:

```
int myFlags;

myFlags = cout.flag(); // returns flag bitfield
myFlags |= ios::skipws; // ORs in skipws flag
cout.flag( myFlags ); // resets flags
```

Unless you really need to work at this level, you're better off sticking with `setf()` and `unsetf()`. Just thought you'd like to see the whole picture.

Turning independent flags on and off individually is no problem, but things get interesting when flags are grouped. For example, the radix flags determine the default base used to represent numbers in output. The radix flags are `dec`, `oct`, and `hex`, representing decimal, octal, and hexadecimal formats, respectively. The problem here is that only one of these flags should be turned on at a time. If you use `setf()`, you could easily turn all three flags on, producing unpredictable results.

To handle grouped flags, `setf()` makes use of a second, optional parameter that indicates which group a flag belongs to. For example, the radix flags `dec`, `oct`, and `hex` belong to the group `basefield`. To set the `hex` flag, you make the following call:

```
cout.setf( ios::hex, ios::basefield );
```

This call ensures that when the specified flag is set, the remainder of the fields in the group get unset.

The grouped flags `left`, `right`, and `internal` are part of the `adjustfield` group. They are used in combination with the `width()` member function. `width()` determines the minimum number of characters used in the next numeric or string output operation. If the `left` flag is set, the next numeric or string output operation appears left-justified in the currently specified `width()`. The output is padded with the currently specified `fill()` character. You can use `fill()` to change this padding character. An example should make this formatting feature clearer.

A Formatting Example

Close the current project by selecting **Close Project** from the **Project** menu. When prompted for a project file to open, go into the THIN C++ Projects folder, open the subfolder named Chap 08.04 - formatter, and open the project file named `formatter.π`. Next, run `formatter.π` by selecting **Run** from the **Project** menu. Here's what you'll see:

```
202
202xx
-======101
*****Hello
```

Hit a return to exit `formatter`. Let's take a look at the source code.

The formatter Source Code
`formatter.cp` starts with the standard `#include`:

```
#include <iostream.h>
```

main() starts by displaying the number 202 in the console window:

```
//----------------------------------- main()

void  main( void )
{
  cout << 202 << '\n';
```

As you'd expect, this code produces the following line of output:

```
202
```

Next, `width()` is used to set the current width to 5, and `fill()` is used to make x the padding character:

```
cout.width( 5 );
cout.fill( 'x' );
```

Remember, `width()` applies only to the very next string or numeric output operation, even if it is part of a sequence. The padding character lasts until the next call of `fill()` or until the program exits.

If your output operation produces more characters than the current width setting, don't worry. All your characters will be printed.

Now, the `left` flag is set, asking `iostream` to left-justify the output in the field specified by `width()`:

```
cout.setf( ios::left, ios::adjustfield );

cout << 202 << '\n';
```

When the number 202 is printed again, it appears like this:

```
202xx
```

Then, `width()` is pumped up to 10, `fill()` is changed to =, and the `internal` flag is set. The `internal` flag asks `iostream` to place padding in between a number and its sign, if appropriate, so that it fills the `width()` field:

```
cout.width( 10 );
cout.fill( '=' );
cout.setf( ios::internal, ios::adjustfield );
```

```
cout << -101 << '\n';
```

Printing the number –101 produces the following line of output:

```
-======101
```

Finally, `width()` is reset to 10 (otherwise, it would have dropped to its default of 0), `fill()` is set to *, and the `right` flag is set to right-justify the output:

```
cout.width( 10 );
cout.fill( '*' );
cout.setf( ios::right, ios::adjustfield );

cout << "Hello";
}
```

When the string `"Hello"` is printed, this line of output appears:

```
*****Hello
```

More Flags and Methods

The `showbase` flag is independent. If it is set, octal numbers are displayed with a leading zero and hex output appears with the two leading characters `0x`. The `showpoint`, `uppercase`, and `showpos` flags are also independent. If `showpoint` is set, trailing zeros in floating-point output are displayed. If `uppercase` is set, `E` rather than `e` is used in scientific notation and `X` rather than `x` is used in displaying hex numbers. If `showpos` is set, positive numbers appear with a leading +.

The `scientific` and `fixed` flags belong to the `floatfield` group. If `scientific` is set, scientific notation is used to display floating-point output. If `fixed` is set, standard notation is used. If neither bit is set, the compiler uses its judgment and prints very large or very small numbers using scientific notation and all other numbers using standard notation. To turn off both bits, you pass a zero instead of `fixed` or `scientific`:

```
cout.setf( 0, ios::floatfield );
```

Both the `fixed` and `scientific` flags are tied to the `precision()` member function. `precision()` determines the number of digits displayed after the decimal point in floating-point output:

```
cout.precision( 6 ); // The default for precision...
```

Finally, the `unitbuf` and `stdio` flags are related but not grouped. If `unitbuf` is set, the output buffer is flushed after each output operation. `stdio`, which is only for folks using C I/O, flushes `stdout` and `stderr` after every insertion.

Using Manipulators

`iostream` provides a set of special functions known as **manipulators** that allow you to perform specific I/O operations while you're in the middle of an insertion or an extraction. For example, consider this line of code:

```
cout << "Enter a number: " << flush;
```

This code makes use of the `flush` manipulator. When its turn comes along in the output sequence, the `flush` manipulator flushes the buffer associated with `cout`, forcing the output to appear immediately as opposed to waiting for the buffer to get flushed naturally (sort of like a C++ version of prunes!).

Just as an I/O sequence can appear in different forms, a manipulator can be called in several different ways. Here are two more examples, each of which calls the `flush` manipulator:

```
cout.flush(); // Call as a stream member function
flush( cout );  // Call with the stream as a parameter
```

Use whichever form fits in with the I/O sequence you are currently building. If you plan on calling any manipulators that take parameters, be sure to include the file `<iomanip.h>`. In addition, some `iostream` implementations require you to link with the `math` library to use certain manipulators. Check your development environment manual to be sure.

The Manipulators

`dec()`, `oct()`, and `hex()` turn on the appropriate format flags, thus turning off the rest of the flags in the `basefield` group. `endl()` places a carriage return (`'\n'`) in its output stream and then flushes the stream. `ends()` places a `NULL` character in its output stream and then flushes the stream. `ws()` eats up all the white space in its input stream until it hits either an end-of-file or the first non-white-space character.

None of the manipulators presented so far take any parameters. The six remaining to be discussed all take a single parameter and require the included file `<iomanip.h>`.

`setbase(int b)` sets the current radix to either 8, 10, or 16. `setfill(int f)` is a manipulator version of the `fill()` member function. `setprecision(int p)` is the manipulator version of `precision()`. `setw(int w)` is the manipulator version of `width()`. `setiosflags(long f)` is the manipulator version of `setf()`. `resetiosflags(long f)` is the manipulator version of `unsetf()`.

Here are two manipulator examples. The line

```
cout << setbase( 16 ) << 256 << endl;
```

produces this line of output:

```
100
```

And, the line

```
cout << setprecision( 5 ) << 102.12345;
```

produces this line of output:

```
102.12
```

istrstream and ostrstream

If you've ever worked with the C `stdio` function `sprintf()`, you'll recognize a similar feature in C++. `sprintf()` allows you to perform all the standard I/O functions normally associated with `printf()` and `fprintf()` on an array of characters.

The `istrstream` and `ostrstream` classes offer all the power of their ancestor classes (`istream` and `ostream` and, ultimately, `ios`) and allow you to write formatted data to a buffer that you create in memory. Here's an example.

A strstream Example

Close the current project by selecting **Close Project** from the **Project** menu. When prompted for a project file to open, go into the `THIN C++ Projects` folder, open the subfolder named `Chap 08.05 - strstream`, and open the project file named `strstream.π`. Next, run `strstream.π` by selecting **Run** from the **Project** menu. Here's what you'll see:

```
Number of characters written: 10
Buffer contents: abcdefghi
```

Hit a return to exit `strstream`. Let's take a look at the source code.

The strstream Source Code

`strstream.cp` starts with two `#includes`, the standard `<iostream.h>` and the file required for the `istrstream` and `ostrstream` classes, `<strstrea.h>`.

```
#include <iostream.h>
#include <strstrea.h>
```

The constant `kBufferSize` is used to define the size of the buffer that makes up the `ostrstream` object:

```
const short kBufferSize = 10;
```

`main()` creates a buffer to hold the stream's characters. The `ostrstream` constructor takes two parameters, a pointer to the buffer and the size of the buffer. The variable `i` is used to keep track of the number of characters written to the `ostrstream`:

```
//----------------------------------- main()

void  main( void )
{
  char         buffer[ kBufferSize ];
  ostrstream   ostr( buffer, kBufferSize );
  short        i = 0;
```

Next, a `while` loop uses `ostr` just as it would use `cout`, writing characters to the stream until an end-of-file causes the loop to terminate. `iostream` generates the end-of-file when the `put()` pointer points beyond the last character in the stream's buffer (just like its `ifstream` counterpart). When the loop exits, ten characters, from `a` to `j`, have been written to the stream's buffer:

```
while ( ostr << (char)('a' + i) )
  i++;
```

Now, the number of characters written to the stream is displayed:

```
cout << "Number of characters written: "
    << i << '\n';
```

Here's the output generated by the previous line of code:

```
Number of characters written: 10
```

Next, a NULL terminator is written on the last byte of the stream's buffer, creating a NULL-terminated string in `buffer`:

```
buffer[ kBufferSize - 1 ] = '\0';
```

Finally, the contents of the stream are printed:

```
cout << "Buffer contents: " << buffer;
}
```

The previous line of code results in this line of output:

```
Buffer contents: abcdefghi
```

Just as an `ostrstream` object mirrors the behavior of `cout`, you can create a similar example, using an `istrstream` object, that mirrors the behavior of `istrstream`. The `istrstream` constructor takes the same two parameters as the `ostrstream` constructor.

Together, `istrstream` and `ostrstream` give you a powerful set of tools to use when you work with strings in memory.

Summary

`iostream` offers you a significant capability. You can use the classes and member functions provided to build an ample user interface for your programs. In the event that you're working with a class library that provides a more sophisticated, graphical user interface, you can still use `iostream` to manage your file I/O as well as to manage an in-core string manipulation facility.

Although I've made every effort to present a complete description of `iostream`, there's no substitution for a thorough reading of the `iostream` included files. You'll find complete listings of the four included files `<iostream.h>`, `<fstream.h>`, `<iomanip.h>`, and `<strstrea.h>` in appendices at the back of the book.

Chapter 9 starts off with a relatively new feature of C++ known as *templates* and then moves on to a potpourri of other topics. See you there!

Chapter 9

C++
Potpourri

This chapter takes you down the homestretch, exploring an array of miscellaneous C++ topics. Once you finish this chapter, you'll have completed the first phase of your C++ education.

This Chapter at a Glance

Templates
The Templates Approach
    Defining an Object Using a Template
    A Formal Parameter List Containing More
        Than One Type
    Function Templates
    Function Template Instantiation
    A Template Example
Multiple Inheritance
    A Multiple Inheritance Example
    Static Members
Resolving Ambiguities
    A Multiple-Root Example
    The Virtual Base Class Alternative
    A Virtual Base Class Example
Initialization Versus Assignment
    const and Reference Types
    A Member Initialization List Example
Memberwise Initialization
    A Memberwise Initialization Function
    A Memberwise Initialization Example
Summary

CONGRATULATIONS! YOU'VE REALLY COME A LONG way. By getting to this point in the book, you've built yourself a strong C++ foundation. Now you're ready for a few of the more advanced topics. We'll start off with one of the newest additions to C++, a feature known as **templates**.

Templates   When you design a class, you're forced to make some decisions about the data types that make up that class. For example, if your class contains an array, the class declaration specifies the array's data type. In the following class declaration, an array of shorts is implemented:

```
class Array
{
  private:
    short   arraySize; // Number of array elements
    short   *arrayPtr; // Pointer to the array

  public:
          Array( short size ); // Allocate an array
                               // of size shorts
          ~Array( void ); // Delete the array
};
```

In this class, the constructor allocates an array of arraySize elements, each element of type short. The destructor deletes the array. The data member arrayPtr points to the beginning of the array. To make the class truly useful, you'd probably want to add a member function that gives access to the elements of the array. You might extend the class further by adding a bounds-checking feature.

This Array class works just fine as long as an array of shorts meets your needs. What happens when you decide that an Array of shorts doesn't quite cut it? Perhaps you need to implement an array of longs or, even better, an array of your own, home-brewed data type.

One approach you can use is to make a copy of the Array class (member functions and all) and change it slightly to implement an array of the appropriate type. For example, here's a version of the Array class designed to work with an array of longs:

```
class LongArray
{
  private:
```

```
   short    arraySize; // Number of array elements
   long     *arrayPtr; // Pointer to the array

 public:
   long     Array( short size ); // Allocate an array
                                 // of size longs
   long     ~Array( void );  // Delete the array
};
```

There are definitely problems with this approach. You are creating a maintenance nightmare by duplicating the source code of one class to act as the basis for a second class. Suppose you add a new feature to your `Array` class. Are you going to make the same change to the `LongArray` class?

The Templates Approach

C++ templates allow you to parameterize the data types used by a class or function. Instead of embedding a specific type in a class declaration, you provide a template that defines the type used by that class. An example should make this a little clearer.

Here's a templated version of the `Array` class presented earlier:

```
template <class T>
class Array
{
  private:
    short    arraySize; // Number of array elements
    T        *arrayPtr; // Pointer to the array

  public:
          Array( short size );  // Allocate an array
                                // of size T's
          ~Array( void ); // Delete the array
};
```

The keyword `template` tells the compiler that what follows is not your usual, run-of-the-mill declaration. Following the keyword `template` is a pair of angle brackets that surround the template's **formal parameter list**. This list consists of a series of comma-separated parameters (one parameter is the minimum).

Each parameter is made up of the keyword `class` followed by the parameter name. In this case, the formal parameter list contains a single parameter, `T`. Throughout the body of the class declaration that follows, the template parameters may be used as if they were data types. In the `Array` class, `T` is used to declare the data member `arrayPtr`.

Defining an Object Using a Template

Once your class template is declared, you can use it to create an object. When you define an object using a class template, you have to specify a formal parameter list along with the class name. Here's an example:

```
Array<long>   longArray( 20 );
```

The compiler uses the single parameter, `long`, to convert the `Array` template into an actual class declaration. This declaration is known as a **template instantiation**. The instantiation is then used to create the `longArray` object.

A Formal Parameter List Containing More Than One Type

As mentioned earlier, a template's formal parameter list may contain more than one type. The `class` keyword must precede each parameter, and a parameter name may not be repeated. Here's an example:

```
template <class Able, class Baker>
class MyClass
{
  public:
            MyClass( Able param );
            ~MyClass( void );
    Baker   MemberFunction( Baker param );
};
```

This template takes two formal parameters. The first, `Able`, is used to declare the constructor's single parameter. The second, `Baker`, is used in the declaration of `MemberFunction()` both as a return type and to declare the `MemberFunction()` parameter. Here's a definition of a `MyClass` object:

```
MyClass<long, char *> myObject( 250L );
```

Take a look at the template parameters. The first, `long`, will be substituted for `Able`. The second, `char *`, will be substituted for `Baker`.

Function Templates

The template technique can also be applied to functions. Here's an example of a function template declaration:

```
template <class T, class U>
T MyFunc( T param1, U param2 )
{
  T var1;
  U var2;
    .
    .
    .

}
```

As you'd expect, the declaration starts with the `template` keyword, which is immediately followed by the formal parameter list. The types defined in the formal parameter list are then used freely throughout the remainder of the function declaration. Once again, a type may not be repeated in the formal parameter list, and the formal parameter list must contain at least one parameter.

There is one additional rule that applies to function templates. Each of the formal parameters must appear at least once in the function's signature. Since a function's signature does *not* include the function's return type, you must use each of the formal parameters in the function's parameter list.

> If you use a template to define a function, you must also include the same template information in the function's prototype. Here's a prototype for `MyFunc()`:
>
> ```
> template <class T, class U>
> T MyFunc( T param1, U param2 );
> ```

Function Template Instantiation

When you call a function that has been templated, the compiler uses the parameters passed to the function to determine the types of the formal parameters.

Here's a simple example:

```
template <class T>
void  MyFunc( T param1 );
```

Suppose this function template were called as follows:

```
char  *s;

MyFunc( s );
```

The compiler would match the type of the calling parameter (`char *`) with the type of the receiving parameter (`T`). In this case, an instantiation of the function is created, and the type `char *` is substituted for `T` everywhere it occurs.

Here's another example:

```
template <class T>
void  MyFunc( T *param1 );
```

Suppose this function template were called as follows:

```
char  *s;

MyFunc( s );
```

In this case, the type `char *` would be matched against the formal parameter type `T *`. Again, an instantiation is created, but this time the type `char` is substituted for `T`.

In the case where more than one parameter is used, the type-matching process always starts with the first parameter and moves to the right. Each occurrence of a formal parameter type is checked and a substitute type deduced. Once a substitute type is determined, any further occurrences of that formal parameter must match the first occurrence *exactly*.

Consider this template:

```
template <class T>
void  MyFunc( T param1, T param2 );
```

This call of `MyFunc()` won't compile:

```
short   i;
int     j;

MyFunc( i, j );
```

First, the compiler matches the first parameter and determines that `T` is a `short`. When the compiler moves on to the second parameter, it finds that `T` should be an `int`. Even though an `int` and a `short` are kissin' cousins, since they are not an exact match, the compiler coughs politely and then spits out your code.

If you so desire, you can overload a function template just as you overload any other function. Just remember that every call to a template function must match one and only one of the overloaded functions.

You can also design a nontemplated version of a function to work alongside a templated version. When a function call occurs, the compiler tries to match the parameters against the nontemplated version first. If the parameters match up, the nontemplated function is called. If no match is found, the regular template-matching process is started.

A Template Example

Our first sample program provides a basic demonstration of class and function templates. If THIN C++ is already running, close the current project by selecting **Close Project** from the **Project** menu. If THIN C++ isn't running, launch it by clicking on the THIN Project Manager. Either way, when prompted for a project file to open, go into the THIN C++ Projects folder, open the subfolder named Chap 09.01 - template, and open the project file named template.π. Next, run template.π by selecting **Run** from the **Project** menu. Here's what you'll see:

```
index out of bounds(10)
----
myRay[0]: 1
myRay[1]: 4
myRay[2]: 16
myRay[3]: 64
myRay[4]: 256
myRay[5]: 1024
myRay[6]: 4096
myRay[7]: 16384
myRay[8]: 0
myRay[9]: 0
----
myLongRay[0]: 1
myLongRay[1]: 4
myLongRay[2]: 16
myLongRay[3]: 64
myLongRay[4]: 256
myLongRay[5]: 1024
myLongRay[6]: 4096
myLongRay[7]: 16384
myLongRay[8]: 65536
myLongRay[9]: 262144
```

Hit a return to exit template. Let's take a look at the source code.

The template Source Code

As usual, `template.cp` starts by including `<iostream.h>`. Next, a `const`, which is used at various points in the program, is declared:

```
#include <iostream.h>

const short kNumElements = 10;
```

   `template` declares a class template named `Array`. `Array` implements an array of type `T`, where `T` is the template's single formal parameter:

```
//----------------------------------- Array

template <class T>
class Array
```

`Array` features three data members, all of them `private`. `arraySize` is the number of elements in the array; `arrayPtr` points to the beginning of the array; `errorRetValue` is identical in type to one of the array elements and comes into play when you try to exceed the bounds of the array:

```
{
  private:
    short   arraySize;
    T       *arrayPtr;
    T       errorRetValue;
```

The `Array()` constructor allocates memory for the array, the destructor deletes the allocated memory, and `operator[]()` is used to implement bounds checking:

```
  public:
          Array( short size );
          ~Array( void );
    T     &operator[]( short index );
};
```

In the following code, notice the format used to define a class template member function. The function starts with the `template` keyword, followed by the template's formal parameter list. Next comes the class name, followed by the parameter types surrounded by angle brackets. Finally, the traditional `::` is followed by the function's name and signature:

```
template <class T>
Array<T>::Array( short size )
```

The constructor uses its parameter, `size`, to initialize `arraySize`. Then, an array of `size` elements of type `T` is allocated. Finally, `errorRetValue` is initialized to zero:

```
{
  arraySize = size;
  arrayPtr = new T[ size ];
  errorRetValue = 0;
}
```

The destructor uses an interesting form of `delete` to delete the memory allocated for the array. This statement tells the compiler that the destructor should be applied to every element in the array pointed to by `arrayPtr` (without the `[ ]` operators, the destructor is called only for the first element of the array; while this is not particularly interesting in the case of an array of `shorts`, it is vital in working with an array of objects having a specific destructor):

```
template <class T>
Array<T>::~Array( void )
{
  delete [] arrayPtr;
}
```

`operator[]()` is called whenever an `Array` element is accessed via the `[ ]` operators. `operator[]()` first checks to see whether the index is out of bounds. If it is, an error message is printed and the pseudo-element, `errorRetValue`, is returned (by placing an unusual value in `errorRetValue`, you can clue the calling code to the fact that the array reference was illegal if printing an error message doesn't fit into your error-handling strategy):

```cpp
template <class T>
T &Array<T>::operator[]( short index )
{
  if ( ( index < 0 ) || ( index >= arraySize ) )
  {
    cout << "index out of bounds(" << index << ")\n";
    return( errorRetValue );
  }
```

If the index is in bounds, the appropriate element of the array is returned:

```cpp
  else
    return( arrayPtr[ index ] );
}
```

The next function in the source code is the templated function `Power()`. As you can see, `Power()` is declared using the `template` keyword and a single template type, T. `Power()` takes two parameters of type T and returns a value of type T (the key here is that the type of the two parameters must match *exactly*):

```cpp
//------------------------------------- Power

template <class T>
T Power( T base, T exponent )
```

`Power()` raises the parameter base to the exponent power, and the final result is returned:

```cpp
{
  T i, product = 1;

  for ( i=1; i<=exponent; i++ )
    product *= base;

  return( product );
}
```

main() starts by defining a short version of Array and a long version of Array (you could have declared a class named EraserHead and used Array to create an array of EraserHeads):

```
//------------------------------------  main()

void  main( void )
{
  Array<short>   myRay( kNumElements );
  Array<long>    myLongRay( kNumElements );
  short          i, shortBase = 4;
  long           longBase = 4L;
```

This loop fills the short array with consecutive powers of 4:

```
for ( i=0; i<=kNumElements; i++ )
  myRay[ i ] = Power( shortBase, i );
```

When i is equal to kNumElements, the array runs out-of-bounds, causing an error message to be printed on the console:

```
index out of bounds(10)
```

Next, a separator line is sent to the console:

```
cout << "----\n";
```

This loop prints the value of each element in the short array:

```
for ( i=0; i<kNumElements; i++ )
  cout << "myRay[" << i << "]: " << myRay[ i ]
       << "\n";
```

Here's the output:

```
----
myRay[0]: 1
myRay[1]: 4
myRay[2]: 16
myRay[3]: 64
myRay[4]: 256
```

```
myRay[5]: 1024
myRay[6]: 4096
myRay[7]: 16384
myRay[8]: 0
myRay[9]: 0
```

By the time we get to Power(4, 8) we've reached the limits of a signed short. Our solution? Redo the whole thing using longs. Thank goodness for templates, eh?

This loop uses the same approach to fill the array of longs, but this time we won't let the array run out-of-bounds:

```
for ( i=0; i<kNumElements; i++ )
  myLongRay[ i ] = Power( longBase, (long)i );
```

We print a separator line and then print the elements of the long array:

```
cout << "----\n";

for ( i=0; i<kNumElements; i++ )
  cout << "myLongRay[" << i
    << "]: " << myLongRay[ i ] << "\n";
}
```

Here's the output:

```
----
myLongRay[0]: 1
myLongRay[1]: 4
myLongRay[2]: 16
myLongRay[3]: 64
myLongRay[4]: 256
myLongRay[5]: 1024
myLongRay[6]: 4096
myLongRay[7]: 16384
myLongRay[8]: 65536
myLongRay[9]: 262144
```

Templates are an extremely powerful part of C++. You might not make use of them right away, but as you develop more and more C++ code, you'll use templates to build a set of parameterized utility classes. For example, you'll probably want to create a linked-list template that you can customize to link up objects of varying types.

Multiple Inheritance

Our next topic is a variation on an earlier theme, class derivation. In the examples presented in Chapter 6, each derived class was based on a single base class. That doesn't have to be the case, however. C++ allows you to derive a class from more than one base class, a technique known as **multiple inheritance**. As its name implies, multiple inheritance means that a class derived from more than one base class inherits the data members and member functions from each of its base classes.

Why would you want to inherit members from more than one class? Check out the derivation chain in Figure 9.1. The ultimate base class, known as the **root base class**, in this chain is Computer. The two classes ColorComputer and LaptopComputer are special types of Computers, each inheriting the nonprivate members from Computer and adding members of their own as well.

Here's where multiple inheritance comes into play. The class ColorLaptop is derived from both ColorComputer and LaptopComputer and inherits members from each class. Multiple inheritance allows you to take advantage of two different classes that work well together. If you want a program that models a color, laptop computer and you already have a ColorComputer class that manages color information and a LaptopComputer class that manages information about laptops, why reinvent the wheel? Think of the ColorLaptop class as the best of both worlds—the union of two already designed classes.

A Multiple Inheritance Example

Our second sample program demonstrates multiple inheritance as well as a few additional C++ features that you should find interesting. Close the current project by selecting **Close Project** from the **Project** menu. When prompted for a project file to open, go into the THIN C++ Projects folder, open the subfolder

FIGURE 9.1
*Multiple inheritance
(the boldfaced data
members are inherited).*

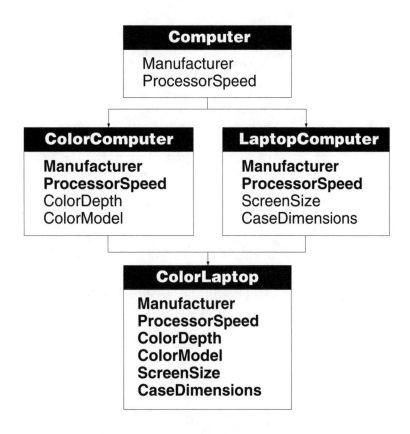

named Chap 09.02 – multInherit, and open the project file
named multInherit.π. Next, run multInherit.π by selecting **Run** from the **Project** menu. Here's what you'll see:

```
shape: Cube
color: Red
objectID: 1
--------
shape: Cylinder
color: Blue
objectID: 2
--------
shape: Sphere
color: Yellow
objectID: 3
--------
```

```
Object(3) destructor called.
HasColor destructor called.
HasShape destructor called.
--------
Object(2) destructor called.
HasColor destructor called.
HasShape destructor called.
--------
Object(1) destructor called.
HasColor destructor called.
HasShape destructor called.
--------
```

Hit a return to exit multInherit. Let's take a look at the source code.

The multInherit Source Code

As usual, multInherit.cp starts by including <iostream.h>:

```
#include <iostream.h>
```

multInherit implements three classes: HasColor, HasShape, and a class derived from these two, Object. The idea here is to create an Object that has a color and a shape. The two enums provide a choice of colors and shapes:

```
enum ColorEnum { red, yellow, blue };
enum ShapeEnum { sphere, cylinder, cube };
```

Later in the program, we'll want to print an Object's color and shape using iostream. This first operator<<() function knows how to print a ColorEnum:

```
//------------------------ ostream overloads

ostream &operator<<( ostream &os, ColorEnum color )
{
  switch ( color )
  {
    case red:
      os << "Red";
```

```
      break;
    case yellow:
      os << "Yellow";
      break;
    case blue:
      os << "Blue";
      break;
    default:
      os << "Unknown";
      break;
  }

  return( os );
}
```

This second operator<<() function knows how to print a ShapeEnum:

```
ostream &operator<<( ostream &os, ShapeEnum shape )
{
  switch ( shape )
  {
    case sphere:
      os << "Sphere";
      break;
    case cylinder:
      os << "Cylinder";
      break;
    case cube:
      os << "Cube";
      break;
    default:
      os << "Unknown";
      break;
  }

  return( os );
}
```

The HasColor class sports a ColorEnum data member, a constructor, and a destructor:

```
//----------------------------------- HasColor

class HasColor
{
  private:
    ColorEnum color;

  public:
         HasColor( ColorEnum objectColor );
         ~HasColor( void );
};
```

The constructor takes a ColorEnum, stores it in the color data member, and then prints an appropriate message:

```
HasColor::HasColor( ColorEnum objectColor )
{
  color = objectColor;

  cout << "color: " << color << "\n";
}
```

The destructor just lets you know it was called. Messages are printed in the constructor and destructor so that you'll be able to follow the order in which they are called during multiple inheritance:

```
HasColor::~HasColor( void )
{
  cout << "HasColor destructor called.\n";
}
```

The HasShape class works just like HasColor but uses a ShapeEnum instead of a ColorEnum:

```
//----------------------------------- HasShape

class HasShape
{
  private:
    ShapeEnum shape;
```

```
    public:
        HasShape( ShapeEnum objectShape );
        ~HasShape( void );
};

HasShape::HasShape( ShapeEnum objectShape )
{
  shape = objectShape;

  cout << "shape: " << shape << "\n";
}

HasShape::~HasShape( void )
{
  cout << "HasShape destructor called.\n"
    << "--------\n";
}
```

The `Object` class is derived from both `HasShape` and `HasColor`. In the following code, notice that the `public` keyword precedes *each* class name on the class title line. `Object` inherits all the nonprivate members from these two classes. In this case, `Object` will inherit only the constructors and destructors from its two base classes (if you wanted access to the `shape` and `color` data members, you'd have to change their protection code from `private` to `protected` or `public`):

```
//------------------------- Object:HasShape,HasColor

class Object : public HasShape, public HasColor
```

The `Object` class has a few data members of its own. `objectID` stores a unique serial number for the `Object`, while `lastObjectID` holds the last serial number assigned for the class:

```
{
  private:
    short        objectID;
    static short lastObjectID;
```

Static Members

We interrupt our regularly scheduled code walk-through to bring you this important message about **static members**. When you declare a data member or member function as `static` (as we do with `lastObjectID`), the compiler creates a single version of the member that is shared by all objects in that class. Why do this? Static members can be very useful. Since a static data member is shared by all objects, you can use it to share information between all objects in a class.

> One way to think of a static member is as a global variable whose scope is limited to the class in which it is declared. This is especially true if the static member is declared as `private` or `protected`.

In this case, `lastObjectID` is incremented every time an `Object` is created. Since `lastObjectID` is not tied to a specific object, it always holds a unique serial number (which also happens to be the number of `Object`s created). To access a static member, you use the class name and the scope operator. For example, to access `lastObjectID`, you refer to it like this:

```
Object::lastObjectID
```

The declaration of a static data member is just that, a declaration. When you declare a `static` within a class declaration, you need to follow it up with a definition in the same scope. Typically, you follow your class declaration immediately with a definition of the static data member, like this:

```
short Object::lastObjectID;
```

If you like, you can use this definition to initialize the member. The scope of the static data member is limited to the file in which it is declared.

> When you're dealing with static members, it's important to keep in mind a rule encountered earlier in the book: Define once, declare often. Typically you stick your class declaration in a `.h` file. This is not the case for your static member *definition*. The definition should appear in the `.cp` file where it will be used.

Although these functions aren't nearly as widely used, you can declare a member function as `static`. Again, the function is not bound to a particular object and is shared with the entire class. If, for example, the class `MyClass` includes a static member function named `MyFunc()`, you call the function by using this syntax:

```
MyClass::MyFunc();
```

Since there is no current object when `MyFunc()` is called, you don't have the advantages of `this`, and any references to other data members or member functions must be done through an object.

Back to multInherit

We now resume our regularly scheduled code walk-through. The `Object()` constructor takes a `ColorEnum` and a `ShapeEnum`, which are mapped to the appropriate base class constructor:

```
    public:
        Object( ColorEnum objectColor,
            ShapeEnum objectShape );
        ~Object( void );
};
```

The `Object()` constructor uses a syntax first laid out in Chapter 6 to map its input parameters to the `HasShape()` and `HasColor()` constructors:

```
Object::Object( ColorEnum objectColor,
  ShapeEnum objectShape ) : HasShape( objectShape ),
  HasColor( objectColor )
```

> The list that follows the constructor's parameter list is called the **member initialization list**. As you can see, a colon *always* precedes a constructor's member initialization list.

The static `lastObjectID` is incremented, and the new serial number is stored in `objectID` and then printed in the console window:

```
{
  objectID = ++lastObjectID;

  cout << "objectID: " << objectID
    << "\n--------\n";
}
```

The destructor prints an appropriate message in the console window:

```
Object::~Object( void )
{
  cout << "Object(" << objectID << ") destructor
    called.\n";
}
```

As described earlier, every static member declaration must be accompanied by a static member definition. Here's `lastObjectID`'s definition. And oh, by the way, we took this opportunity to initialize it to zero (the initialization takes place before any code in this file starts executing):

```
short Object::lastObjectID = 0;
```

`main()` creates three `Object`s, a red cube, a blue cylinder, and a yellow sphere:

```
//--------------------------------------- main()
```

```
void  main( void )
{
  Object  object1( red, cube );
  Object  object2( blue, cylinder );
  Object  object3( yellow, sphere );
}
```

When the red cube is defined, the `HasShape()` constructor is called, then the `HasColor()` constructor, and finally the `Object()` constructor:

```
shape: Cube
color: Red
objectID: 1
```

When the blue cylinder is defined, the same sequence is repeated:

```
shape: Cylinder
color: Blue
objectID: 2
```

The same sequence is also repeated for the yellow sphere:

```
shape: Sphere
color: Yellow
objectID: 3
```

The order of the `HasColor()` and `HasShape()` constructor calls is determined by the order of their appearance in the `Object()` constructor's member initialization list:

```
Object::Object( ColorEnum objectColor, ShapeEnum
  objectShape ) : HasShape( objectShape ),
  HasColor( objectColor )
```

Try switching the order of `HasShape()` and `HasColor()` in the member initialization list, like this:

```
Object::Object( ColorEnum objectColor, ShapeEnum
  objectShape ) : HasColor( objectColor ),
  HasShape( objectShape )
```

When the program exits, the three `Object`s are deleted automatically. Notice that the order of the destructor calls is exactly opposite to the order of the constructor calls:

```
Object(3) destructor called.
HasColor destructor called.
HasShape destructor called.
--------
Object(2) destructor called.
HasColor destructor called.
HasShape destructor called.
--------
Object(1) destructor called.
HasColor destructor called.
HasShape destructor called.
```

I think it would be intriguing to use these classes to implement a virtual reality world of blocks. You could create objects with all kinds of attributes, including proximity attributes. For example, you could put a red cylinder on top of a blue cube. If the program truly mirrored reality, you'd have trouble putting a cylinder on top of a sphere (it would roll off) and if you picked up an `Object` with another `Object` on top of it, the top `Object` would move as well. Just a thought. Ah, well, on to the next subject.

Resolving Ambiguities

Deriving a class from more than one base class brings up an interesting problem. Suppose the two base classes from our previous example, `HasShape` and `HasColor`, each have a data member with the same name (which is perfectly legal, by the way). Let's call this data member `clone`. Now suppose that an `Object` object is created, derived from both `HasShape` and `HasColor`. When this `Object` refers to `clone`, which `clone` does it refer to, the one inherited from `HasShape` or the one from `HasColor`?

As it turns out, the compiler would complain if the `Object` class referred to just plain `clone` because it can't resolve this ambiguity. To get around this problem, you can access each of the two `clone`s by referring to

```
HasShape::clone
```

or

`HasColor::clone`

Here's another interesting problem brought on by multiple inheritance. Take a look at the derivation chain in Figure 9.2. Notice that the `Derived` class has two paths of inheritance back to its ultimate base class, `Root`.

FIGURE 9.2

Four classes in a derivation chain.

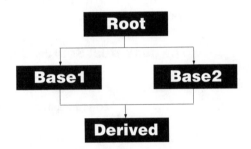

Since `Derived` is derived from both `Base1` and `Base2`, when a `Derived` object is created, `Base1` and `Base2` objects are created as well. When the `Base1` object is created, a `Root` object is created. When the `Base2` object is created, a second `Root` object is created.

Why is this a problem? Suppose `Root` contains a data member destined to be inherited by `Derived`. When `Derived` refers to the `Root` data member, which of the two `Root` objects contains the data member `Derived` is referring to? Sounds like another ambiguity to me.

A Multiple-Root Example

Before we resolve this latest ambiguity, here's an example that shows what happens when a derived class has two paths back to its root class. Close the current project by selecting **Close Project** from the **Project** menu. When prompted for a project file to open, go into the THIN C++ Projects folder, open the subfolder named Chap 09.03 – nonVirtual, and open the project file named nonVirtual.π. Now, run nonVirtual.π by selecting **Run** from the **Project** menu. Here's what you'll see:

```
Root constructor called
Base1 constructor called
Root constructor called
Base2 constructor called
Derived constructor called
```

Hit a return to exit nonVirtual. Let's take a look at the source code.

The nonVirtual Source Code

As usual, nonVirtual.cp starts by including <iostream.h>:

```
#include <iostream.h>
```

nonVirtual declares the four classes shown in Figure 9.2. Root consists of a constructor that prints a message letting you know it was called:

```
//------------------------------------ Root

class Root
{
  public:
    Root( void );
};

Root::Root( void )
{
  cout << "Root constructor called\n";
}
```

Base1 is derived from Root. Its constructor also prints a useful message:

```
//------------------------------------ Base1

class Base1 : public Root
{
```

```
  public:
    Base1( void );
};

Base1::Base1( void )
{
  cout << "Base1 constructor called\n";
}
```

Base2 is also derived from Root. Its constructor also prints a message in the console window:

```
//------------------------------------- Base2

class Base2 : public Root
{
  public:
    Base2( void );
};

Base2::Base2( void )
{
  cout << "Base2 constructor called\n";
}
```

Derived is derived from both Base1 and Base2. Just like all the other classes, Derived has its constructor print a message in the console window just to let you know it was called:

```
//------------------------------------- Derived

class Derived : public Base1, public Base2
{
  public:
    Derived( void );
};

Derived::Derived( void )
{
  cout << "Derived constructor called\n";
}
```

main() starts the constructor roller coaster by creating a Derived object.

```
//----------------------------------- main()

void  main( void )
{
  Derived    myDerived;
}
```

Since Base1 is listed first in the Derived derivation list, a Base1 object is created first. Since Base1 is derived from Root, it causes a Root object to be created. The Root constructor is called and then the Base1 constructor is called, resulting in the following two lines of output:

```
Root constructor called
Base1 constructor called
```

Next, this process is repeated as a Base2 object is created. Since Base2 is also derived from Root, it causes a *second* Root object to be created. Once the Root constructor is called, control returns to Base2 and its constructor is called:

```
Root constructor called
Base2 constructor called
```

Once the Base2 object is created, control returns to the Derived class and the Derived constructor is called:

```
Derived constructor called
```

The Virtual Base Class Alternative

Once again, think about the problem raised by this last example. If the Root class contained a data member, how would the Derived object access the data member? Which of the two Root objects would contain the *real* copy of the data member?

The answer to this problem lies in the use of **virtual base classes**. Back in Chapter 6's whatAmI program, we declared a member function as `virtual` to allow a derived class to override the function. Basically, when a virtual function is called, the compiler follows the derivation chain down from the root class to the most derived class and looks at each level for a function matching the virtual function. The lowest-level matching function is the one that is called.

Virtual functions are extremely useful. Here's why. Suppose you're writing a program that implements a window-based user interface. Let's say that your standard window is broken into several areas (we'll call them panes) and that each pane is broken into subpanes. When the time comes to draw the contents of your window, your `Window` class's `Draw()` member function is called. If your `Pane` class also has a `Draw()` member function *and* if the `Window` version of `Draw()` is declared as `virtual`, the `Pane`'s `Draw()` is called instead.

This same logic applies to your `SubPane` class and its `Draw()` function. If it is derived from `Pane`, the `SubPane`'s `Draw()` is called instead of the `Pane`'s `Draw()`. This strategy allows you to override an existing class with a new class whose actions are more appropriate or more efficient.

A similar technique can be used to remove the ambiguity brought up when a derived class has two different paths back to one of its ancestor classes. In our earlier example, `Root` was the root class, and `Base1` and `Base2` were derived from `Root`. Finally, `Derived` was derived from both `Base1` and `Base2`. When we created a `Derived` object, we ended up creating two `Root` objects. Thus the ambiguity.

By declaring `Root` as a virtual base class, we're asking the compiler to merge the two `Root` object creation requests into a single `Root` object (you'll see how to mark a class as `virtual` in a moment). The compiler gathers every reference to the virtual base class from the different constructor member initialization lists and picks the one that's tied to the deepest constructor. That reference is used, and all the others are discarded. This will become clearer as you walk through the next sample program.

To create a virtual base class, you must insert the `virtual` keyword in the member initialization lists between the virtual base class and the potentially ambiguous derived class. You don't need to mark every class between `Root` and `Derived` as long as the compiler has no path between `Root` and `Derived` that doesn't contain at least one `virtual` reference. The general strategy is to mark all *direct* descendants of the virtual base class. In this case, we'd need to place the `virtual` keyword in both the `Base1` and `Base2` member initialization lists.

Here's an example:

```
class Base1 : public virtual Root
{
  public:
    Base1( void );
};
```

The `virtual` keyword can appear either before or after the `public` keyword.

Once the `virtual` keywords are in place, the compiler ignores all member initialization list references to the `Root` class constructor except the deepest one. This sample `Derived` constructor includes a reference to the `Root` constructor:

```
Derived::Derived( short param ) : Root( param )
{
  cout << "Derived constructor called\n";
}
```

Even if the `Base1` and `Base2` constructors map parameters to the `Root` constructor, their mappings are superseded by the deeper, `Derived` constructor. By overriding the constructor mappings, the compiler makes sure that only a single object of the virtual base class (in this case, `Root`) is created.

A Virtual Base Class Example

This next example brings these techniques to life. Close the current project by selecting **Close Project** from the **Project** menu. When prompted for a project file to open, go up to the THIN C++ Projects folder, open the subfolder named Chap 09.04 – virtual, and open the project file named virtual.π. Next, run virtual.π by selecting **Run** from the **Project** menu. Here's what you'll see:

```
Root constructor called
Base1 constructor called
Base2 constructor called
Derived constructor called
------
num = 3
```

Hit a return to exit virtual. Let's take a look at the source code.

The virtual Source Code

As usual, virtual.cp starts by including <iostream.h>:

```
#include <iostream.h>
```

This version of the Root class includes a data member named num:

```
//------------------------------------- Root

class Root
{
  protected:
    short num;

  public:
        Root( short numParam );
};
```

The `Root()` constructor takes a single parameter and uses it to initialize num (as you read through the code, try to figure out where the value for this parameter comes from):

```
Root::Root( short numParam )
{
  num = numParam;

  cout << "Root constructor called\n";
}
```

`Base1` is derived from `Root`, but it treats `Root` as a virtual base class:

```
//------------------------------------  Base1

class Base1 : public virtual Root
{
  public:
    Base1( void );
};
```

Notice that the `Base1()` constructor asks the compiler to call the `Root()` constructor and passes it a value of 1. Will this call take place?

```
Base1::Base1( void ) : Root( 1 )
{
  cout << "Base1 constructor called\n";
}
```

`Base2` also declares `Root` as a virtual base class. Now there's no path down from `Root` that's not marked as `virtual`:

```
//------------------------------------  Base2

class Base2 : public virtual Root
{
  public:
    Base2( void );
};
```

The `Base2()` constructor asks the compiler to pass a value of 2 to the `Root()` constructor. Is this the value that is passed on to the `Root()` constructor?

```
Base2::Base2( void ) : Root( 2 )
{
  cout << "Base2 constructor called\n";
}
```

The `Derived` class doesn't need the `virtual` keyword (although it wouldn't hurt things if `virtual` were used here):

```
//---------------------------------- Derived

class Derived : public Base1, public Base2
{
  public:
        Derived( void );
    short GetNum( void );
};
```

The `Derived()` constructor also asks the compiler to pass a value on to the `Root()` constructor. Since `Derived` is the deepest class, this is the constructor mapping that takes precedence. The `Root` data member num should be initialized with a value of 3:

```
Derived::Derived( void ) : Root( 3 )
{
  cout << "Derived constructor called\n";
}
```

This function makes the value of num available to `main()`. Why can't `main()` reference num directly? `Derived` inherits num and `main()` doesn't:

```
short Derived::GetNum( void )
{
  return( num );
}
```

main() creates a Derived object, causing a sequence of constructor calls:

```
//------------------------------------ main()

void   main( void )
{
  Derived    myDerived;
```

Notice that the Root constructor is called only once:

```
Root constructor called
Base1 constructor called
Base2 constructor called
Derived constructor called
```

Finally, the value of num is printed (drum roll, please):

```
  cout << "------\n"
    << "num = " << myDerived.GetNum();
}
```

As you've already guessed, num has a value of 3, showing that the Base1 and Base2 constructor initializations are overridden by the deeper, Derived constructor initialization:

```
------
num = 3
```

Initialization Versus Assignment

When you think about initialization, you might think of a line of code like this, where the variable i is defined and *initialized* to a value of 21:

```
short   i = 21;
```

In the following code i is defined and then a value of 21 is assigned to i:

```
short    i;

i = 21;
```

The point here is that the compiler thinks of initialization and assignment as two completely different operations. Every constructor is broken into two parts, the initialization part and the assignment part. The initialization part takes place in the *member initialization list*. The assignment part takes place in the *body* of the constructor. The remainder of this section discusses things you should know about initialization and assignment as they relate to object construction.

const and Reference Types

When a `const` is defined, a value is tied to it at initialization. In the strictest sense of the word, you can't *assign* a value to a `const`. This code will compile:

```
const short kMaxNameLength = 20;
```

This code won't compile:

```
const short kMaxNameLength;

kMaxNameLength = 20; // Aaack!
```

The same holds true for a reference type. A reference type must be given a value at initialization. This code compiles just fine:

```
short    number = 20;
short    &numberAlias = number;
```

This code, on the other hand, is destined for failure:

```
short    &numberAlias; // Error: Must be
                       // initialized!!
```

You can declare a class data member as a `const` or a reference type, but beware! You can't provide these data members their initial value via an assignment statement. Instead, you must use the member initialization list to do your dirty work for you. Here's an example:

```
class MyClass
{
  private:
    const short    kMaxNameLength;
    short          &numberAlias;
    short          number;

  public:
    MyClass( short  constValue );
};

MyClass::MyClass( short constValue ) :
  kMaxNameLength( constValue ), numberAlias( number )
{
  // kMaxNameLength is set to constValue
  // numberAlias references number
}
```

Up until this point, we've used the member initialization list to map parameters from the constructor to a base class. In this example, we use the member initialization list to initialize some members. How appropriate!

If you include a data member name in the member initialization list and follow the name by an expression surrounded by parentheses, the compiler uses the expression to initialize the data member. In the previous chunk of code, `kMaxNameLength` is initialized to the value in `constValue` and `numberAlias` is set to reference `number`. As you can see, the member initialization list is pretty useful.

A Member Initialization List Example

Here's a working version of the previous chunk of code. Close the current project by selecting **Close Project** from the **Project** menu. When prompted for a project file to open, go into the THIN C++ Projects folder, open the subfolder named Chap 09.05 – init, and open the project file named init.π. Next, run init.π by selecting **Run** from the **Project** menu. Here's what you'll see:

```
Before: number = 10
After:  number = 20
```

Hit a return to exit init. Let's take a look at the source code.

The init Source Code

As usual, init.cp starts by including <iostream.h>:

```
#include <iostream.h>
```

The declaration of MyClass is pretty much the same as the one you just saw. To simplify things, all the data members are declared as public. Also, the constructor is filled out to make things a little more interesting:

```
//----------------------------------- MyClass

class MyClass
{
  public:
    const short    kMaxNameLength;
    short          &numberAlias;
    short          number;

    MyClass( short  constValue );
};
```

The constructor takes a single parameter, a value used to initialize our const variable. The member initialization list is used to initialize kMaxNameLength and numberAlias:

```
MyClass::MyClass( short constValue ) :
  kMaxNameLength( constValue ), numberAlias( number )
```

We start off by assigning number the value stored in kMaxNameLength:

```
{
  number = kMaxNameLength;
```

To prove that kMaxNameLength is initialized properly, we print out the value in number:

```
cout << "Before: number = "
  << number << "\n";
```

This results in the following line of output:

```
Before: number = 10
```

Next, to prove that numberAlias references number, numberAlias is incremented by 10:

```
numberAlias += 10;
```

Now, we print out the value of number again:

```
cout << "After:  number = "
  << number << "\n";
}
```

Just as we'd hoped, number now has a value of 20:

```
After:  number = 20
```

main( ) has a pretty simple job—just to create a MyClass object and pass a value of 10 to its constructor:

```
//------------------------------------- main()

void  main( void )
{
  MyClass    myObject( 10 );
}
```

Memberwise Initialization

In certain instances, a special form of initialization, known as **memberwise initialization**, is used to initialize a newly created object. Basically, memberwise initialization is the technique of copying the contents of one object, data member by data member, into another object.

Memberwise initialization is a convenient way to make a copy of an object. Here's one way to do this:

```
MyClass obj1( 20 );
MyClass obj2 = obj1; // Uses memberwise initialization
```

The first line of code defines an object of class `MyClass` and passes the number 20 to its constructor. The second line creates another `MyClass` object, but instead of calling the constructor, the second object becomes an exact duplicate of the first object.

There are several other ways to achieve memberwise initialization. If you pass an object by value as a parameter, the compiler creates a local copy of your parameter, using memberwise initialization to initialize the copy. Also, if you write a function that returns an object, memberwise initialization is used to copy the returned object into the object receiving the returned object.

Memberwise initialization is easy to use and it *is* convenient, but there's a catch. Memberwise initialization makes an exact copy of an object, *including any and all pointers*. Suppose you declare a `Name` class that holds someone's first and last names:

```
class Name
{
  private:
    char  *last;
    char  *first;

  public:
    Name( char *firstParam, char *lastParam );
};
```

Suppose also that the `Name()` constructor allocates the memory for `last` and `first`, based on the size of the two constructor parameters. This being the case, you might define a `Name` like this:

```
Name  yourAuthor( "Dave", "Mark" );
```

What happens if you define a second `Name` by using the memberwise initialization syntax?

```
Name   aCopy = yourAuthor;
```

Now, `yourAuthor` and `aCopy` share some common memory. Both copies of `last` point to the same block of memory, and both copies of `first` point to the same block of memory. If you `delete` one of the objects, the other object is left with a dangling pointer. That can be a problem.

A Memberwise Initialization Function

You can provide a memberwise initialization function for any of your classes. Before the compiler does a memberwise copy, it first checks to see whether your class includes an overloaded version of your constructor having the form

```
MyClass( const MyClass& )
```

where `MyClass` is the class being copied.

def'ə nish' ən

> This special constructor is known as a **copy constructor**.

If you provide a copy constructor, it is called whenever memberwise initialization is called for. Your copy constructor should copy the current object into the object passed by reference as a parameter. If the object to be copied contains any pointers, you may want to reallocate the necessary memory in the copy instead of blindly copying the pointers.

A Memberwise Initialization Example

Here's a working version of the previous chunk of code. Close the current project by selecting **Close Project** from the **Project** menu. When prompted for a project file to open, go into the THIN C++ Projects folder, open the subfolder named Chap 09.06 - memberWise, and open the project file named memberWise.π. Next, run memberWise.π by selecting **Run** from the **Project** menu. Here's what you'll see:

```
Original constructor...
Copy constructor...
Original constructor...
Name: Dave Mark
Name: Dave Mark
Name: Scott Knaster
```

Hit a return to exit memberWise. Let's take a look at the source code.

The memberWise Source Code

memberWise.cp starts by including <iostream.h> and <string.h>:

```
#include <iostream.h>
#include <string.h>
```

The Name class includes two data members, last and first:

```
//------------------------------------- Name

class Name
{
  private:
    char  *last;
    char  *first;
```

The first Name() constructor is for regular Name objects; the second constructor is our copy constructor:

```
public:
      Name( char *firstParam, char *lastParam );
      Name( const Name& original );
```

The `operator()()` function is used to display the data members of the current `Name` object:

```
void  Name::operator()( void );
```

The `Name` class's `operator=()` function provides a service similar to the `Name()` copy constructor. When the compiler encounters an expression of the form

```
myObject = yourObject
```

where both operands belong to the same class, it performs a memberwise copy of the right operand to the left operand. If the class in question provides an `operator=()` function in the proper form, the `operator=()` function is called in lieu of performing the memberwise copy. Use the `Name operator=()` function as a template for your own versions:

```
    Name   &Name::operator=( const Name& original );
};
```

The regular `Name()` constructor uses `new` to allocate memory for `first` and `last`:

```
Name::Name( char *firstParam, char *lastParam )
{
  first = new char[ strlen(firstParam) + 1 ];
  last = new char[ strlen(lastParam) + 1 ];
```

Next, `strcpy()` is called to copy the two parameters into their associated data members:

```
  strcpy( first, firstParam );
  strcpy( last, lastParam );
```

Then, a message is printed to let us know which constructor we're in:

```
  cout << "Original constructor...\n";
}
```

When the copy constructor is called, the current object is the new `Name` object. The parameter passed in is the original `Name` object from which the data is being copied:

```
Name::Name( const Name& original )
{
  first = new char[ strlen(original.first) + 1 ];
  last = new char[ strlen(original.last) + 1 ];

  strcpy( first, original.first );
  strcpy( last, original.last );
```

Once again, a message is printed telling us which constructor we're in:

```
  cout << "Copy constructor...\n";
}
```

Again, the `operator()()` function prints the current `Name`:

```
void  Name::operator()( void )
{
  cout << "Name: " << first << " " << last << "\n";
}
```

The `operator=()` function starts by checking to see whether the left and right operands are the same object, as in this expression:

```
myObject = myObject;
```

Why is this case special? As you'll see, before we copy the right operand to the left operand, we **delete** any memory allocated to the left operand. If the left and right objects are the same object, we'll lose data if we **delete** before we copy:

```
Name  &Name::operator=( const Name& original )
{
  if ( this == &original )
    return( *this );
```

Once we know we're dealing with two different objects, we start by deleting any previously allocated memory. Remember, the left-hand operand is the current object; the right hand operand is passed in as the parameter `original`:

```
delete first;
delete last;
```

The next four lines are lifted right from the copy constructor:

```
first = new char[ strlen(original.first) + 1 ];
last = new char[ strlen(original.last) + 1 ];

strcpy( first, original.first );
strcpy( last, original.last );
```

Finally, we return the current object as the result of the = operation:

```
    return( *this );
}
```

`main()` starts by creating an original `Name`, reflecting the identity of your hard-working author:

```
//-------------------------------------- main()

void  main( void )
{
    Name  yourAuthor( "Dave", "Mark" );
```

This results in a call of the original constructor, and the following message appears in the console window:

```
Original constructor...
```

Next, another `Name` is created using the copy constructor:

```
Name  aCopy = yourAuthor;
```

This results in the following line of output:

```
Copy constructor...
```

The third `Name` object is used to test our `operator=( )` function:

```
Name   anotherAuthor( "Scott", "Knaster" );
```

This results in the following line of output:

```
Original constructor...
```

When `yourAuthor( )` is called, the contents of the original `Name` are printed:

```
yourAuthor();
```

Here's the result:

```
Name: Dave Mark
```

When `aCopy( )` is called, the contents of the copy are printed:

```
aCopy();
```

Here's the result:

```
Name: Dave Mark
```

Next, the = operator is used to copy `anotherAuthor` to `aCopy`. Before the copy is done, `aCopy` has the name *Dave Mark* and `anotherAuthor` has the name *Scott Knaster*.

```
aCopy = anotherAuthor;

aCopy();
}
```

This call of `aCopy( )` results in the following line of output:

```
Name: Scott Knaster
```

If you have any doubts about memberwise initialization, add some additional output statements to the program to verify that a copied object has its own unique memory allocated for it. To do this, print the addresses of `first` and `last` in both the original and the copy.

Summary   OK, time to break out the good champagne (grab a Perrier if you're driving). You have now officially made it through the basics of C++. Although there are still many interesting things to learn, you've mastered the essentials and you're ready to code. Chapter 10 offers a look at some C++ class libraries and development environments. Let's rip!

Chapter 10

Moving On

Now that you've mastered the basics of C++ programming, you're ready to develop some applications. This chapter takes a look at a variety of Macintosh development environments and class libraries.

This Chapter
at a Glance

The User Interface
The Macintosh Toolbox
   Accessing the Macintosh Toolbox
Class Libraries
   Class Library Economics
   Waiting for Bedrock
   What Next?
Books and Other Reference Material
   Inside Macintosh
   THINK Reference
   The Macintosh C Programming Primer
   Macintosh Programming Secrets
   Unofficial C++ Style Guide
   The Bibliography
Go Get 'Em...

WHAT DOES IT TAKE TO DEVELOP A C++ APPLICATION? The answer depends on the computer and operating system under which your application will ultimately run. Are you building a program destined for a text-based environment like DOS or Unix? Are you writing an application that will run only on a Macintosh? Are you trying to write an application that will run on a variety of platforms?

The User Interface

If you can live within the confines of a text-oriented user interface, almost any C++ development environment will work for you. By taking advantage of the `iostream` library, you can build a C++ application with a completely portable user interface. The upside here is that you can develop an application on a Macintosh, copy the source code to a PC, and recompile, and (with some minor retooling, perhaps) you'll have a perfectly acceptable DOS application.

The down side is that a text-oriented user interface is so limited. The console works, but it isn't pretty. (If you tried to fob off an `iostream`-based user interface on seasoned Macintosh users, they'd likely run you out of town.) Most graphical user interfaces (GUIs, pronounced "gooeys") require strict adherence to a set of **interface guidelines**. In the Macintosh world, these guidelines are described in *Inside Macintosh*, and in the *Macintosh Human Interface Guidelines* (both of these are listed in the bibliography at the back of the book). The Windows' environment has its own interface guidelines, as do GUIs such as Motif and OpenLook.

If you can live within the confines of `iostream`, you'll have the ultimate in application portability. If you want to create an application with the look and feel of the environment it's running under, you'll have some extra work to do. First, you must become an expert user of the destination environment. You'll need to recognize each of the elements that make up that environment's user interface, as well as the proper behavior of each element. When a window is in front, does it look different than when it is behind another window? What's the proper way to disable a menu item? Where do scroll bars usually appear? How do you resize a window? When you've mastered this **interface vocabulary**, you're ready to design your application's interface.

If you plan to develop an application that will run on more than one platform, you have even more work to do. First, you must absorb the interface vocabulary for each platform you plan to support. Next, you'll have to make some decisions about your user interface. Your programming task will be simpler if you build your interface by using elements common to all of the platforms your application will run on. For example, unless all of the candidate platforms support pop-up menus, you might consider leaving them out of your interface. Each special case that you support will make your software more difficult to maintain.

The Macintosh Toolbox

For the moment, let's assume that you wish to use your newfound C++ talents to build a Macintosh application with all of the user-interface elements that Mac users have come to know and love. Fortunately, every Macintosh that rolls off the assembly line comes with a slew of user-interface functions built right in. Collectively, these user-interface routines are known as the **Macintosh Toolbox**. The more than 2000 routines that make up the Macintosh Toolbox are stored on board the Macintosh, burned into the Mac's **read-only memory (ROM)**.

The Macintosh Toolbox contains functions that create windows on the screen and others that draw text in these windows. There are functions for drawing shapes, lines, and dots in color and in black and white. There's a set of functions that allow you to implement your own pull-down menus. The Mac Toolbox is huge.

Every program that supports the standard Macintosh interface relies on the Mac Toolbox. That's why Macintosh programs have such a consistent look and feel. Take a look at the pull-down menu in Figure 10.1. Although the item names may be different, this menu bears a striking resemblance to every other Macintosh pull-down menu because the same Mac Toolbox routines are used to implement all Macintosh pull-down menus. When Mac programmers want to implement a pull-down menu, they always turn to this set of functions, collectively known as the *Menu Manager*. The Menu Manager has a set of rules it follows to create a pull-down menu. For example, a standard Macintosh menu is always drawn using the **Chicago** font. The **Chicago** font is built into every Macintosh ROM, from the tiniest PowerBook to the mighty Quadra.

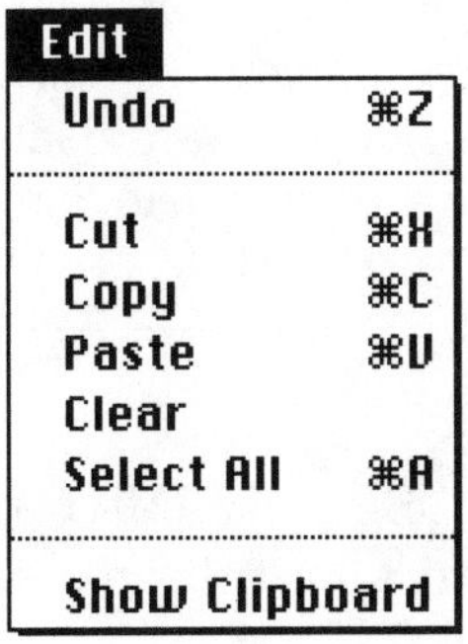

FIGURE 10.1
*An **Edit** menu. This one comes from the Finder.*

Edit	
Undo	⌘Z
Cut	⌘X
Copy	⌘C
Paste	⌘V
Clear	
Select All	⌘A
Show Clipboard	

The Mac Toolbox is divided into a series of managers. As you learn to implement a standard Macintosh interface, you'll learn about the functions that make up each manager. For example, you'll learn how to use the functions that make up the *Window Manager* to create and maintain your program's windows. You'll use the *Control Manager* to manage scroll bars, push buttons, and other standard Macintosh controls, like the ones shown in Figure 10.2.

FIGURE 10.2

A set of radio buttons, a push button, and a scroll bar. Each of these is created and maintained via the Control Manager.

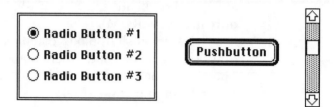

Accessing the Macintosh Toolbox

Every Macintosh development environment worth its salt provides a mechanism for calling each and every Mac Toolbox function. In the THINK C and THINK C++ environments, this mechanism is implemented via the `MacTraps` library. Many of the most popular Macintosh programs were written using nothing more than THINK C and `MacTraps` (OK, and maybe some pizza and Snapple).

The official name of Symantec's C++ environment is *Symantec C++ for Macintosh*. Almost everyone I know calls it "THINK C++," but your friendly neighborhood software dealer might not respond to anything but the complete name. Incidentally, THINK C's offical name is "THINK C 6.0." Just thought you'd like to know.

Since THINK C++ also comes with the `MacTraps` library, you can take full advantage of the Macintosh Toolbox from inside your THINK C++ application. In fact, you might design a set of classes and have each one implement a different piece of the Macintosh user interface. You might build one group of classes to create and manage windows and another group of classes to implement your program's menus.

This approach is just fine, though it might take you a fair amount of time to implement all of the Toolbox pieces that you'll need. An alternative is to take advantage of one of the existing class libraries.

Class Libraries

A **class library** is a collection of predefined classes. There are several class libraries designed specifically to simplify the process of creating a Macintosh application. Probably the most famous of these class libraries is Apple's MacApp, which contains classes that implement every nook and cranny of the Mac Toolbox. The MacApp classes are organized in a treelike hierarchy, known as an **application framework**. This application framework is much more than just an object-oriented translation of the Toolbox. Think of it as a generic application, complete with menu and window-handling code in place and ready to go. Rather than starting from scratch, your job is to customize this generic application, shaping its look and behavior to suit your design. For the most part, you do this by deriving new classes from the existing MacApp classes and then adding your own classes as the need arises.

Another popular class library is the THINK Class Library (TCL), brought to you by Symantec, the folks responsible for THIN and THINK C++. The TCL classes are also organized hierarchically as an application framework. Just as with MacApp, you start with a generic TCL application and then customize it to suit your needs.

To allow it to work with both THINK C and THINK C++, the TCL was written in C with special C++-like extensions. So, if you work with the TCL, you won't be able to use C++ features like overloading, default arguments, and multiple inheritance. Since the TCL is so popular, I'd say that most programmers don't have much trouble living with these limitations.

Class Library Economics

Which class library should you choose—MacApp or TCL? Both of these libraries are Macintosh specific, so you won't be able to use them to create a Unix or Windows application. Some people feel that MacApp is more robust, and, since MacApp has been around longer, this makes sense. MacApp supports true C++, while TCL puts some definite restrictions on C++ compatibility. On the other hand, consider the economics of programming with each library.

To make full use of MacApp, you need to purchase Apple's Macintosh Programmer's Workshop (MPW), a Unixlike development environment. You also need to buy MacApp as well as a C++ compiler (either CFront or Symantec's C++ for MPW). Finally, you need at least 16 megabytes if you want a little elbow room. Overall, this is a pretty pricey proposition. According to my APDA catalog, the latest MPW/C++ bundle costs $575 and the latest version of MacApp costs $350 if you have a CD-ROM drive, $395 on floppies, for a total ranging from $925 to $970. Ouch!

To make full use of the TCL, you have only one thing to buy—either THINK C or THINK C++, both of which come with their respective versions of the TCL. THINK C lives comfortably in 4 megabytes of RAM, while THINK C++ needs about 8. THINK C 6.0 lists for $299, and *Symantec C++ for Macintosh* lists for $499 (the street price of each is definitely lower). If saving money is your chief objective, the THINK Class Library is your best bet.

APDA is the Apple Programmers and Developers Association, a branch of Apple that sells all kinds of cool developer goodies. If you don't have a current APDA catalog, get one immediately. You can reach APDA at:

- (800) 282-2732 in the United States
- (800) 637-0029 in Canada
- (716) 871-6555 internationally
- (716) 871-6511 by fax

Waiting for Bedrock

Just when you thought you had this class library thing figured out, along comes a new wrinkle—Bedrock. Bedrock is the class library that is being developed jointly by Apple and Symantec and is scheduled for release in late 1993. Bedrock is intended as *the* standard cross-platform class library, capable of generating applications that will run on the Macintosh as well as under Windows and Unix. While you *can* use Bedrock exclusively for the creation of Macintosh applications, the beauty of Bedrock is that by changing a few settings, you can use the same source code to generate applications that will run on multiple platforms.

Although several good cross-platform development systems are available that support the Macintosh, Windows, and Unix, none of them have the gold seal of approval that goes along with being developed by Apple and Symantec. In my opinion, Bedrock is the future of Macintosh development.

What Next?

If Bedrock is the future, where does that leave MacApp and the TCL? Apple and Symantec have promised to create a migration path from both MacApp and the TCL to Bedrock. So, if you invest your time learning either one of these class libraries, your investment will pay off handsomely when you make the switch to Bedrock.

If you do decide to order THINK C++, make sure you take advantage of the money-saving coupon in the back of the book.

Books and Other Reference Material

Once you've decided on a class library, you'll be ready to turn your sights to the Macintosh Toolbox. If you're new to the Toolbox, you'll be glad to know that there's a lot of reading material available to help ease you through the Toolbox learning curve.

Inside Macintosh

If there is one item found on every Macintosh programmer's bookshelf, it's a well-worn copy of *Inside Macintosh*, Apple's official Macintosh programmer's reference guide. It covers the Toolbox in depth, describing each of the Toolbox managers along with their respective functions, including each functions' parameters and each function's place in the Mac universe.

When the Macintosh was first introduced, Apple also published the first two volumes of *Inside Macintosh*. As new Macintosh models were released, Apple put out new volumes of *Inside Macintosh* to keep programmers abreast of the latest developments.

The six volumes of the original *Inside Macintosh* truly stood the test of time, lasting from 1984 until now. In 1992, however, Apple decided to give the whole series a facelift, and the new *Inside Macintosh* was born. Instead of being organized historically, the new series is organized by topic. For example, *Inside Macintosh: Files* tells you everything you need to know about the Macintosh Hierarchical File System (HFS). Other books in the series include *Macintosh Toolbox Essentials*, *Overview*, *Processes*, and *Memory*. I suggest you start by picking up a copy of *Overview* and of *Macintosh Toolbox Essentials*. Then, add *Inside Macintosh* volumes as the need arises.

THINK Reference

One resource that I just can't live without is THINK Reference from Symantec. THINK Reference is a data base tool that contains a relatively comprehensive summary of the Toolbox, broken down in a variety of ways. With THINK Reference, you can list all of the Window Manager's functions and data structures or you can display a detailed listing of one of the Menu Manager's routines. THINK Reference is awesome!

The *Macintosh C Programming Primer*

When *Inside Macintosh* was written, Pascal was the primary Macintosh programming language. Because of this, all of the function descriptions and examples presented in *Inside Macintosh* were written in Pascal. In addition, *Inside Macintosh* was written as a reference and not a tutorial. It becomes indispensable once you understand the basics of Toolbox programming; its not the ideal reading material for getting you started.

There is a book that helps bridge the gap for first-time Macintosh programmers. The *Macintosh C Programming Primer*, by Dave Mark and Cartwright Reed, offers a step-by-step tour through the mysteries of the Toolbox. The *Mac Primer* walks you through each of the Toolbox managers, punctuating each chapter with a variety of sample programs. The *Mac Primer* takes the sting out of learning to program using the Mac Toolbox.

The *Mac Primer* also offers a lot of advice for programmers who want to get involved with the Macintosh development community. Whether you are interested in developing your own best-selling Macintosh application or you just want to hook up with other Macintosh developers, the *Mac Primer* can help. Inside, you'll find descriptions of Apple's developer relations programs, designed to help you get your products out the door. You can read about AppleLink, Apple's internal electronic mail system that you can be a part of. There are descriptions of technical reference material available from Apple as well as from third parties.

In general, Cartwright and I tried to put everything into the *Mac Primer* that we were looking for when we were first learning to program the Macintosh. We hope you enjoy it.

Macintosh Programming Secrets

A book that I frequently turn to is Scott Knaster's excellent *Macintosh Programming Secrets*. This book is chock-full of Macintosh programming tips, tricks, and techniques. Scott takes his years of experience as an Apple employee and puts them to good use, revealing some of the deep, dark secrets that only a Mac aficionado could know. Once you've mastered the basics of Macintosh Toolbox programming, give this book a try.

Unofficial C++ Style Guide

In 1990, Apple's technical magazine *develop* featured an article called "Unofficial C++ Style Guide." I love this article and think you will too. You'll find a copy of it in Appendix G. Take the time to read the style guide. It is packed with useful, even critical, information that no C++ programmer can afford to be without. Hats off to David Goldsmith and Jack Palevich, the authors of this article. Great stuff!

Though the style guide was written with MacApp in mind, its contents apply just as well to the TCL. As an example, when the style guide refers to a specific class name, it uses MacApp's class-naming convention, starting each class name with T. Since the TCL starts all of its classes with C, you just substitute the leading Ts for Cs when reading for the TCL.

The Bibliography

Be sure to check out the bibliography in Appendix I, where you'll find a list of books that will help ease your transition into Macintosh C++ programming. Now that you've mastered the basics of C++, you should pick up a good reference guide to help complete your education. *The C++ Programming Language* by Bjarne Stroustrup (the principal architect of C++) is a must. C++ *Primer* by Stanley Lippman is also very helpful. Make sure you get the second edition of both books.

Go Get 'Em...   Well, that's it. I hope you enjoyed reading *Learn C++ on the Macintosh* as much as I enjoyed writing it. Above all, I hope you are excited about C++. Now go out there and write some source code!

Appendix A

Glossary

abstract class: A base class whose sole purpose is to provide a basis for derived classes. You'll never create an object based on an abstract class.

access code: One of `public`, `private`, or `protected`, the access code defines which of your program's functions has access to the specified data member or function.

access function: A function designed specifically to provide access to a data member. See *setter* or *getter function*.

application framework: A collection of classes that implement a generic application. Typically, the classes in an application framework act as placeholders. The programmer overloads various parts of the framework to give the application the desired look and feel.

automatic object: An object created by definition. Memory for an automatic object is allocated and deallocated automatically.

base class: A class used as the basis for the declaration of a second class, known as a derived class. The derived class inherits all the non-`private` members of the base class.

bundling: A technique that lets you represent more than one piece of information under a single name. Classes and structs are both examples of bundling mechanisms.

class: A C++ structure that bundles together data and functions, known as data members and member functions.

class derivation: The technique of deriving classes based on other classes.

class library: A collection of classes, typically used to implement a platform's user interface. Many class libraries come in the form of an application framework.

constructor function: A member function having the same name as its class. The constructor function is typically used to initialize an object's data members. Constructors should not be used to allocate memory. Instead, use the two-stage construction technique.

copy constructor: A constructor designed for the sole purpose of providing an alternative to memberwise initialization for copying one object to another.

current object: The object that launched the current member function. The members of the current object may be referred to without using the normal object notation. `this` is always a pointer to the current object.

data member: One of the data elements of a class.

declaration: A statement that creates a reference to an object or function, without actually allocating memory for the object or function.

default argument initializer: A function argument with an associated default value. If the function is called and no value is passed in corresponding to the argument, the argument is initialized to its default value.

definition: A statement that causes memory to be allocated for a variable or function. A function prototype is a declaration. The entire function, including curly braces and all the statements between, is known as the function definition.

derivation chain: The chain of classes running from a root class, through a sequence of derived classes, to the ultimate derived class, which is the last class in the derivation chain.

derived class: A class declared using a base class. The derived class inherits all the non-`private` members of its base class.

destructor function: A member function having the same name as its class preceded by the ~ character. The destructor function is typically used to delete any member allocated for an object.

extraction operator: The >> operator, part of `iostream`, that allows you to extract data from a stream.

formal parameter list: The list of type placeholders following the `template` keyword in a function or class template.

formatting flags: A series of flags maintained by the `ios` class used to control various iostream formatting features.

function name overloading: A feature that allows you to create several functions with the same name, but having different signatures. Each call of an overloaded function is compared against the available signatures and the matching function is called. If no match is found, the compiler reports an error.

getter function: A function designed specifically to return the value of a data member.

inheritance: The technique wherein a derived class receives access to members of its base class.

inline function: A function declared using the `inline` keyword. The body of an inline function is actually copied into the calling function, allowing you to bypass the overhead normally associated with calling a function.

insertion operator: The `<<` operator, part of `iostream`, that allows you to insert data into a stream.

interface guidelines: A document that guides you through the process of designing a user interface for a specific platform. The Macintosh user interface guidelines are found in *Macintosh Human Interface Guidelines*, published by Addison-Wesley Publishing Co..

interface vocabulary: A language that describes the elements in a platform's user interface. The terms scroll bar, window, and pull-down menu are all part of the Macintosh interface vocabulary.

Macintosh Toolbox: The more than 2000 routines built into every Macintosh computer. These routines give Macintosh applications their unique Macintosh look and feel.

manipulator: A special function, provided as part of the `iostream` library, that allows you to perform a specific I/O operation while you are in the middle of in insertion or extraction.

member function: One of the functions declared as part of a class.

member initialization list: The list that optionally follows a constructor's parameter list, used to initialize an object's members. The member initialization list is always preceded by a `:`.

memberwise assignment: The process of copying the value of the data members of one object to the data members of another object belonging to the same class, one at a time.

memberwise initialization: A special form of initialization used to copy one object to another. The first object's data members are copied to those of the second, one at a time.

multiple inheritance: The technique of defining a class derived from more than one class.

object: A specialized variable, defined as a member of a class, having data members and member functions. Some people extend the definition of object to include any C++ entity that occupies memory.

operator overloading: Similar to function overloading, the technique of assigning more than one meaning to one of the built-in C++ operators. Overloaded operators rely on functions having the name `operator`, followed by the name of the operator being overloaded. For example, the function `operator+()` overloads the + operator.

project: A collection consisting of a project file and all the other files that contribute to a particular program.

project file: A file used by Symantec's development environments to manage all of a program's source and object code. By convention, project files usually end in ".π".

project window: A window that appears when you open a project using the Think Project Manager. The window that describes all the source code file and library files that make up the project.

read-only memory (ROM): Computer memory that can only be read from, not written to. On a Macintosh, the ROM is used to store the Macintosh Toolbox.

reference variable: A variable designed to act as an alias to another variable of the exact same type. To denote a variable as a reference variable, precede its name with an & in its definition. Reference variables must be initialized (set to alias another variable) at the same time they are defined.

root base class: The ultimate base class in a derivation chain.

scope: A variable's scope defines the availability of the variable throughout the rest of the program.

scope operator: The scope operator, `::`, precedes a variable, telling the compiler to look outside the current block for a variable of the same name. The scope operator is also used to refer to a class' static members.

setter function: A function designed specifically to set the value of a data member.

signature: A function's parameter list. A function's name and signature combine to distinguish it from all other functions. A function's return type is not part of its signature.

smart pointer: An overloaded version of the `->` operator, used to walk down a chain of pointers.

state bits: A series of bits that reflect the current status of a stream. The bits are `goodbit`, `eofbit`, `failbit`, and `badbit`.

static member: A data member or member function declared using the `static` keyword. A static data member is shared by the entire class, rather than allocated for each object of the class. A static member function is also shared by the entire class and therefore has no current object when it is called. The `this` pointer is unavailable in a static member function.

template: A function or class definition containing a series of placeholders, each of which represents a type that isn't provided until the function is called or until an object of the class is defined.

template instantiation: A function or class defined based on a template.

two-stage construction: An alternative to a single constructor. The second constructor is named by placing the letter `I` in front of the class name. The `I` constructor is used to perform an object's memory allocation, which is inappropriate for the object's constructor.

virtual base class: A root base class having all derived classes marked using the `virtual` keyword. This ensures that a derived class having more than one path back to the virtual base class will not instantiate more than one copy of the root base class.

Appendix B

Source Code Listings

```cpp
#include <iostream.h>

//--------------------------------------- Item

class Item
{
    private:
        float     price;

    public:
                    Item( float itemPrice );
        float     operator()( float taxRate );
};

Item::Item( float itemPrice )
{
    price = itemPrice;
}

float Item::operator()( float taxRate = 0 )
{
    return( ((taxRate * .01) + 1) * price );
}
```

313

```
//--------------------------------------- main()

void   main( void )
{
    Item   stimpyDoll( 36.99 );

    cout << "Price of Stimpy doll: $" << stimpyDoll();
    cout << "\nPrice with 4.5% tax:  $" << stimpyDoll( 4.5 );
}
```

cin
(Chapter 4)

```
#include <iostream.h>

const short  kMaxNameLength = 40;

void   main( void )
{
    char   name[ kMaxNameLength ];
    short  myShort;
    long   myLong;
    float  myFloat;

    cout << "Type in your first name: ";
    cin >> name;

    cout << "Short, long, float: ";
    cin >> myShort >> myLong >> myFloat;

    cout << "\nYour name is: " << name;
    cout << "\nmyShort: " << myShort;
    cout << "\nmyLong: " << myLong;
    cout << "\nmyFloat: " << myFloat;
}
```

cout
(Chapter 4)

```
#include <iostream.h>

void   main( void )
{
    char   *name = "Dr. Crusher";

    cout << "char:    " << name[ 0 ] << '\n'
         << "short:   " << (short)(name[ 0 ]) << '\n'
         << "string:  " << name << '\n'
         << "address: " << (unsigned long)name;
}
```

derived (Chapter 6)

```cpp
#include <iostream.h>


//------------------------------------- Base

class Base
{
//      Data members...
   protected:
      short baseMember;

//      Member functions...
   public:
      void  Base::SetBaseMember( short baseValue );
};

void  Base::SetBaseMember( short baseValue )
{
   baseMember = baseValue;
}


//------------------------------------- Base:Derived

class Derived : public Base
{
//      Data members...
   private:
      short derivedMember;

//      Member functions...
   public:
      void  Derived::SetDerivedMember( short derivedValue );
      void  Derived::PrintDataMembers( void );
};

void  Derived::SetDerivedMember( short derivedValue )
{
   derivedMember = derivedValue;
}

void  Derived::PrintDataMembers( void )
{
   cout << "baseMember was set to "
      << baseMember << '\n';

   cout << "derivedMember was set to "
      << derivedMember << '\n';
}
```

```
//------------------------------------- main()

void   main( void )
{
    Derived        *derivedPtr;

    derivedPtr = new Derived;

    derivedPtr->SetBaseMember( 10 );

    derivedPtr->SetDerivedMember( 20 );

    derivedPtr->PrintDataMembers();
}
```

employee (Chapter 5)

```
#include <iostream.h>
#include <string.h>

const short  kMaxNameSize = 20;

class Employee
{
//        Data members...
    private:
        char    employeeName[ kMaxNameSize ];
        long    employeeID;
        float   employeeSalary;

//        Member functions...
    public:
                Employee( char *name, long id, float salary );
                ~Employee( void );
        void    PrintEmployee( void );
};

Employee::Employee( char *name, long id, float salary )
{
    strcpy( this->employeeName, name );
    this->employeeID = id;
    this->employeeSalary = salary;

    cout << "Creating employee #" << employeeID << "\n";
}

Employee::~Employee( void )
{
    cout << "Deleting employee #" << employeeID << "\n";
}
```

```
void  Employee::PrintEmployee( void )
{
   cout << "-----\n";
   cout << "Name:    " << employeeName << "\n";
   cout << "ID:      " << employeeID << "\n";
   cout << "Salary: " << employeeSalary << "\n";
   cout << "-----\n";
}

void  main( void )
{
   Employee  employee1( "Dave Mark", 1, 200.0 );
   Employee  *employee2;

   employee2 = new Employee( "Steve Baker", 2, 300.0 );

   employee1.PrintEmployee();
   employee2->PrintEmployee();

   delete employee2;
}
```

equals (Chapter 7)

```
#include <iostream.h>
#include <string.h>


//------------------------------------- String

class String
{
   private:
      char     *s;
      short    stringLength;

   public:
               String( char *theString );
      void     operator()( void );
      String&String::operator=( const String& fromString );
};

String::String( char *theString )
{
   stringLength = strlen( theString );
   s = new char[ stringLength + 1 ];

   strcpy( s, theString );
}
```

```
void  String::operator()( void )
{
   cout << "String address: " << (unsigned long)s << "\n";
}

String&String::operator=( const String& fromString )
{
   delete this->s;

   this->stringLength = fromString.stringLength;

   s = new char[ this->stringLength + 1 ];

   strcpy( this->s, fromString.s );

   return( *this );
}


//------------------------------------ main()

void  main( void )
{
   String    captain( "Picard" );
   String    doctor( "Crusher" );

   captain();
   doctor();

   cout << "-----\n";

   doctor = captain;

   captain();
   doctor();
}
```

formatter (Chapter 8)

```
#include <iostream.h>


//------------------------------------ main()

void  main( void )
{
   cout << 202 << '\n';

   cout.width( 5 );
```

```
        cout.fill( 'x' );
        cout.setf( ios::left, ios::adjustfield );

        cout << 202 << '\n';

        cout.width( 10 );
        cout.fill( '=' );
        cout.setf( ios::internal, ios::adjustfield );

        cout << -101 << '\n';

        cout.width( 10 );
        cout.fill( '*' );
        cout.setf( ios::right, ios::adjustfield );

        cout << "Hello";
}
```

friends (Chapter 5)

```
#include <iostream.h>
#include <string.h>

const short  kMaxNameSize = 20;

class Employee;

class Supervisor
{
//       Data members...
    private:
        char    supervisorName[ kMaxNameSize ];
        long    supervisorID;
        float   supervisorSalary;

//       Member functions...
    public:
            Supervisor( char *name, long id, float salary );
            ~Supervisor( void );
        void  PayRaise( Employee *luckyPerson );
};

class Employee
{
    friend class Supervisor;

//       Data members...
    private:
        char    employeeName[ kMaxNameSize ];
```

```
                    long   employeeID;
                    float employeeSalary;

//          Member functions...
          public:
                    Employee( char *name, long id, float salary );
                    ~Employee( void );
             void   PrintEmployee( void );
};

Employee::Employee( char *name, long id, float salary )
{
    strcpy( this->employeeName, name );
    this->employeeID = id;
    this->employeeSalary = salary;

    cout << "Creating employee #" << employeeID << "\n";
}

Employee::~Employee( void )
{
    cout << "Deleting employee #" << employeeID << "\n";
}

void   Employee::PrintEmployee( void )
{
    cout << "-----\n";
    cout << "Name:    " << employeeName << "\n";
    cout << "ID:      " << employeeID << "\n";
    cout << "Salary: " << employeeSalary << "\n";
    cout << "-----\n";
}

Supervisor::Supervisor( char *name, long id, float salary )
{
    strcpy( this->supervisorName, name );
    this->supervisorID = id;
    this->supervisorSalary = salary;

    cout << "Creating supervisor #" << supervisorID << "\n";
}

Supervisor::~Supervisor( void )
{
    cout << "Deleting supervisor #" << supervisorID << "\n";
}

void   Supervisor::PayRaise( Employee *luckyPerson )
{
    luckyPerson->employeeSalary *= 1.10;
}
```

```
void   main( void )
{
   Employee      *employeePtr;
   Supervisor    *supervisorPtr;

   employeePtr = new Employee( "Dave Mark", 1000, 200.0 );
   supervisorPtr = new Supervisor( "Carlos Derr", 1002, 600.0 );

   employeePtr->PrintEmployee();
   supervisorPtr->PayRaise( employeePtr );
   employeePtr->PrintEmployee();

   delete employeePtr;
   delete supervisorPtr;
}
```

gramps (Chapter 6)

```
#include <iostream.h>

//--------------------------------------- Gramps

class Gramps
{
//        Data members...

//        Member functions...
   public:
              Gramps( void );
              ~Gramps( void );
};

Gramps::Gramps( void )
{
   cout << "Gramps' constructor was called!\n";
}

Gramps::~Gramps( void )
{
   cout << "Gramps' destructor was called!\n";
}


//-------------------------------- Pops:Gramps

class Pops : public Gramps
{
//        Data members...
```

```
//        Member functions...
   public:
             Pops( void );
             ~Pops( void );
};

Pops::Pops( void )
{
   cout << "Pops' constructor was called!\n";
}

Pops::~Pops( void )
{
   cout << "Pops' destructor was called!\n";
}


//------------------------------ Junior:Pops

class Junior : public Pops
{
//        Data members...

//        Member functions...
   public:
             Junior( void );
             ~Junior( void );
};

Junior::Junior( void )
{
   cout << "Junior's constructor was called!\n";
}

Junior::~Junior( void )
{
   cout << "Junior's destructor was called!\n";
}


//------------------------------------ main

void  main( void )
{
   Junior    *juniorPtr;

   juniorPtr = new Junior;

   cout << "----\n";

   delete juniorPtr;
}
```

**hello++
(Chapter 2)**

```
#include <iostream.h>

void  main( void )
{
    cout << "Hello, world!";
}
```

**init
(Chapter 9)**

```
#include <iostream.h>

//-------------------------------------- MyClass

class MyClass
{
    public:
        const short     kMaxNameLength;
        short           &numberAlias;
        short           number;

        MyClass( short  constValue );
};

MyClass::MyClass( short constValue )
    : kMaxNameLength( constValue ), numberAlias( number )
{
    number = kMaxNameLength;

    cout << "Before: number = "
        << number << "\n";

    numberAlias += 10;

    cout << "After:  number = "
        << number << "\n";
}


//-------------------------------------- main()

void  main( void )
{
    MyClass     myObject( 10 );
}
```

inline
(Chapter 4)

```
#include <iostream.h>

inline long power( short base, short exponent );

void  main( void )
{
    cout << "power( 2, 3 ): " <<
         power( 2, 3 ) << "\n";

    cout << "power( 3, 6 ): " <<
         power( 3, 6 ) << "\n";

    cout << "power( 5, 0 ): " <<
         power( 2, 0 ) << "\n";

    cout << "power( -3, 4 ): " <<
         power( -3, 4 ) << "\n";
}

inline long power( short base, short exponent )
{
    long  product = 1;
    short i;

    if ( exponent < 0 )
       return( 0 );

    for ( i=1; i<=exponent; i++ )
       product *= base;

    return( product );
}
```

memberWise
(Chapter 9)

```
#include <iostream.h>
#include <string.h>

//--------------------------------------- Name

class Name
{
    private:
       char  *last;
       char  *first;
```

```
    public:
            Name( char *firstParam, char *lastParam );
            Name( const Name& original );
      void  Name::operator()( void );
      Name  &Name::operator=( const Name& original );
};

Name::Name( char *firstParam, char *lastParam )
{
   first = new char[ strlen(firstParam) + 1 ];
   last = new char[ strlen(lastParam) + 1 ];

   strcpy( first, firstParam );
   strcpy( last, lastParam );

   cout << "Original constructor...\n";
}

Name::Name( const Name& original )
{
   first = new char[ strlen(original.first) + 1 ];
   last = new char[ strlen(original.last) + 1 ];

   strcpy( first, original.first );
   strcpy( last, original.last );

   cout << "Copy constructor...\n";
}

void  Name::operator()( void )
{
   cout << "Name: " << first << " " << last << "\n";
}

Name   &Name::operator=( const Name& original )
{
   if ( this == &original )
      return( *this );

   delete first;
   delete last;

   first = new char[ strlen(original.first) + 1 ];
   last = new char[ strlen(original.last) + 1 ];

   strcpy( first, original.first );
   strcpy( last, original.last );

   return( *this );
}
```

```
//--------------------------------------- main()

void  main( void )
{
   Name   yourAuthor( "Dave", "Mark" );
   Name   aCopy = yourAuthor;
   Name   anotherAuthor( "Scott", "Knaster" );

   yourAuthor();
   aCopy();

   aCopy = anotherAuthor;

   aCopy();
}
```

**menu
(Chapter 7)**

```
#include <iostream.h>
#include <string.h>

const short kMaxNameLength = 40;

//--------------------------------------- MenuItem

class MenuItem
{
   private:
      float      price;
      char       name[ kMaxNameLength ];

   public:
                 MenuItem( float itemPrice, char *itemName );
      float      GetPrice( void );
      float      operator+( MenuItem item );
      float      operator+( float subtotal );
};

MenuItem::MenuItem( float itemPrice, char *itemName )
{
   price = itemPrice;
   strcpy( name, itemName );
}

float MenuItem::GetPrice( void )
{
   return( this->price );
}
```

```
float MenuItem::operator+( MenuItem item )
{
    cout << "MenuItem::operator+( MenuItem item )\n";

    return( this->GetPrice() + item.GetPrice() );
}

float MenuItem::operator+( float subtotal )
{
    cout << "MenuItem::operator+( float subtotal )\n";

    return( this->GetPrice() + subtotal );
}


//------------------------------------- operator+()

float operator+( float subtotal, MenuItem item )
{
    cout << "operator+( float subtotal, MenuItem item )\n";

    return( subtotal + item.GetPrice() );
}


//------------------------------------- main()

void  main( void )
{
    MenuItem chicken( 8.99, "Chicken Kiev with salad" );
    MenuItem houseWine( 2.99, "Riesling by the glass" );
    MenuItem applePie( 3.99, "Apple Pie a la Mode" );

    cout << "\nTotal: " <<
        chicken + houseWine + applePie
        << "\n\n";

    cout << "\nTotal: " <<
        chicken + (houseWine + applePie);
}
```

multInherit (Chapter 9)

```
#include <iostream.h>

enum ColorEnum { red, yellow, blue };
enum ShapeEnum { sphere, cylinder, cube };

//------------------------- ostream overloads
```

```
ostream &operator<<( ostream &os, ColorEnum color )
{
    switch ( color )
    {
        case red:
            os << "Red";
            break;
        case yellow:
            os << "Yellow";
            break;
        case blue:
            os << "Blue";
            break;
        default:
            os << "Unknown";
            break;
    }

    return( os );
}

ostream &operator<<( ostream &os, ShapeEnum shape )
{
    switch ( shape )
    {
        case sphere:
            os << "Sphere";
            break;
        case cylinder:
            os << "Cylinder";
            break;
        case cube:
            os << "Cube";
            break;
        default:
            os << "Unknown";
            break;
    }

    return( os );
}


//---------------------------------------- HasColor

class HasColor
{
    private:
        ColorEnum color;

    public:
```

```
                        HasColor( ColorEnum objectColor );
                        ~HasColor( void );
};

HasColor::HasColor( ColorEnum objectColor )
{
    color = objectColor;

    cout << "color: " << color << "\n";
}

HasColor::~HasColor( void )
{
    cout << "HasColor destructor called.\n";
}


//-------------------------------------- HasShape

class HasShape
{
    private:
        ShapeEnum shape;

    public:
                HasShape( ShapeEnum objectShape );
                ~HasShape( void );
};

HasShape::HasShape( ShapeEnum objectShape )
{
    shape = objectShape;

    cout << "shape: " << shape << "\n";
}

HasShape::~HasShape( void )
{
    cout << "HasShape destructor called.\n"
        << "---------\n";
}


//-------------------------- Object:HasShape,HasColor

class Object : public HasShape, public HasColor
{
    private:
        short           objectID;
        static short    lastObjectID;
```

```
    public:
            Object( ColorEnum objectColor,
                ShapeEnum objectShape );
            ~Object( void );
};

Object::Object( ColorEnum objectColor, ShapeEnum objectShape ) :
    HasShape( objectShape ), HasColor( objectColor )
{
    objectID = ++lastObjectID;

    cout << "objectID: " << objectID
        << "\n---------\n";
}

Object::~Object( void )
{
    cout << "Object(" << objectID << ") destructor called.\n";
}

short Object::lastObjectID = 0;


//------------------------------------- main()

void  main( void )
{
    Objectobject1( red, cube );
    Objectobject2( blue, cylinder );
    Objectobject3( yellow, sphere );
}
```

**new
(Chapter 7)**

```
#include <iostream.h>
#include <stddef.h>


//------------------------------------- Blob

class Blob
{
    public:
        void  *operator new( size_t blobSize );
        void  operator delete( void *blobPtr, size_t blobSize );
};

void  *Blob::operator new( size_t blobSize )
{
```

```
        cout << "new: " << blobSize << " bytes.\n";
        return NULL;
}

void   Blob::operator delete( void *blobPtr, size_t blobSize )
{
        cout << "delete: " << blobSize << " bytes.\n";
}



//-------------------------------------- main()

void   main( void )
{
    Blob   *blobPtr;

    blobPtr = new Blob;

    delete blobPtr;
}
```

**newTester
(Chapter 4)**

```
#include <iostream.h>
#include <new.h>

void   NewFailed( void );

char   gDone = false;
char   *gSpareBlockPtr = NULL;

void   main( void )
{
    char   *myPtr;
    long   numBlocks = 0;

    cout << "Installing NewHandler...\n";

    set_new_handler( NewFailed );
    gSpareBlockPtr = new char[20480];

    while ( gDone == false )
    {
        myPtr = new char[1024];
        numBlocks++;
    }

    cout << "Number of blocks allocated: " << numBlocks;
}
```

```
void  NewFailed( void )
{
   if ( gSpareBlockPtr != NULL )
   {
      delete gSpareBlockPtr;
      gSpareBlockPtr = NULL;
   }

   gDone = true;
}
```

nonVirtual (Chapter 9)

```
#include <iostream.h>


//--------------------------------------- Root

class Root
{
   public:
      Root( void );
};

Root::Root( void )
{
   cout << "Root constructor called\n";
}


//--------------------------------------- Base1

class Base1 : public Root
{
   public:
      Base1( void );
};

Base1::Base1( void )
{
   cout << "Base1 constructor called\n";
}


//--------------------------------------- Base2

class Base2 : public Root
{
   public:
```

```
        Base2( void );
};

Base2::Base2( void )
{
    cout << "Base2 constructor called\n";
}


//------------------------------------- Derived

class Derived : public Base1, public Base2
{
    public:
        Derived( void );
};

Derived::Derived( void )
{
    cout << "Derived constructor called\n";
}


//------------------------------------- main()

void   main( void )
{
    Derived        myDerived;
}
```

overload (Chapter 4)

```
#include <iostream.h>

void   Display( short shortParam );
void   Display( long longParam );
void   Display( char *text );

void   main( void )
{
    short  myShort = 3;
    long   myLong = 12345678L;
    char   *text = "Make it so...";

    Display( myShort );
    Display( myLong );
    Display( text );
}
```

```
void   Display( short shortParam )
{
   cout << "The short is: " << shortParam << "\n";
}

void   Display( long longParam )
{
   cout << "The long is:  " << longParam << "\n";
}

void   Display( char *text )
{
   cout << "The text is:  " << text << "\n";
}
```

**overload
(Chapter 8)**

```
#include <iostream.h>
#include <fstream.h>
#include <string.h>

const short kMaxNameLength = 40;

//---------------------------------------- MenuItem

class MenuItem
{
   private:
      float      price;
      char       name[ kMaxNameLength ];

   public:
      void       SetName( char *itemName );
      char       *GetName( void );
      void       SetPrice( float itemPrice );
      float      GetPrice( void );
};

void   MenuItem::SetName( char *itemName )
{
   strcpy( name, itemName );
}

char   *MenuItem::GetName( void )
{
   return( this->name );
}
```

```
void  MenuItem::SetPrice( float itemPrice )
{
    price = itemPrice;
}

float MenuItem::GetPrice( void )
{
    return( this->price );
}


//------------------------  iostream operators


istream &operator>>( istream &is, MenuItem &item )
{
    float itemPrice;
    char  itemName[ kMaxNameLength ];

    is.getline( itemName, kMaxNameLength );
    item.SetName( itemName );

    is >> itemPrice;
    item.SetPrice( itemPrice );

    is.ignore( 1, '\n' );

    return( is );
}

ostream &operator<<( ostream &os, MenuItem &item )
{
    os << item.GetName() << " ($"
       << item.GetPrice() << ") ";

    return( os );
}


//-------------------------------------- main()

void  main( void )
{
    ifstream readMe( "Menu Items" );
    MenuItem item;

    while (  readMe >> item )
       cout << item << "\n";
}
```

**protoTester
(Chapter 4)**

```
#include <iostream.h>

void  MyFunc( short param1,
              short param2 = 0,
              short param3 = 0 );

void  main( void )
{
   MyFunc( 1 );
   MyFunc( 1, 2 );
   MyFunc( 1, 2, 3 );
}

void  MyFunc( short param1,
              short param2,
              short param3 )
{
   cout << "MyFunc( " << param1
      << ", " << param2
      << ", " << param3
      << " )\n";
}
```

**readMe
(Chapter 8)**

```
#include <iostream.h>
#include <fstream.h>

void  main( void )
{
   ifstream  readMe( "My File" );
   char      c;

   while ( readMe.get( c ) )
      cout << c;
}
```

**reference
(Chapter 4)**

```
#include <iostream.h>

void  CallByValue( short valueParam );
void  CallByReference( short &refParam );

void  main( void )
```

```
{
    short  number = 12;
    long   longNumber = 12L;

    cout << "&number:       " <<
        (unsigned long)&number << "\n";

    cout << "&longNumber: " <<
        (unsigned long)&longNumber << "\n\n";

    CallByValue( number );
    cout << "After ByValue: " << number << "\n\n";

    CallByReference( number );
    cout << "After ByRef( short ): " << number << "\n\n";

    CallByReference( longNumber );
    cout << "After ByRef( long ): " << longNumber << "\n";
}

void  CallByValue( short valueParam )
{
    cout << "&valueParam: " <<
        (unsigned long)&valueParam << "\n";
    valueParam *= 2;
}

void  CallByReference( short &refParam )
{
    cout << "&refParam:     " <<
        (unsigned long)&refParam << "\n";
    refParam *= 2;
}
```

**scopeTester
(Chapter 4)**

```
#include <iostream.h>

short myValue = 5;

void  main( void )
{
    short yourValue = myValue;

    cout << "yourValue: " << yourValue << "\n";

    short myValue = 10;
    yourValue = myValue;
```

```
        cout << "yourValue: " << yourValue << "\n";

        yourValue = ::myValue;
        cout << "yourValue: " << yourValue << "\n";
}
```

smartPtr (Chapter 7)

```
#include <iostream.h>
#include <string.h>

const short kMaxNameLength = 40;


//-------------------------------------- Name

class Name
{
    private:
        char    first[ kMaxNameLength ];
        char    last[ kMaxNameLength ];

    public:
                Name( char *lastName, char *firstName );
        void    DisplayName( void );
};

Name::Name( char *lastName, char *firstName )
{
    strcpy( last, lastName );
    strcpy( first, firstName );
}

void    Name::DisplayName( void )
{
    cout << "Name: " << first << " " << last;
}


//-------------------------------------- Politician

class Politician
{
    private:
        Name    *namePtr;
        short   age;

    public:
                Politician( Name *namePtr, short age );
```

```
         Name   *operator->( void );
};

Politician::Politician( Name *namePtr, short age )
{
   this->namePtr = namePtr;
   this->age = age;
}

Name   *Politician::operator->( void )
{
   return( namePtr );
}


//------------------------------------- main()

void   main( void )
{
   Name            myName( "Clinton", "Bill" );
   Politician  billClinton( &myName, 46 );

   billClinton->DisplayName();
}
```

square (Chapter 6)

```
#include <iostream.h>


//------------------------------------- Rectangle

class Rectangle
{
//      Data members...
   protected:
      short height;
      short width;

//       Member functions...
   public:
            Rectangle( short heightParam, short widthParam );
      void  DisplayArea( void );
};

Rectangle::Rectangle( short heightParam, short widthParam )
{
   height = heightParam;
   width = widthParam;
}
```

```
void   Rectangle::DisplayArea( void )
{
   cout << "Area is: " <<
       height * width << '\n';
}


//-------------------------------------- Rectangle:Square

class Square : public Rectangle
{
//        Data members...

//        Member functions...
   public:
             Square( short side );
};

Square::Square( short side ) : Rectangle( side, side )
{
}


//-------------------------------------- main()

void   main( void )
{
   Square    *mySquare;
   Rectangle *myRectangle;

   mySquare = new Square( 10 );
   mySquare->DisplayArea();

   myRectangle = new Rectangle( 10, 15 );
   myRectangle->DisplayArea();
}
```

**stateBits
(Chapter 8)**

```
#include <iostream.h>

#define true 1
#define false 0

void   main( void )
{
   char   done = false;
   char   c;
   short  number;
```

```
            while ( ! done )
            {
                cout << "Type a number: ";
                cin >> number;

                if ( cin.good() )
                {
                    if ( number == 0 )
                    {
                        cout << "Goodbye...";
                        done = true;
                    }
                    else
                        cout << "Your number is: " << number << "\n\n";
                }
                else if ( cin.fail() )
                {
                    cin.clear();

                    cin.get( c );
                    cout << c << " is not a number...";
                    cout << "Type 0 to exit\n\n";
                }
                else if ( cin.bad() )
                {
                    cout << "\nYikes!!! Gotta go...";
                    done = true;
                }
            }
        }
```

strstream (Chapter 8)

```
#include <iostream.h>
#include <strstrea.h>

const short kBufferSize = 10;

//------------------------------------- main()

void  main( void )
{
    char         buffer[ kBufferSize ];
    ostrstream   ostr( buffer, kBufferSize );
    short        i = 0;

    while ( ostr << (char)('a' + i) )
        i++;
```

```
        cout << "Number of characters written: "
             << i << '\n';

        buffer[ kBufferSize - 1 ] = '\0';

        cout << "Buffer contents: " << buffer;
}
```

subscript (Chapter 7)

```
#include <iostream.h>
#include <string.h>

const short kMaxNameLength = 40;

//-------------------------------------- Name

class Name
{
    private:
        char  nameString[ kMaxNameLength ];
        short nameLength;

    public:
              Name( char *name );
        void  operator()( void );
        char  &operator[]( short index );
};

Name::Name( char *name )
{
    strcpy( nameString, name );
    nameLength = strlen( name );
}

void  Name::operator()( void )
{
    cout << nameString << "\n";
}

char& Name::operator[]( short index )
{
    if ( ( index < 0 ) || ( index >= nameLength ) )
    {
        cout << "index out of bounds!!!\n";
        return( nameString[ 0 ] );
    }
    else
        return( nameString[ index ] );
}
```

```
//--------------------------------------- main()

void   main( void )
{
    Name   pres( "B. J. Clinton" );

    pres[ 3 ] = 'X';
    pres();

    pres[ 25 ] = 'Z';
    pres();
}
```

template (Chapter 9)

```
#include <iostream.h>

const short kNumElements = 10;

//--------------------------------------- Array

template <class T>
class Array
{
    private:
        short arraySize;
        T     *arrayPtr;
        T     errorRetValue;

    public:
            Array( short size );
            ~Array( void );
        T   &operator[]( short index );
};

template <class T>
Array<T>::Array( short size )
{
    arraySize = size;
    arrayPtr = new T[ size ];
    errorRetValue = 0;
}

template <class T>
Array<T>::~Array( void )
{
    delete [] arrayPtr;
}
```

```
template <class T>
T   &Array<T>::operator[]( short index )
{
    if ( ( index < 0 ) || ( index >= arraySize ) )
    {
        cout << "index out of bounds(" << index << ")\n";
        return( errorRetValue );
    }
    else
        return( arrayPtr[ index ] );
}


//--------------------------------------- Power

template <class T>
T   Power( T base, T exponent )
{
    T   i, product = 1;

    for ( i=1; i<=exponent; i++ )
        product *= base;

    return( product );
}


//--------------------------------------- main()

void   main( void )
{
    Array<short>    myRay( kNumElements );
    Array<long>     myLongRay( kNumElements );
    short           i, shortBase = 4;
    long            longBase = 4L;

    for ( i=0; i<=kNumElements; i++ )
        myRay[ i ] = Power( shortBase, i );

    cout << "----\n";

    for ( i=0; i<kNumElements; i++ )
        cout << "myRay[" << i << "]: " << myRay[ i ] << "\n";

    for ( i=0; i<kNumElements; i++ )
        myLongRay[ i ] = Power( longBase, (long)i );

    cout << "----\n";

    for ( i=0; i<kNumElements; i++ )
```

```
            cout << "myLongRay[" << i
                << "]: " << myLongRay[ i ] << "\n";
        }
```

time (Chapter 7)

```
#include <iostream.h>

//--------------------------------------- Time

class Time
{
//      Data members...
    private:
        short hours;
        short minutes;
        short seconds;

//      Member functions...
    public:
                Time( short h, short m, short s );
        void    NormalizeTime( void );
        void    Display( void );
        Time    *operator+( Time aTime );
        void    operator*=( short num );
};

Time::Time( short h, short m, short s )
{
    seconds = s;
    minutes = m;
    hours = h;

    NormalizeTime();
}

void  Time::NormalizeTime( void )
{
    hours += ((minutes + (seconds/60)) / 60);

    minutes = (minutes + (seconds/60)) % 60;

    seconds %= 60;
}

void  Time::Display( void )
{
```

```
        cout << "(" << hours << ":" << minutes
             << ":" << seconds << ")\n";
    }

Time    *Time::operator+( Time aTime )
{
    short  h;
    short  m;
    short  s;
    Time   *tempTimePtr;

    h = hours + aTime.hours;
    m = minutes + aTime.minutes;
    s = seconds + aTime.seconds;

    tempTimePtr = new Time( h, m, s );

    return( tempTimePtr );
}

void   Time::operator*=( short num )
{
    hours *= num;
    minutes *= num;
    seconds *= num;

    NormalizeTime();
}


//------------------------------------- main()

void   main( void )
{
    Time   firstTime( 1, 10, 50 );
    Time   secondTime( 2, 24, 20 );
    Time   *sumTimePtr;

    firstTime.Display();
    secondTime.Display();

    cout << "---------\n";

    sumTimePtr = firstTime + secondTime;
    sumTimePtr->Display();

    cout << "*       2\n";
    cout << "---------\n";

    (*sumTimePtr) *= 2;
    sumTimePtr->Display();
}
```

virtual (Chapter 9)

```
#include <iostream.h>

//------------------------------------ Root

class Root
{
    protected:
        short num;

    public:
                Root( short numParam );
};

Root::Root( short numParam )
{
    num = numParam;

    cout << "Root constructor called\n";
}


//------------------------------------ Base1

class Base1 : public virtual Root
{
    public:
        Base1( void );
};

Base1::Base1( void ) : Root( 1 )
{
    cout << "Base1 constructor called\n";
}


//------------------------------------ Base2

class Base2 : public virtual Root
{
    public:
        Base2( void );
};

Base2::Base2( void ) : Root( 2 )
{
    cout << "Base2 constructor called\n";
}
```

```
//-------------------------------------- Derived

class Derived : public Base1, public Base2
{
   public:
              Derived( void );
        short GetNum( void );
};

Derived::Derived( void ) : Root( 3 )
{
   cout << "Derived constructor called\n";
}

short Derived::GetNum( void )
{
   return( num );
}


//-------------------------------------- main()

void  main( void )
{
   Derived       myDerived;

   cout << "-------\n"
        << "num = " << myDerived.GetNum();
}
```

whatAmI
(Chapter 6)

```
#include <iostream.h>

//-------------------------------------- Shape

class Shape
{
//       Data members...

//       Member functions...
   public:
      virtual void WhatAmI( void );
};

void  Shape::WhatAmI( void )
{
   cout << "I don't know what kind of shape I am!\n";
}
```

```
//-------------------------------------- Shape:Rectangle

class Rectangle : public Shape
{
//       Data members...

//       Member functions...
   public:
       void   WhatAmI( void );
};

void   Rectangle::WhatAmI( void )
{
   cout << "I'm a rectangle!\n";
}


//-------------------------------------- Shape:Triangle

class Triangle : public Shape
{
//       Data members...

//       Member functions...
   public:
       void   WhatAmI( void );
};

void   Triangle::WhatAmI( void )
{
   cout << "I'm a triangle!\n";
}


//-------------------------------------- main()

void   main( void )
{
   Shape *s1, *s2, *s3;

   s1 = new Rectangle;
   s2 = new Triangle;
   s3 = new Shape;

   s1->WhatAmI();
   s2->WhatAmI();
   s3->WhatAmI();
}
```

fstream.h

```
// IOStreams Package
// Steve Teale April 1992
// Copyright Symantec Corp 1990-1992. All Rights Reserved.

#ifndef __FSTREAM_H
#define __FSTREAM_H

#include <iostream.h>


class filebuf : public streambuf {
// This is a streambuf class specialized for handling files.
// The get and put pointers are locked together so that reads and writes
// happen at the same offset into the file.

   public:
      enum { openprot = 0644 };

      filebuf();
      // The default constructor. Creates a filebuf that is not associated
      // with any file. open() or attach() can then be used to connect
      // to a file.

      filebuf(int file_descriptor, int io_mode = ios::in|ios::out
        #if M_UNIX || M_XENIX
           );
        #else
           |ios::translated);
```

```
     #endif
// Constructs a filebuf for the open file attached to the argument
// file descriptor. More comprehensive io_mode information can
// be specified e.g. ios::app, if required

filebuf(int descriptor, char *memory, int length,
    int io_mode = ios::in|ios::out
    #if M_UNIX || M_XENIX
        );
    #else
        |ios::translated);
    #endif
// Constructs a filebuf for the open file attached to the
// file_descriptor, and sets the buffer to "memory", which is of
// "length" bytes in size. If memory is 0 or length is <= 0,
// it is taken as a request that the file be unbuffered.

~filebuf();

filebuf *attach(int file_descriptor,
    int io_mode = ios::in|ios::out
    #if M_UNIX_ || M_XENIX
        );
    #else
        |ios::translated);
    #endif
// Attaches an open file to a filebuf. Returns "this" if successful,
// 0 if the filebuf is already attached to a file.

filebuf *close();
// Flushes output, closes the file, and detaches the file from this
// filebuf. Clears the error state unless there is an error flushing
// the output. Will always close the file and detach it from the
// filebuf, even if there are errors.

int fd() const { return file; };
// Returns the file descriptor for the connected file. If the
// filebuf is closed or not attached to a file, returns EOF.

int is_open() const { return file != EOF; };
// Returns non-zero when this filebuf is attached to a file,
// otherwise returns zero.

filebuf *open(const char *name, int io_mode,
    int protection = openprot);
// Opens the file "name", and connects it to this filebuf.
// io_mode is a bit-mask containing one or more of the values of
// enum open_mode:
// ios::in       Open for reading.
// ios::out      Open for writing.
```

```
// ios::ate        Position to the end-of-file.
// ios::app        Open the file in append mode.
// ios::trunc      Truncate the file on open.
// ios::nocreate   Do not attempt to create the file if itdoes not exist.
// ios::noreplace  Cause the open to fail if the file exists.
// ios::translate  Convert CR/LF to newline on input and vice versa on output

   streampos seekoff(streamoff offset, ios::relative_to,
      int which);
   // Relative seek the get and put pointers within the file.
   // The get and put pointers of a filebuf always point to the
   // same byte of the file.

   streambuf *setbuf(char *memory, int length);
   // Set the buffer to use "memory", of "length" bytes.
   // If memory == 0 or length <= 0, it is taken as a request that
   // I/O to the file be unbuffered.

   int sync();
   // Flush any bytes in the get buffer, and re-position the file so
   // that is appears they were never read. Write any bytes in the
   // put buffer to the file.

   #if __ZTC__ > 0x214
      int overflow(int c);
   #else
      int overflow(int c = EOF);
   #endif
   // Flush bytes in the put area to the file.

   int underflow();
   // Get more bytes for reading.

protected:
   int doallocate();

   int pbackfail(int c);
   // Called to atempt recovery if putback attempted at
   // start of get buffer

private:
   void buffer_setup();
   // Internal. Set up I/O buffer.

   int newlines();
   // count newline chars in the get buffer

   int syncin();
   int syncout();
   // two halves of sync() function
```

```
    int fillbuf();
    int flushbuf();
    // Functions which actually transfer to/from the file

    int file;
    // File descriptor for the associated file.

    short mode;
    // I/O mode from the argument to open().

    char unbuf[2];
    //. pseudo buffer for unbuffered operation

    char *gptr_;
    char *egptr_;
    // Save old gptr() & egptr() while using the
    // pushback buffer.

    char pushback_buf[4];
    // Reserve buffer for pushback.
    // Only used if there is no room for pushback in
    // the regular buffer.

    char do_not_seek;
    // Set if the file (device) does not support seeks.
    // This is set for a TTY, or a Unix pipe.

    char own_file_descriptor;
    // Set if the file descriptor is from open, and
    // the file should be closed by the destructor.

    static const int lseek_consts[3];
    // A look up table for the lseek constants from
    // the appropriate C header file
};


class fstream_common : virtual public ios {
// Features common to ifstream, ofstream, and fstream.

  public:
    void attach(int file_descriptor, int io_mode);
    // Attach the filebuf to the argument file descriptor, error state
    // set to ios::failbit|ios::badbit on failure.

    void close();
    // Flush the filebuf, and close the file attached to it. Error state

    // set ios::failbit|ios::badbit if rdbuf()->sync() fails. File closed
    // regardless.
```

```
      void open(const char *name, int io_mode,
         int protection = filebuf::openprot);
      // Open a file, and attach it to the filebuf. Error state set to
      // ios::failbit|ios::badbit on failure

      void setbuf(char *memory, int length)
         {
            buffer.setbuf(memory, length);
         }
      // Use the argument memory, of the given length, as the I/O buffer.

      filebuf *rdbuf() { return &buffer; }
      // Note that fstream_common::rdbuf returns a filebuf*
      // instead of a streambuf*.

   protected:
      fstream_common();
      filebuf buffer;
};


class ifstream : public fstream_common, public istream {
   public:
      ifstream();
      // Create an ifstream not attached to any file.

   ifstream(const char *name, int io_mode = ios::in | ios::nocreate
      #if M_UNIX || M_XENIX
         ,int protection = filebuf::openprot);
      #else
         | ios::translated, int protection = filebuf::openprot);
      #endif
   // Open the argument file and create an ifstream attached to it.

   ifstream(int file_descriptor, int io_mode = ios::in
      #if M_UNIX || M_XENIX
         );
      #else
         | ios::translated);
      #endif
   // Create an ifstream attached to the argument file descriptor.

   ifstream(int file_descriptor, char *memory, int length,
      int io_mode = ios::in
      #if M_UNIX || M_XENIX
         );
      #else
         | ios::translated);
      #endif
   // Create an ifstream attached to the argument file descriptor, and
   // using the argument memory as the I/O buffer.
```

```
  ~ifstream();

  void attach(int file_descriptor, int io_mode = ios::in
    #if M_UNIX || M_XENIX
      )
    #else
      | ios::translated)
    #endif
  {
    fstream_common::attach(file_descriptor, io_mode);
  }

  void open(const char *name, int io_mode = ios::in
    #if M_UNIX || M_XENIX
      ,int protection = filebuf::openprot)
    #else
      | ios::translated, int protection = filebuf::openprot)
    #endif
  {
    fstream_common::open(name, io_mode, protection);
  }
};


class ofstream : public fstream_common, public ostream {

  public:
    ofstream();
    // Create an ofstream not attached to any file.

  ofstream(const char *name, int io_mode = ios::out
    #if M_UNIX || M_XENIX
      ,int protection = filebuf::openprot);
    #else
      | ios::translated, int protection = filebuf::openprot);
    #endif
  // Open the argument file and create an ofstream attached to it.

  ofstream(int file_descriptor, int io_mode = ios::out
    #if M_UNIX || M_XENIX
      );
    #else
      | ios::translated);
    #endif
  // Create an ofstream attached to the argument file descriptor.

  ofstream(int file_descriptor, char *memory, int length,
    int io_mode = ios::out
    #if M_UNIX || M_XENIX
      );
    #else
```

```
       | ios::translated);
    #endif
// Create an ofstream attached to the argument file descriptor, and
// using the argument memory as the I/O buffer.

    ~ofstream();

    void attach(int file_descriptor, int io_mode = ios::out
       #if M_UNIX || M_XENIX
          )
       #else
          | ios::translated)
       #endif
    {
       fstream_common::attach(file_descriptor, io_mode);
    }

    void open(const char *name, int io_mode = ios::out
       #if M_UNIX_ || M_XENIX
          ,int protection = filebuf::openprot)
       #else
          | ios::translated, int protection = filebuf::openprot)
       #endif
    {
       fstream_common::open(name, io_mode, protection);
    }
};


class fstream : public fstream_common, public iostream {

    public:
       fstream();

// Create an fstream not attached to any file.

    fstream(const char *name, int io_mode = ios::in|ios::out
       #if M_UNIX || M_XENIX
          ,int protection = filebuf::openprot);
       #else
          | ios::translated, int protection = filebuf::openprot);
       #endif
    // Open the argument file and create an fstream attached to it.

    fstream(int file_descriptor, int io_mode = ios::in | ios::out
       #if M_UNIX || M_XENIX
          );
       #else
          | ios::translated);
       #endif
    // Create an fstream attached to the argument file descriptor.
```

```
fstream(int file_descriptor, char *memory, int length,
    int io_mode = ios::in | ios::out
    #if M_UNIX || M_XENIX
        );
    #else
        | ios::translated);
    #endif
// Create an fstream attached to the argument file descriptor, and
// using the argument memory as the I/O buffer.

~fstream();

void attach(int file_descriptor, int io_mode = ios::in | ios::out
    #if M_UNIX || M_XENIX
        )
    #else
        | ios::translated)
    #endif
{
    fstream_common::attach(file_descriptor, io_mode);
}

void open(const char *name, int io_mode = ios::in | ios::out
    #if M_UNIX || M_XENIX
        ,int protection = filebuf::openprot)
    #else
        | ios::translated, int protection = filebuf::openprot)
    #endif
{
    fstream_common::open(name, io_mode, protection);
}
};
#endif   // __FSTREAM_H
```

iomanip.h

```
// IOStreams Package
// Steve Teale April 1992
// Copyright Symantec Corp 1990-1992. All Rights Reserved.
#ifndef __IOMANIP_H
#define __IOMANIP_H
#include <iomdefs.h>
ios &_iomanip_resetiosflags(ios&, long);
inline SMANIP<long> resetiosflags(long f)
   { return SMANIP<long>(_iomanip_resetiosflags,f); }
ios &_iomanip_setfill(ios&, int);
inline SMANIP<int> setfill(int filler)
   { return SMANIP<int>(_iomanip_setfill,filler); }
ios &_iomanip_setiosflags(ios&, long);
inline SMANIP<long> setiosflags(long f)
   { return SMANIP<long>(_iomanip_setiosflags,f); }
ios &_iomanip_setprecision(ios&, int);
inline SMANIP<int> setprecision(int n)
   { return SMANIP<int>(_iomanip_setprecision,n); }
ios &_iomanip_setw(ios&, int);
inline SMANIP<int> setw(int w)
   { return SMANIP<int>(_iomanip_setw,w); }
ios &_iomanip_setbase(ios&, int);
inline SMANIP<int> setbase(int n)
   { return SMANIP<int>(_iomanip_setbase,n); }
#endif  // __IOMANIP_H
```

```
// IOStreams Package
// Steve Teale April 1992
// Copyright Symantec Corp 1990-1992. All Rights Reserved.
#ifndef __IOSTREAM_H
#define __IOSTREAM_H
#include <stddef.h>
#include <2comp.h>
#define seek_dir relative_to
#ifndef EOF
const int EOF = -1;
#endif
const int _ios_default_decimal_precision = 6;
const int _ios_n_extended_format_words = 10;
// This is the number of extended format state words reserved for use
// by derived classes and user inserters. This value should be reasonably
// small, as it inflates the size of each instance of ios.


class streampos {
friend class streamoff;

public:
   streampos(long elems, size_t elemsize = 1) : ne(elems), es(elemsize) {}
   operator long() const { return (ne == -1)? EOF: ne*es; }

private:
   long ne;
   size_t es;
};
```

```
class streamoff {

public:
   streamoff(long elems, size_t elemsize = 1) : ne(elems), es(elemsize) {}
   streamoff(streampos &a) : ne(a.ne), es(a.es) {}
   size_t stepsize() const { return es; }
   long steps() const { return ne == -1? 0: ne; }
   streamoff& operator += (long o) { ne += o; return *this; }
   streamoff& operator -= (long o) { ne -= o; return *this; }
   operator long() const { return steps()*es; }

private:
   long ne;
   size_t es;
};


class streambuf;
class ostream;
class istream;


class ios {
// This is the base class for istream and ostream, and all of their
// derivations.
friend ostream &endl(ostream &);

public:
   enum io_state {
      goodbit=0,
      // No errors - everything hunky dory!

      eofbit=1,
      // Normally set when underflow failed because there was no more file.

      failbit=2,
      // An error has ocurred, but it is probably recoverable, and the
      // stream is still in a useable state

      badbit=4
      // A fatal error has ocurred
   };

   // This is called seek_dir in the AT & T version, which is misleading.
   // A define is included above for compatibility. These enumerators are
   // used to specify relative seeks in streams.
   enum relative_to {
      beg,
      // For seek operations relative to the beginning of the stream (file),
      cur,
      // relative to the current position in the stream (file),
```

```
    end
    // and relative to the end of the stream (file)
};

// The following enumeration applies to file related derivatives.
enum open_mode {
    in=0x1,
    // Input allowed

    out=0x2,
    // Output allowed

    ate=0x4,
    // A seek to the end of the file to be performed during open.

    app=0x8,
    // All writes are to the end of the file - implies out

    trunc=0x10,
    // Existing contents of the file to be discarded. Implies out
    // unless ate or app specified as well.

    nocreate=0x20,
    // Open will fail if the file does not already exist

    noreplace=0x40,
    // Open will fail if the file does already exist

    translated = 0x80
    // CR/LF pairs to be translated to newline characters on input
    // and newline characters to be translated to CR/LF pairs on
    // output (the normal behaviour for DOS)
};

// The formatting state is a bit-mask used to control some of the
// inserters and extractors. All of the bits of the format state
// can be manipulated by flags(), setf(), and unsetf(). Some

// specialized parts of the formatting state can be manipulated
// by fill(), width(), and precision() . Here are the meanings
// of the various bits:
enum format_mode {
    skipws = 0x1,
    // Skip past leading white space when extracting.
    // Since zero-width fields are considered an
    // error by the numeric extractors, attempting
    // to extract white-space into a number without
    // this bit set will set an error flag.

    left = 0x2,
    // Left-adjust values when inserting (fill on the right).
```

```
right = 0x4,
// Right-adjust values when inserting (fill on the left).

internal = 0x8,
// When inserting, fill _between_ the numeric sign or
// base indicator and the value.

dec = 0x10, oct = 0x20, hex = 0x40,
// Default radix for integers. If neither dec, octal,
// or hex is set, integer inserters use base 10, and
// integer extractors interpret numbers according to the
// C++ lexical convention: "0x" precedes a base-16 number,
// and a number with a leading zero is base-8.

showbase = 0x80,
// If this is set, base-16 numbers will be inserted with a
// leading "0x", and base-8 numbers will have a leading zero.

showpoint = 0x100,
// If this is set, the floating-point inserters will print a
// decimal point and trailing zeroes, even when the trailing
// places are not significant.

uppercase = 0x200,
// If this is set, "E" instead of "e" will be used to indicate
// the exponent of a floating point number, and "A" through "F"
// will be used to represent base-16 numerals instead of "a"
// through "f".
//
// If uppercase and showbase are both set, the string "0X"
// instead of "0x" will be used to indicate a base-16 number.

showpos = 0x400,
// If this is set, positive numbers will be inserted with a
// leading "+".

scientific = 0x800,
// If this is set, the floating-point inserters will print a
// number with one digit before the decimal point, and the
// number of digits after the decimal point equal to the
// value of precision(). The character "e" will introduce the
// exponent.

fixed = 0x1000,
// If this is set, the floating-point inserters will use
// precision() to determine the number of digits after the
// decimal point.
//
// If neither scientific or fixed is set, numbers with
// exponents smaller than -4 or greater than precision() will
// be printed as if scientific were set. Other numbers will
// be printed using zeroes to explicitly show the decimal place.
```

```
      unitbuf = 0x2000,
      // When this is set, a flush is performed after each insertion
      // (by ostream::osfx()). This is more efficient than using
      // unbuffered output, but provides most of the same advantages.

      stdio = 0x4000
      // When this is set, streams using stdiobufs will flush stdout and
      // stderr after each insertion.
      // Note that it is not possible to use bit 0x8000 in this way,
      // as this evaluates to an enumerator with a negative value and
      // lots of bits set.
   };    // end enum format_mode
static const long stickywidth; static const long spacing;
   enum format_mode_mask {
      defaults = right|skipws, basefield = dec|oct|hex,
      adjustfield = left|right|internal, floatfield = scientific|fixed
   };

public: // just a reminder!
   ios(streambuf *buffer);
   // Construct an ios associated with the argument streambuf.
   // "buffer" should not be null.
   virtual ~ios();

//////////////////////////////////////////////////////////////
//
// Functions to interrogate/set the error state

   int good() const { return error_state == 0; };
   // If there are no error bits set, this returns non-zero, otherwise
   // it returns zero.

   int eof() const { return error_state & eofbit; };
   // If eofbit is set in the error state, this return non-zero, otherwise
   // it returns zero. This indicates that end-of-file has been reached
   // while reading the character stream.

   int fail() { return error_state & (badbit | failbit); }
   // If badbit or failbit is set in the error state, return non-zero.
   // Otherwise, return zero. Failbit generally indicates that some

   // extraction has failed, but the stream may still be used once
   // failbit has been cleared.

   int bad() const { return error_state & badbit; }
   // Returns non-zero if badbit is set in the error state. This
   // indicates some unrecoverable error, generally an I/O error.

   int operator!() const
   {
     return error_state & (badbit|failbit);
```

```
}
// Return non-zero if badbit or failbit is set in the error state,
// which allows expressions of the form:
//   if ( !cout )

operator void*()
{
    return (error_state & (badbit|failbit))?
        0: this;
}
// Convert an ios to a value that can be compared to zero, but can
// not be easily used accidentally. The return value is a void pointer
// that will be zero if failbit or badbit is set in the error state,
// and non-zero otherwise. This allows an iostream to be used
// in conditional expressions that test its state, as in:
// if ( cin ) and if ( cin >> variable )

int rdstate() const { return error_state; };
// Returns the current error state.

void clear(int new_state = 0) { error_state = new_state; }
// Stores "new_state" as the error state.
//
// To set a bit without clearing others requires something like
// clear(bits_to_set | rdstate()) .

/////////////////////////////////////////////////////////////// //
// Functions to set/interrogate various options

    char fill(char new_value)
    {
        char old_value = padding_character;
        padding_character = new_value;
        return old_value;
    }
// Sets the fill character, and returns the old value. This is the
// character used to pad output when the left, right, or internal
// adjustments are in effect.

    char fill() const { return padding_character; }
// Returns the fill character.

    int precision(int new_value)
    {
        int old_value = decimal_precision;
        decimal_precision = new_value >= 0?
            new_value: _ios_default_decimal_precision;
        return old_value;
    }
// Sets the decimal precision, and returns the old value.
// This controls the number of digits inserted after the decimal
// point by the floating-point inserter.
```

```
int precision() const { return decimal_precision; }
// Returns the current decimal precision.

ostream *tie(ostream * new_value)
{
   ostream *old_value = tied_ostream;
   tied_ostream = new_value;
   return old_value;
};
// Facilitate automatic flushing of iostreams.
// Associate this ios to an ostream such that the ostream will be
// flushed before this ios makes a request for characters, or flushes
// output characters. These ties exist by default:
//   cin.tie(cout);
//   cout.tie(cerr);
//   cout.tie(clog);
//
// For other instances of ios, the tie is set to zero by default.
// This returns the old value.

long flags() const { return format_state; }
// Return the format state flags.

long flags(long new_value)
{
   long old_value = format_state;
   format_state = new_value;
   return old_value;
}
// Sets the format state flags, returning the old values.

long setf(long bits_to_set, long mask = 0) {
   long old_value = format_state; format_state =
      (format_state & ~mask) | bits_to_set;
   return old_value;
}
// Clears the bits corresponding to mask in the format state, and
// then sets only those bits from the value of bits_to_set.

long unsetf(long bits_to_clear)
{
   long old_value = format_state;
   format_state &= ~bits_to_clear;
   return old_value;
};
// Clears flags in the format state.

ostream *tie() const { return tied_ostream; };
// Return the current "tied" ostream.

int width(int new_value);
// Sets the field width used by inserters.
```

```
// When the width is zero, inserters will use only as many characters
// as necessary to represent a value. When the width is non-zero,
// inserters will insert at least that many characters, using the
// fill character to pad out the field. Inserters will never truncate,
// so they may output more characters than the current width.

int width() const { return field_width; };
// Returns the current width.
```

```
///////////////////////////////////////////////////////////////
//
// Other utilities
```

```
streambuf *rdbuf() { return buf; }
// Returns a pointer to the streambuf associated with this ios.

static void sync_with_stdio();
// Use this when mixing C and C++ in the same program.
// It resets cin, cout, cerr, and clog to use stdiobufs, and
// thus makes I/O to these streams compatible with the C stdio.
// Invoking this degrades performance.
```

```
///////////////////////////////////////////////////////////////
//
// Functions to manipulate user defined format flags and control
// words.
```

```
static int bitalloc();
// Returns an int with one previously-unallocated bit set.
// This allows users who need an additional format flag to
// get one. Note that this allocation is global for class ios,
// not local to any instance of class ios.

static int xalloc();
// Returns a previously-unused index into an array of words usable
// as format-state variables by derived classes.

long &iword(int index)
{
    return extended_format_words[index].l;
}
// Returns a reference to one of the auxillary format state words
// reserved for use by derived classes and user inserters, where
// index is a value returned by xalloc().

void* &pword(int index)
{
    return extended_format_words[index].vp;
};
// Returns a reference to a pointer to one of the auxillary format
// state words reserved for use by derived classes and user
// inserters, where index is a value returned by xalloc().
```

```
protected:
   void set_buffer(streambuf *b) { buf = b; }

private:
   streambuf *buf;
   ostream *tied_ostream;
   long format_state;
   char error_state;
   char padding_character;
   short   decimal_precision;
   short   field_width;
   union {
      void *vp;
      long l;
      } extended_format_words[_ios_n_extended_format_words];
   ios(const ios&);
   ios &operator=(const ios&);
   // These copying functions are private so that the compiler
   // will complain about an attempt to assign an ios. It is not
   // actually defined. Instead of copying an ios, assign a pointer
   // to it.
};

/////////////////////////////////////////////////////////////////
// Manipulator functions

ios &dec(ios&);
// Set the default integer radix to 10.
// Invoke this (and the other manipulators) this way:
// stream >> dec;
// stream << dec;

ios &hex(ios&);
ios &oct(ios&);
ios &defaults(ios&);


class streambuf {
// Streambuf abstracts the operations used to perform I/O on a character
// stream such as a computer terminal, a file or a string.
//
// The two basic operations are "get", which fetches characters from the
// stream, and "put", which places characters on the stream. Some streambufs
// are unidirectional, in which case they support the "get" operation but
// not "put", or vice-versa.
//
// Some streambufs are bi-directional, with the "get" and "put" offsets
// at different locations in the stream. Some streambufs may implement
// a circular buffer between the "get" and "put" offsets, as in a FIFO.
// Some streambufs lock the "get" and "put" offset together, as in a UNIX file.
// Some streambufs provide buffered I/O on the underlying character streams
// for efficiency.
```

```
//
// Streambufs contain a buffer, a get area, and a put area. Usually, the
// get area and put area overlap the buffer, but do not overlap each other.

public:
    streambuf();
    // The default constructor.

    streambuf(char *memory, int length);
    // Constructs a streambuf, possibly using the argument buffer.
    virtual ~streambuf();

    void dbp();
    // Write debugging information about the streambuf on file
    // descriptor 1. Nothing about the form of that information
    // is specified.

    int in_avail() const { return _egptr - _gptr; }
    // Return the number of characters that can be read immediately
    // with a guarantee that no errors will be reported.

    int out_waiting() const { return _pptr - _pbase; }
    // Return the number of characters that have not
    // been flushed away, or EOF if there are no characters.

    virtual streambuf *setbuf(char *memory, int length);
    // Requests that this streambuf use the argument memory buffer.
    // Special case: a null memory argument, or a length argument that is
    // zero or negative, is taken as a request that this streambuf be
    // unbuffered.
    //
    // If the request to set the buffer is honored, return "this",
    // otherwise return 0.
    //
    // * Use of this interface, except by a derived class of streambuf,
    // is discouraged. It is not protected for compatibility with the
    // original stream package in Stroustrup.
    //
    // The default version of this member will honor the request if no
    // buffer has been allocated.

    virtual streampos  seekpos(streampos position,
        int which=ios::in|ios::out);
    // Performs an absolute seek of the get or put pointers, or both, to
    // "position". Position is an implementation-dependent value which
    // should not have arithmetic performed on it. "which" signifies what
    // pointer is to be affected: ios::in signifies the get pointer, and
    // ios::out signifies the put pointer. The two "which" values may be
    // or-ed together, in which case the operation affects both pointers.
    //
    // * The default version of this member returns
    //        seekoff(position, ios::beg, which)
```

```
// thus is is only necessary for a derived class to define
// seekoff(), and use the inherited seekpos().

virtual streampos seekoff(streamoff offset, ios::relative_to pos,
   int which=ios::in|ios::out);
// Performs a relative seek of the get or put pointers, or both, by
// "offset". Position is a byte offset, and may be negative.
// "pos" may be ios::beg, which signifies a seek relative to
// the beginning of the stream; ios::cur, which signifies a seek
// relative to the current position in the stream; and ios::end, which
// signifies a seek relative to the end of the stream.
// "which" signifies what pointer is to be affected: ios::in
// signifies the get pointer, and ios::out signifies the put pointer.
// The two "which" values may be or-ed together, in which case the
// operation affects both pointers.
// * The default version of this member always returns EOF.

int sgetc()
{
   return _gptr < _egptr?
      (unsigned char) *_gptr: underflow();
}
// Returns the character at the get pointer, without moving the get
// pointer.

int sbumpc()
{
   return _gptr < _egptr?
      (unsigned char) *_gptr++: sbumpc_special();
}
// Moves the get pointer forward one character, and return the
// character it moved past.

int sgetn(char *buffer, int count);
// Fetch the "count" characters following the get pointer, and
// stores them in "buffer". If there are less than "count" characters,
// the number remaining are fetched. The get pointer is repositioned
// after the fetched characters, and the number of characters fetched
// is returned.

int snextc()
{
   return _gptr+1 < _egptr?
      ((unsigned char) *(++_gptr)): underflow();
}
// Skip past the character at the get pointer, and return the
// character after that, or EOF.

int sputbackc(char c)
{
   return _gptr > _gbase?
      (*(--_gptr) = c, 0): pbackfail(c & 0x00ff);
```

```
}
// Move the get pointer back one character. If c is not the last
// character retrieved, the effect is undefined. In this implementation
// it should work

int sputc(int c)
{
   return _pptr < _epptr?
      (*_pptr++ = c, 0): overflow(c & 0x00ff);
}
// Store c on the character stream, advancing the "put" pointer.
// Return EOF when an error occurs.

int sputn(const char *string, int length);
// Store "n" characters on the character stream, advancing the "put"
// pointer past the stored characters. Return the number of characters
// stored, which may be less than "n" if there is an error.

void stossc()
{
   if (_gptr < _egptr) ++_gptr;
}
// Skip the "get" pointer forward, wasting one character of input.
// If the get pointer is already at the end of the sequence
// this has no effect.

virtual int sync();
// Make the external character stream and the streambuf consistent
// with each other. This usually means:
// 1. If there are characters in the get area, return them to the
//    stream, or throw them away. Re-position the stream so that
//    it appears that the characters that had been in the get area
//    had never been taken from the stream.
// 2. If there are characters in the put area, store them to the
//    stream. Re-position the stream immediately after the characters
//    just stored.
// 3. Return EOF if there's an error, otherwise return some other
//    value.
//       * The default version of this member will return 0 if the get area
//         is empty, otherwise it returns EOF.

virtual int overflow(int c = EOF);
// This is called to store characters in the character stream, usually
// when the put area is full. It generally stores all of the characters
// that are in the put area, stores c if it is not EOF, and calls
// setp() to establish a new put area. It should return EOF if it
// has an error, otherwise return some other value.

virtual int underflow();
// This is called to read characters from the character stream,
// usually when the get area is empty. It should read one or more
```

```
// characters, and place them in the get area. It should return the
// first character in the get area, without incrementing the get
// pointer. It should return EOF if there's a problem.

protected:
    // Buffer base and one past the end
    char *base() const { return _base; }
    char *ebuf() const { return _ebuf; }
    // Get pointer, pushback limit, and one past end of put area
    char *gptr() const { return _gptr; }
    char *eback() const { return _gbase; }
    char *egptr() const { return _egptr; }
    // Put pointer, and one past end of put area
    char *pbase() const { return _pbase; }
    char *pptr() const { return _pptr; }
    char *epptr() const { return _epptr; }
    int blen() const { return _ebuf-_base; }
    // Return the size in characters of the buffer.

    int allocate();
    // Try to set up the buffer. If one already exists or unbuffered() is
    // non-zero, return 0 without doing anything. If something goes wrong,
    // return EOF. Otherwise, return 1. This function is only called by
    // virtual members of the base class streambuf, thus you can override
    // everything that uses it.

    virtual int doallocate();
    // This is called when allocate() determines that space is needed.
    // This function must call setb() to set up the buffer, and return
    // a non-eof value, or return EOF if it can not get space.
    // This function is only called if unbuffered() is zero, and base()
    // is zero.
    //
    // * The default version allocates a buffer using operator new.

    virtual int pbackfail(int c);
    // This is called by sputbackc() when the get pointer is equal to
    // the base of the get area, and there is thus no space to put back
    // characters. It may try to re-arrange the buffer so that it is
    // possible to put back characters, and then put back c. If it
    // succeeds it should return c, otherwise it should return EOF.
    // * The default version of this member always returns EOF.

    void setg(char *base, char *get, char *end)
    {
        _gbase = base;
        _gptr = get;
        _egptr = end;
    }
    // Sets the base of the get area, the get pointer, and the end of
    // the get area.
```

```
    void setp(char *base, char *end)
    {
      _pbase = _pptr = base;
      _epptr = end;
    }
    // Sets the base of the put area, the put pointer, and the end of
    // the put area.

    void setb(char *base, char *end, int own = 0);
    // Sets the base and end of the buffer. If own is true, then this
    // streambuf will delete base in its destructor or if setb() is called
    // again.

    void gbump(int n) { _gptr += n; }
    void pbump(int n) { _pptr += n; }
    int unbuffered() const { return _unbuffered; }
    void unbuffered(int u) { _unbuffered = u; }

private:
    char *_base;
    char *_ebuf;
    char *_gbase;
    char *_gptr;
    char *_egptr;
    char *_pbase;
    char *_pptr;
    char *_epptr;
    char _unbuffered;
    char _owned;
    char unbuf[2];
    // This is big enough to deal with the translated case when unbuffered

    int sbumpc_special();
    // Called by sbumpc() when get_pointer == get_area_end.
    // Simply calls overflow(), increments the get pointer, and
    // returns the value returned by overflow(). It's here so that
    // the special-case code does not have to be inlined.
};


class ostream : virtual public ios {
// This is the class used for formatted character output.
// The various "operator << (...)" members are called "inserters", because
// they insert information into the character stream.
//
// Unless otherwise noted, all of the functions here that do output set
// the error state on failure.
//
// Where the inserters perform conversions of numbers to a readable string,
// the conversion is affected by the format state flags in ios::flags().
```

```
public:
    ostream(streambuf * buffer);
    // Construct an ostream associated with the argument streambuf.

    virtual ~ostream();

    ostream &flush();
    // Flush any characters queued for output.

    int opfx();
    // Perform output-prefix operations.
    // If the error state is non-zero, return zero immediately.
    // If there is a tied ostream (see ios::tie()), flush it.
    // Return non-zero. If you define your own inserter that directly
    // manipulates the streambuf instead of calling other inserters,
    // it should call this when it starts.

    void osfx();
    // Perform output-suffix operations.
    // If ios::unitbuf is set in the format state, flush output.
    // If ios::stdio is set, flush stdio and stderr.
    // If you define your own inserter that directly manipulates the
    // streambuf, it should call this just before returning.
    // All of the inserters in ostream call this.
    // The binary put() and write() functions do not call this.

    ostream &put(char c);
    // Inserts a character

    ostream &seekp(streampos position);
    // Absolute seeks the output stream to "position".

    ostream &seekp(streamoff offset, seek_dir direction);
    // Relative seeks the output stream. See streambuf::seekoff()

    streampos tellp();
    // Returns the current position in the output stream.

    ostream &write(const void *data, size_t size);
    size_t pcount() { return write_count; }
    // Inserts the block of "size" bytes starting at "data". Does not
    // perform any formatting. The number of characters successfully
    // output can be determined by a following call to ostream::pcount().

    ostream &operator<<(const char *string);
    ostream &operator<<(const signed char *string)
        { return operator<<((const char *) string); }
    ostream &operator<<(const unsigned char *string)
        { return operator<<((const char *) string); }
    // Insert a null-terminated string.
```

```
   ostream &operator<<(char c);
   ostream &operator<<(signed char c)
      { return operator<<((char) c); }
   ostream &operator<<(unsigned char c)
      { return operator<<((char) c); }
   // Insert a single character.

   ostream &operator<<(short v)
      { return _2Comp::insert(*this,&v,sizeof(short),1); }
   ostream &operator<<(int v)
      { return _2Comp::insert(*this,&v,sizeof(int),1); }
   ostream &operator<<(long v)
      { return _2Comp::insert(*this,&v,sizeof(long),1); }
   ostream &operator<<(unsigned short v)
      { return _2Comp::insert(*this,&v,sizeof(unsigned short),0); }
   ostream &operator<<(unsigned v)
      { return _2Comp::insert(*this,&v,sizeof(unsigned),0); }
   ostream &operator<<(unsigned long v)
      { return _2Comp::insert(*this,&v,sizeof(unsigned long),0); }
#if macintosh
   ostream &operator<<(float v) { return operator<<((long double) v); }
   ostream &operator<<(double v) { return operator<<((long double) v); }
   ostream &operator<<(long double);
#else
   ostream &operator<<(float v) { return operator<<((double) v); }
   ostream &operator<<(double);
#endif

   ostream &operator<<(void *);
   // Convert a pointer to a hex integer, and insert.

   ostream &operator<<(streambuf *source);
   // Insert all of the characters that can be fetched from the streambuf.

   ostream &operator<<(ostream &(*manipulator)(ostream &))
      { return (*manipulator)(*this); }
   // Parameterless manipulators are implemented by providing an

   // inserter for the type pointer to function taking an ostream reference
   // argument and returning an ostream reference.  The specified function
   // is simple executed for the current ostream.

   ostream &operator<<(ios &(*manipulator)(ios &))
   {
      (*manipulator)(*this);
      return *this;
   }
   // Similar facility to insert a pointer to function taking an ios
   // reference argument.
```

```
      // This isn't in the draft standard, but it is so useful in the
      // implementation of inserters that it is made public here.
      int pad(int where, int wide);

protected:
      ostream();
      // ios will be initialized by derived class

private:
      size_t write_count;
      // Records number of bytes actually put out by a write()

      void eof_fail() { clear(ios::badbit | ios::failbit | ios:: eofbit); }
      // Internal. Set error flags after an output EOF error.

#if macintosh
      int fixed_point(long double, char *);
#else
      int fixed_point(double, char *);
#endif
// Internal. Convert double to fixed-point string.

#if macintosh
      int sci_notation(long double, char *, int &);
#else
      int sci_notation(double, char *, int &);
#endif
// Internal. Convert double to scientific-notation string.

      int adjust(int bit_to_test, int field_width);
      // Manages padding

      void flush_stdio();
      // Called by osfx() if ios::stdio is set.  This function is in a
      // separate module to prevent the stdio stuff from being pulled
      // in when it is not required.
};

// The following functions provide parameterless inserters of the
// type noted above. They have to be real functions because we
// need to take their address.

ostream &ends(ostream&);
// Ends a string by inserting a null character. Use this on strstreams
// before you call ostrstream::freeze() .
//
// stream << "whatever" << ends;

ostream &flush(ostream&);
// Flushes output on an ostream.
//
// stream << "whatever" << flush
```

```
ostream &endl(ostream &);
// Inserts the appropriate new-line character(s) for the system, and flushes
// output. On Unix the new-line character is inserted. On DOS, the
// carriage-return and new-line characters are inserted. Thus, using endl
// instead of '\n' or "\r\n" is more portable.
//
// stream << "whatever" << endl;

ostream &stickywidth(ostream &);
// Sets the state so that width is not reset after each insertion
// unlatch this by a call to width() or use setw manipulator.

ostream &spacing(ostream &);
ostream &nospacing(ostream &);
// Sets the state so that a space is output after any item which
// makes a call to osfx() except the endl manipulator.

ostream &fixed(ostream &);
ostream &scientific(ostream &);
ostream &showpoint(ostream &);
ostream &floating(ostream &);
ostream &uppercase(ostream &);
// Manipulate the floating point format, floating sets the default state.

ostream &leftjust(ostream &);
ostream &rightjust(ostream &);
ostream &internal(ostream &);
ostream &showbase(ostream &);
// Set a justify mode

// types used by istream dfa extractor function
typedef void (*translate_function_t)(void *, const char *, void *);
typedef int (*helper_function_t)(int, char, void *);


class istream : virtual public ios {
// This is the class used for character input.
// The various "operator>>(...)" members are called "extractors", because
// they extract information from the character stream.
//  * Where the extractors perform conversions of a string to a number,
// the conversion is affected by the format state flags in ios::flags() .
// Each of the extractors calls ipfx() first, and returns immediately if
// ipfx returns zero. Extractors indicate errors by setting bits of the
// error state. ios::failbit means the input characters weren't a
// representation of the required type. ios::badbit means that the I/O
// system failed to get the required characters.
//  * The unformatted extractors (get(), getline()) will set ios::failbit
// only if they are not able to extract at least one character.
//  * Caveat: The ATT version ignores overflow. This version attempts to set
// the error flags on overflow.
```

```
public:
    static int is_white_space(char c);
    // Internal. Return 1 if the argument character is white-space,
    // otherwise return 0.

    istream(streambuf *buffer);
    // Construct a new istream associated with the argument streambuf.

    virtual ~istream();

    size_t gcount() { return read_count; }
    // Return the number of characters extracted by the last unformatted
    // input function. Other input functions may call the unformatted
    // input functions, so this counter is only accurate immediately
    // after a call to an unformatted input function.

    istream &get(char *data, int length, char delimiter = '\n');
    istream &get(signed char *data, int length, char delimiter = '\n');
    istream &get(unsigned char *data, int length, char delimiter = '\n');
    // Both of these extract up to "length" characters, storing them in
    // "data". If a character equal to "delimiter" is seen, it is pushed
    // back on the input stream and extraction stops.

    istream &get(char &destination);
    istream &get(signed char &destination);
    istream &get(unsigned char &destination);
    // Extract a single character.

    istream &get(streambuf &destination, char delimiter = '\n');
    // Call ipfx(0), and if the result is non-zero, get characters until
    // the delimiter is seen or EOF, and stuff the characters into the
    // streambuf. Doesn't extract the delimiter character. Only sets
    // ios::badbit if it can't extract at least one character.

    int get();
    // Get one character, and return it in an int. Return EOF if there's
    // an error.

    istream &getline(char *data, int length, char delimiter = '\n');
    istream &getline(signed char *data, int length, char delimiter = '\n');
    istream &getline(unsigned char *data, int length, char delimiter = '\n');
    // These two are like get(char *data, int length, char delimiter),
    // except that they extract the terminating delimiter instead of
    // pushing it back.

    istream &ignore(int length = 1, int delimiter = EOF);
    // Extract and throw away up to "length" characters. Extraction
    // stops if "delimiter" is extracted, or at EOF. If "delimiter"
    // is EOF, it won't match any character, and thus will not stop
    // extraction.
```

```
int ipfx(int need = 0);
// Perform input-prefix operations.
// The argument "need" is the number of characters that will be
// required, or 0 if you don't know how many you'll need. The
// formatted input functions call this with 0, and the unformatted
// input functions call it with 1.
// * If the error state is non-zero, this returns zero immediately.
// Otherwise, it returns non-zero when finished.
// If there is a tied stream (see ios::tie()) and need is 0 or greater
// than the number of immediately available characters, the tied
// iostream is flushed.
// * If ios::skipws is set in the format state, and "need" is zero,
// leading white-space characters are thrown away and the stream
// is advanced to the first available character.
// This returns zero if there is an error while skipping a
// white-space character, otherwise it returns non-zero.

int peek();
// Calls ipfx(1). If that returns zero, or if the input character
// stream is at EOF, return EOF. Otherwise return the next character
// without extracting it from the input stream.

istream &putback(char c);
// Attempt to push the last character read back onto the input stream.
// "c" must be the last character read. This does not call ipfx(), but
// it will return without doing anything if the error state is
// non-zero.

istream &read(void *data, int size);
// Extracts a block of "size" bytes and stores them at "data".
// If EOF is reached before "size" bytes are extracted,
// ios::failbit is set. The number of characters actually
// extracted is available as the return value of istream::gcount().

istream &seekg(streampos position);
// Absolute-seek the input character stream to "position".

istream &seekg(streamoff offset, seek_dir direction);
// Relative-seek the input character stream by "offset" relative to
// the current position.

int sync();
// Establishes consistency between the internal data structure
// and the external character source. This usually means that
// characters that were buffered for input are thrown away, and
// the file pointer is decremented so that it appears that the
// buffered characters were never read.

streampos tellg();
// Return the current file position. The value returned is a magic
// cookie that is usable only as an argument to seekg(streampos).
// Don't perform arithmetic on the return value.
```

```
istream &operator>>(char *);
istream &operator>>(signed char *s)
   { return operator>>((char *) s); }
istream &operator>>(unsigned char *s)
   { return operator>>((char *) s); }
// For the string extractors, characters are extracted until a
// white-space is seen. The white-space is pushed back on the
// incoming character stream. If width() is non-zero, it is taken
// as the size of the argument character array, and no more than
// width()-1 characters are extracted. A terminating null character
// is ALWAYS stored, even when nothing else is done because of
// the error state.

istream &operator>>(char &);
// Extracts a single character, similar to get()
#if macintosh
   istream &operator>>(signed char &c)
      { return operator>>((char) c); }
   istream &operator>>(unsigned char &c)
      { return operator>>((char) c); }
#else
   istream &operator>>(signed char &c)
      { return _2Comp::extract(*this,&c,1); }
   istream &operator>>(unsigned char &c)
      { return _2Comp::extract(*this,&c,1); }
#endif

// Extract byte wide integers -128 - +127 and 0 - 255 respectively
istream &operator>>(short &v)
   { return _2Comp::extract(*this,&v,sizeof(short)); }
istream &operator>>(int &v)
   { return _2Comp::extract(*this,&v,sizeof(int)); }
istream &operator>>(long &v)
   { return _2Comp::extract(*this,&v,sizeof(long)); }
istream &operator>>(unsigned short &v)
   { return _2Comp::extract(*this,&v,sizeof(unsigned short)); }
istream &operator>>(unsigned int &v)
   { return _2Comp::extract(*this,&v,sizeof(unsigned int)); }
istream &operator>>(unsigned long &v)
   { return _2Comp::extract(*this,&v,sizeof(unsigned long)); }
istream &operator>>(float &);
istream &operator>>(double &);
#if macintosh
   istream &operator>>(long double &);
#endif

istream &operator>>(streambuf*);
// Calls ipfx(0), and if the result is non-zero, extracts characters
// and stuffs them into the argument streambuf until EOF is reached.
// Only sets ios::badbit if it can't get at least one character.
```

```
    istream &operator>>(istream &(*manip)(istream&))
    {
       (*manip)(*this);
       return *this;
    }
    // Provides an pseudo extractor which allows for parameterless
    // manipulators. The target type is pointer to function returning
    // istream reference and taking istream reference argument.

    istream &operator>>(ios &(*manip)(ios&))
    {
       (*manip)(*this);
       return *this;
    }
    // Similar facility to manipulate an ios object directly

protected:
    istream();  // derived class will initialize ios directly

private:
    friend istream &_2Comp::extract(istream&, void *, int);

// The extract function provides for general type translation using
// a character set string and a DFA transition table
    istream &extract(void *type, const char *okchars, int *tt,
       translate_function_t tf, helper_function_t hf, void *tds);
       size_t read_count;
};

istream &ws(istream&);
// Manipulator to skip white-space, positioning the input
// character stream to the first available non-white-space
// character.


class iostream : public istream, public ostream {
// A stream that supports both insertion and extraction.

public:
    iostream(streambuf *buf);
    // Construct an iostream associated with the argument streambuf.
    virtual ~iostream();

protected:
    iostream(); // derived class will initialize ios directly
};

// Iostream classes that support assignment.
//
// They're used for cin, cout, cerr, and clog, but you should not use them for
// anything else. Instead, use a regular stream and assign a pointer to it.
```

```
class istream_withassign : public istream {
public:
   istream_withassign();
   istream_withassign(streambuf *);
   ~istream_withassign();
   istream_withassign &operator=(istream &);
   istream_withassign &operator=(istream_withassign &s)
      {return operator=((istream &)s);}
   istream_withassign &operator=(streambuf *);

private:
   short assigned_to;
};


class ostream_withassign : public ostream {
public:
   ostream_withassign();
   ostream_withassign(streambuf *);
   ~ostream_withassign();
   ostream_withassign &operator=(ostream &);
   ostream_withassign &operator=(ostream_withassign &s)
      {return operator=((ostream &)s);}
   ostream_withassign &operator=(streambuf *);

private:
   short assigned_to;
};


class iostream_withassign : public iostream {
public:
   iostream_withassign();
   iostream_withassign(streambuf *);
   ~iostream_withassign();
   iostream_withassign &operator=(ios &);
   iostream_withassign &operator=(iostream_withassign &s)
      {return operator=((ios &)s);}
   iostream_withassign &operator=(streambuf *);

private:
   short assigned_to;
};

extern istream_withassign cin;
extern ostream_withassign cout;
extern ostream_withassign cerr;
#ifdef __XENIX__
extern ostream_withassign   clog;
#endif
```

```
class IosTie {
public:
   IosTie(ios *a, ostream *b) {a->tie(b);
   #if THINK_CPLUS
      ios::sync_with_stdio(); #endif
      } };


class IosUnitbuf {
public:
IosUnitbuf(ios *a) { a->setf(ios::unitbuf); }
};
#endif  // __IOSTREAM_H
```

strstrea.h

```
// IOStreams Package
// Steve Teale April 1992
// Copyright Symantec Corp 1990-1992. All Rights Reserved.

#ifndef __SSTREAM_HPP
#define __SSTREAM_HPP

#include <iostream.hpp>

const int default_allocation = 32;

class strstreambuf : public streambuf {
// This is a streambuf that holds a character array, and I/O is to that
// character array instead of a file or some external character stream.
// There is a dynamic-allocation mode that allocates space for characters
// as needed. Get, put, and seeks are supported within the character array.
// The call freeze() returns a pointer to the array, so that the data may
// be read by conventional string-handling routines.

public:
    // state flags
    enum sstream_flags {
        statmem = 1,
        // Set if the buffer was set with an argument to the constructor or
        // setbuf, and I should not do dynamic allocation if it runs out of
        // space.
```

```
    frozen = 2,
    // Set when the buffer is frozen.

    merged = 4,
    // Set if the get and put areas are considered to be overlapped. This
    // will be the case if the strstreambuf is dynamic, or if a simultaneous
    // seek of both the get and put pointers has been done.

    rdonly = 0x10
    // Puts are not allowed.
};

strstreambuf(int chunksize = default_allocation);
// Create a strstreambuf in dynamic-allocation mode, with the initial
// allocation at least "chunksize" bytes long, defaulted to default
// allocation

strstreambuf(char *memory, int length = 0, char *start_of_put_area = 0);
// Create a strstreambuf using the static buffer at "memory".
// If "length" is positive, that is taken as the length of the
// buffer. If it is zero, the length is taken from strlen(memory).
// If "length" is negative, the buffer is assumed to be of infinite
// length.
//
// The get pointer is initialized to "memory". If "start_of_put_area"
// is zero, the get area covers the entire buffer and a put will be
// considered an error. If "start_of_put_area" is non-zero, the
// get area consists of the bytes between "memory" and
// "start_of_put_area" - 1, and the put area consists of the bytes
// between "start_of_put_area" and the end of the buffer.

strstreambuf(unsigned char *memory, int length = 0,
   unsigned char *start_of_put_area = 0);
// Same as above, but for an unsigned character buffer.

strstreambuf(void * (*allocate_function)(size_t), void (*free_function)(void *),
   int chunksize = default_allocation);
// Create a streambuf in dynamic allocation mode. Use
// void * allocate_function(size_t length) to allocate memory,
// and void free_function(void * memory) to free it. Allocation
// chunk size can be specified.

~strstreambuf();

void freeze(int on = 1);
void unfreeze() { freeze(0); }
// If the argument is non-zero, "freeze" the strstreambuf. This
// inhibits automatic deletion of the current character buffer.
// This is only important in dynamic-allocation mode. Stores into
// the buffer are invalid when it is "frozen". Calling this with
// a zero argument "un-freezes" the buffer. Deleting a strstreambuf
// will not de-allocate a frozen buffer - you must delete it yourself.
```

```
    int pcount() const { return pptr()-pbase(); }
    // Return the number of characters inserted. Not accurate after
    // a seek.

    char *str();
    // Freeze the buffer and return a pointer to its first byte.
    // The pointer may be null if no bytes have been stored and the
    // buffer is in dynamic-allocation mode. The buffer may be "un-frozen"
    // by calling freeze(0). Deleting a strstreambuf will not de-allocate
    // a frozen buffer - you must delete it yourself.

    streambuf *setbuf(char *memory, int length);
    // The memory argument is not used. The next time the streambuf
    // does dynamic allocation, it will allocate at least "length" bytes.
    // This function in fact sets the allocation granularity.

#if __ZTC__ > 0x214
    int overflow(int c = EOF);
#else
    int overflow(int c);
#endif

    int underflow();
    streampos seekoff(streamoff offset, ios::seek_dir direction,
        int which =ios::in|ios::out);
    int sync();
    // All of these are virtual functions derived from streambuf.
    // There's more documentation on them in iostream.h.

protected:
    int doallocate();

private:
    short sflags;
    int chunk;
    // The minimum amount to allocate when doing dynamic allocation.

    void *(*allocate_function)(size_t size);
    // Points to the function used to allocate memory.

    void (*free_function)(void *memory);
    // Points to the function used to free memory.

    void buffer_setup(char *memory, int length,
        char *start_of_put_area);
};


class istrstream : public istream {
// A class of istream that takes as input a character array, and extracts
// information from it.
```

```
public:
    istrstream(char *memory, int length = 0);
    // Create an istrstream attached to the character array at "memory",
    // of length "length". If length is zero, strlen() is used, if length
    // is negative, the stream is considered to be of a length equivalent
    // to the maximum value of type size_t.

    ~istrstream();
    strstreambuf *rdbuf() { return &buffer; }

private:
    strstreambuf buffer;
};


class ostrstream : public ostream {
// A class of ostream that inserts information into a character array.

public:
    ostrstream();
    // Create an ostrstream in dynamic-allocation mode.

    ostrstream(char *memory, int length, int mode=ios::out);
    // Create an ostrstream attached to the character array at "memory",
    // of length "length". If ios::ate or ios::app is set in "mode",
    // the buffer is assumed to contain a null-terminated string, and
    // the put area begins at the null character. Otherwise the put
    // area will begin at "memory".

    ~ostrstream();

    int pcount() const { return buffer.pcount(); }
    // Returns the number of bytes that have been put into the buffer.

    char *str();
    // Freezes the buffer, and returns a pointer to the first byte of the
    // buffer. Once the buffer is frozen it will not be deleted by
    // the destructor of the stream: it becomes the user's responsibility
    // to delete it.

    void unfreeze();
    // Unfreeze the buffer and unconditionally clear the state flags.

    strstreambuf *rdbuf() { return &buffer; }

private:
    strstreambuf buffer;
};
```

```
class strstream : public iostream {
// A class of iostream that inserts and extracts information in a character array.

public:
    strstream();
    // Create a strstream in dynamic-allocation mode.

    strstream(char *memory, int length = 0, int mode = ios::in|ios::out);
    // Create a strstream attached to the character array at "memory",

    // of length "length". If length is zero, then "memory" is assumed to
    // contain a null terminated string, and the langth is taken from
    // strlen. If ios::ate or ios::app is set in "mode", the buffer is
    // assumed to contain a null-terminated string, and the put area begins
    // at the null character. Otherwise the put area will begin at "memory".

    ~strstream();

    char *str();
    // Freezes the buffer, and returns a pointer to the first byte of the
    // buffer. Once the buffer is frozen it will not be deleted by
    // the destructor of the stream: it becomes the user's responsibility
    // to delete it.

    void unfreeze();
    // Unfreeze the buffer and unconditionally clear the state flags.

    strstreambuf *rdbuf() { return &buffer; }

private:
    strstreambuf buffer;
};
#endif // __SSTREAM_HPP
```

Appendix G

Unoffical C++ Style Guide

by Dave Goldsmith and Jack Palevich

This article is reprinted with permission from develop, The Apple Technical Journal, *Issue 2, April 1990. It's an enhanced version of an internal, informal Apple style guide written by David Goldsmith. Jack Palevich edited the original document to bring it into this form. The opinions expressed in this document are David's and/or Jack's; they are not necessarily those of Apple Computer.*

develop *provides an in-depth look at code and techniques that show the "Apple way" of doing things. Each issue comes with a CD that contains the source code for that issue, as well as all back issues, Technical Notes, sample code, and other useful software and documentation. Subscriptions to* develop *and back issues are available through APDA; call 1-800-282-2732.*

C++ is fast emerging as the premier object-based language of the 1990s. Its expressive power combined with its down-and-dirty C heritage makes it a natural choice for writing Macintosh applications. But beware: all is not sweetness and light. Harnessing C++'s power without getting tripped up by some of its less savory features isn't all that easy. Here are guidelines that make it easier to write, debug, and change C++ programs.

When we first started using C++ several years ago, we learned the hard way—by trial and error—a lot of what we're about to tell you. After thousands of hours of C++ programming, we've formed strong opinions about the best way to use C++. In this unofficial style guide we tell you which features to use and which ones to avoid. Following our techniques will lead to programs that are easier to write, debug, and change. You may not agree with all of our guidelines—some are more a matter of taste than of science—but we hope you'll find them useful and enlightening.

Part 1: Style

In this part you'll find fairly simple advice on formatting source files. Even if you prefer to use a different style in your own work, you may be interested to see how we handle these standard matters of style.

Source File Conventions

Use the following conventions to keep your source files easy to read, easy to use, and legally protected.

Include a copyright notice. To protect your intellectual property rights, include the following line at the front of every file you create:

```
// Copyright © 1990 ~~~Your name or company~~~.
// All rights reserved.
```

You can make the © by typing Option-g. The "All rights reserved" is specifically for our foreign friends. (We bet you thought all you had to say was "Copyright." Ha!) In addition, any binary files you ship should contain a copyright notice somewhere.

If you modify a file in more than one calendar year, you must list every year in which you modified it. For example,

```
// Copyright © 1988-1990 ~~~Your name or company~~~.
// All rights reserved.
```

Add helpful comments. We won't go into a lengthy discussion of comment style here. We'll only say it's good to have them. Also, comments that describe something subtle about the source are more helpful than comments like assign a to b.

Be careful about omitting argument names in function prototypes. It's OK to omit dummy argument names in function prototypes, but only if the meaning is clear without them. It's almost always necessary to include argument names when you have more than one argument of the same type, as it's impossible to figure out which one is which otherwise.

```
double cosine(double angle);        // Prototype with
                                    // argument name.
double cosine(double);              // Reasonable
                                    // omission of
                                    // arg. name.
TPoint::TPoint(short h, short v);   // Easy to
                                    // understand.
TPoint::TPoint(short, short);       // Impossible to
                                    // figure out.
```

If you are getting compiler warnings of the form "warning: foo not used" where foo is an argument to a function, leaving the argument name out of the function header for the function's implementation will stop the warning. Whether or not an argument name appears in the function's declaration has no bearing on the warning.

```
void f(short foo, long bar);        // Prototype.
void f(short /* foo */, long bar)   // Implementation.
  {
  bar = 7;
  }
```

Put only related classes in one file. To keep your class definitions under control and to make life easier for those trying to decipher them, follow the lead of the MPW {CIncludes} files. Limit each header file to a single class definition or a set of related class definitions. MPW C has always followed this convention, for example, Windows.h, Controls.h versus Toolbox.h.

On the implementation side, put only one class implementation in a given source file (classes private to the implementation of the class may be declared and implemented in the same source file). Name the file after the class, but without the initial *T*—for example, put the class TMyView in MyView.c.

Make it easy to use your header files. Trying to figure out whether you've included all the necessary antecedents for a header file is a pain. To save your clients this pain, enclose the definitions in your header with code that looks like the following:

```
#ifndef __MYCLASS__
#define __MYCLASS__
#include "prerequisite1.h"
#include "prerequisite2.h"
... definitions for MyClass
#endif
```

Now you can include your header's prerequisites without caring whether they've already been included elsewhere (assuming that everyone follows this convention). The name of the preprocessor variable should be all uppercase and consist of the file name (without .h) surrounded by two underlines on either side.

To speed up compilation, you can even do this in your files that use foo.h:

```
#ifndef __FOO__
#include "foo.h"
#endif
```

which skips the overhead of reading and parsing foo.h.

Store files in Projector. As soon as a file is published for use by others (for example, you stick it on a file server so others can use it), you should start storing it in Projector. Projector is part of

MPW 3.0. It consists of a collection of built-in MPW commands and windows that help programmers (both individuals and teams) control and account for changes to all the files (documentation, source, applications, and so forth) associated with a software project. This lets you recreate old versions if necessary, and makes sure things don't get lost.

Since the whole point of using Projector is to make it easier for those who follow you in the great chain of software being, please use the features that will make their lives easier. Try to maintain a proper set of versions (for example, don't remove your file from Projector and then add it again—that loses all the revisions), and use the comment features when you check things in and out.

Naming Conventions

To make C++ even more readable, you should adopt a consistent set of naming conventions. Here at Apple we use the following conventions:

Type names. *All* type names begin with a capital letter. In addition, class names begin with a *T* for base classes, and an *M* for mix-in classes. See "Multiple Inheritance" in Part 2. Examples: Boolean, TView, MAdjustable. Never use C types directly; see below.

Member names. Member names should begin with an *f*, for "field." Member function names need only begin with a capital letter. Examples: fVisible, Draw.

Global names. Names of global variables (*including* static members of classes) should begin with a *g*. Examples: gApplication, TGame::gPlayingField.

Local and parameter names. Names of local variables and function arguments should begin with a word whose initial letter is lowercase. Examples: i, thePort, aRegion.

Constant names. Names of constants should begin with a *k*. Example: kSaveDialogResID.

Abbreviations. It's best to avoid abbreviations, especially ad hoc ones. Inconsistent use of abbreviations makes it hard for clients to remember the correct name of a function or variable. Abbreviations are OK as long as they are consistent and universal. For example, don't use VisibleRegion some places and VisRgn others; use one or the other throughout.

Multiple-word names. In any name that contains more than one word, the first word should follow the convention for the type of the name, and subsequent words should immediately follow, with the first letter of each word capitalized. Do not use underscores in names. Here are multiple-word examples of each type:

`TSortedList`	class name
`fSubViews`	data member of class
`DrawContents`	function member of class
`gDeviceList`	global or static data member
`theCurrentSize`	local or parameter
`kMaxStringLength`	constant

Names with global scope. Any name with global scope (for example, class names, typedefs, constants, globals) should have a distinctive and unique name. This will help avoid name conflicts. Names like Short and Number are fairly nondescript and likely to wind up conflicting with identifiers from other header files accidentally (this is a big problem with MPW and the ROM interfaces today). Better in these cases would be kShortLived (to follow our advice on constant names) or StringLength (more descriptive of the function). When you name something with global scope, think about the fact that it's in a global name space and someone may have to figure out what it is without context. Use more specific names rather than more general ones.

C++ relieves this problem somewhat by adding enumerations with class scope and static members. Enumerations declared inside classes are accessible using qualification, as in

```
class TFoo {
public:
  enum {kFred, kBarney};
  ...
};
```

```
i = TFoo::kFred;
```

This lets you put constants associated with different classes into different name spaces, somewhat like when C changed a few years back so that structure members from different structs were in different name spaces.

Static members let you put ordinary functions and global variables associated with a class into the scope of the class. For example:

```
class TView {
public:
   static void Initialize();
   static const TView kWhizzyView;
   static const long kMagicNumber;
...
};
TView::Initialize();
...TView::kWhizzyView...
i = TView::kMagicNumber;
```

Putting such global functions and variables into the scope of the class helps avoid name collisions. In fact, we frown on the use of ordinary globals: most global functions and variables should be static members of some class. The same with constants; they should be made members of an enumeration inside a class, if possible. Of course, global variables that are not constants of the sort shown above shouldn't be public at all; instead, access should be through static or normal member functions:

```
class TFoo {
public:
   static Boolean gWhoopeeFlag;   // BAD!
}
TFoo::gWhoopeeFlag = TRUE;        // BAD!
```

The Preprocessor

One of the most powerful features of the C and C++ languages is the C preprocessor.

Don't use it.

Except for include files and conditional compilation, C++ has features that supersede most of the techniques that used the preprocessor. Sometimes you need to use the preprocessor to accomplish things you can't with C++, but far less often than with straight C.

Use const for constants. Don't use #define for symbolic constants. Instead, C++ defines the const storage class. As with #define symbols, these are evaluated at compile time. Unlike #define symbols, they follow the C scope rules and have types associated with them. You can also use enums. For example:

```
#define kGreen 1                    // No no
const int kGreen = 1;               // Better
enum Color {kRed, kGreen, kBlue}; // Best
```

This prevents a host of problems. With #define symbols, for example, if you accidentally redefine a name, the compiler will silently change the meaning of your program. With const or enums, you'll get an error message. Even better, with enums you can put the identifiers in the scope of an enclosing class; see "Naming Conventions," earlier. As an extra bonus, each enumeration defined is treated as a separate type for purposes of type-checking (much like the way scalars are handled in Pascal).

Unlike in ANSI C, objects in C++ that are declared const and initialized with compile-time expressions are themselves compile-time constants (but only if they are of integral type). Thus, they can be used as case labels and such.

Use enum for a set of constants. If your constants define a related set, don't use separate const definitions. Instead, make your constants an enumerated type. For example:

```
// Bleah.
const int kRed = 0;
const int kBlue = 1;
const in kGreen = 2;
// Allll Riiiight!
enum ColorComponent {kRed, kBlue, kGreen};
```

This causes ColorComponent to become a distinct type that is type-checked by the compiler. Values of type ColorComponent will be automatically converted to int as needed, but integers cannot be changed to ColorComponents without a cast. If you need to assign particular numerical values, you can do that too:

```
enum ColorComponent {kRed = 0x10, kGreen = 0x20,
  kBlue = 0x40};
```

Where possible, the type declaration should occur within the scope of a class. Then, references to the constants outside of the class's member functions must be qualified:

```
class TColor {
public:
  ColorComponent enum {kRed, kGreen, kBlue};
...
}
foo = TColor::kRed;
```

Note that the enum type name is not local to the class, only the actual constants. The enum type name should not be qualified.

Use inline for macro functions. Function macros are another source of fun problems in C programs, like this classic example:

```
#define SQUARE(x) ((x)*(x))
SQUARE(y++);
```

C++ allows functions to be declared inline (see also "Inline Functions" in Part 2), which completely obviates the need for function macros. Like const, inline functions follow the C++ scope rules and allow argument type-checking. Both member functions and nonmember functions can be declared inline. So the preceding example becomes

```
inline int Square(int x)
{
  return x*x;
};
Square(y++);
```

which does the right thing, and is actually more efficient than the macro version (as well as being correct).

Use the preprocessor only in these cases. As stated earlier, the preprocessor is necessary for #include files, and preprocessor symbols are necessary for conditional compilation.

Use of const

Both ANSI C and C++ add a new modifier to declarations, const. You use this modifier to declare that the specified object cannot be changed. The compiler can then optimize code, and also warn you if you do something that doesn't match the declaration. Here are some examples of const declarations:

```
const int *foo;
```

This is a modifiable pointer to constant integers. foo can be changed, but what it points to cannot be.

```
int *const foo;
```

This is a constant pointer to modifiable integers. The pointer cannot be changed (once initialized), but the integers it points to can be changed at will.

```
const int *const foo;
```

This is a constant pointer to a constant integer. Neither the pointer nor the integer it points to can be changed.

Note that const objects can be assigned to non-const objects (thereby making a copy), and the modifiable copy can of course be changed. However, *pointers* to const objects *cannot* be assigned to pointers to non-const objects, although the converse is allowed. Both of these assignments are legal:

```
(const int *) = (int *);
(int *) = (int *const);
```

Both of these assignments are illegal:

```
(int *) = (const int *);
(int *const) = (int *);
```

When const is used in an argument list, it means that the argument will not be modified. This is especially useful when you want to pass an argument by reference, but you don't want the argument to be modified. For example:

```
void BlockMove(const void* source,
   void* destination, size_t length);
```

Here we are explicitly stating that the source data will not be modified, but that the destination data will be modified. (Of course, if the length is 0, then the destination won't actually be modified.)

All of these rules apply to class objects as well; you can declare something (const TView *). There used to be a hole in the language, however: you could call any member function of an object using a const pointer to it, and that member function could modify the object (since there was no way to declare which member functions modify the object). For example, this was legal:

```
const TView *aView;
...
aView->ModifySomething();
```

To plug this hole, member functions that will be called for const objects must now be declared const; see the 1985-1989 paper discussed in the sidebar "Background Reading" for details. The syntax looks like this:

```
class TFoo {
public:
   void Bar1() const;
   void Bar2();
};
...
const TFoo *fp;
fp->Bar1(); // legal
fp->Bar2(); // illegal (actually, just a warning
            // for now)
```

Note that inside a const member function, the pointer has type const TFoo *, so you really can't change the object. You could cast the pointer to be just a TFoo *, but then you may be surprising your clients. Even though you think that your change to the object is not externally visible (that is, it doesn't change the state of the object as far as clients are concerned; one example is an internal cache), it can have an impact. If your object is being used by an interrupt routine that "reads" it, your client may assume that it's OK to call a const member function, since he or she thinks the object isn't going to change. However, if the internal state of the object changes anyway, access by multiple "readers" will cause its state to become corrupted.

Another example is an object placed in ROM. The client thinks it's all right to call a const member function of the object, and then gets a bus error because the attempted write access fails.

The bottom line is that if you attempt to cast your this pointer to a non-const version inside a const member function, you had better think through the implications of this for your clients, and you had better document it.

Part 2: Using Language Features

In this part you'll find advice on using particular features of the C++ language. The topics are arranged roughly in order of increasing difficulty.

Global Variables (!)

Static class members are the same as global variables (actually, better). Static class members do have one major advantage over regular globals: scope. Regular globals (that is, static extern variables) have global scope. That means there are potential name collisions with globals from any other include file the developer may use. Static class members, however, have full scoping: they're qualified by the name of their class, and don't conflict with any identifier outside the class. They can also be protected. If you were going to have a simple global, consider a static member instead.

Be careful about static initialization. If you design a class that depends on some other facility in its constructor, be careful about order dependencies in static initialization. The order in which static constructors (that is, the constructors of objects with static storage class) get called is undefined. You cannot count on one object being initialized before another. Therefore, if you have such a dependency, you must either document that your class cannot be used for static objects, or you must use "lazy evaluation" to defer the dependency until later.

Inline Functions

We mentioned inline functions under "The Preprocessor," earlier. Never use them. Well, hardly ever. The main reason is that they get compiled into your caller's code. This makes them a tad difficult to override. Also, you have to ship their source code to everyone. There are, however, a few times when it's OK to use them.

Use an inline function if it expands to call to something else. If your inline function just calls something else that isn't inline, that's fine, as long as the other function *has identical semantics*. An example: You might have a class that defines a virtual function IsEqual, which compares two objects for equality. It also has an inline definition for operator ==, as a notational convenience. Since operator == just turns around and calls the IsEqual function, it's OK for it to be inline and not virtual. This does not apply if your function just happens to have a one-line implementation.

Use an inline function if efficiency is very, very important and you'll never change it. Of course, the other time it's OK to use inline is if efficiency is extremely important. Note that code size may increase due to duplication of code. *You may actually decrease system performance by making something inline*, since you're increasing the amount of code that must fit in memory. Also, once a function is more than a couple of lines long, the function call overhead is a very small fraction of the total time, and you are not buying much by making it inline.

An example is addition for a complex number type; here, the efficiency consideration together with the low probability of a future change makes an inline implementation a good idea. The complex number implementation shipped with C++ makes addition and subtraction inlines (fairly short), but makes multiplication and division regular functions (they are longer, so the overhead for a call is less important and the code size issue is more important).

If you don't *know* (that is, God has told you in person) that your implementation must be inline, *don't make it inline*. Build it normally and then *measure* the performance. Experience has shown again and again that programmers spend lots of time optimizing code that hardly ever gets executed, while totally missing the real bottlenecks. The empirical approach is much more reliable. Experience has also shown that a better algorithm or smarter data structures will buy you a lot more performance than code tweaking.

Don't write inlines in declarations. C++ has two ways of declaring an inline member function (of course). One is to declare the member function normally and then supply an inline function definition later in the same header file. The other is to write the function definition directly in the class declaration. Never use this latter form; always declare the function normally and then put an inline definition at the end of the file. That way, it's much easier to change between inline and regular implementations of a function, and it's no less efficient. The fact that something is inline should not be made obvious in the class declaration, since clients may start counting on it.

```
class TFoo {
public:
  int TweedleDee() { return 1; }; // Bad!
  int TweedleDum();               // Good!
};

inline int TFoo::TweedleDum()
{
  return 2;
};
```

Unspecified and Default Arguments

It's possible to partially circumvent the strong type-checking C++ imposes on function arguments. You should avoid doing this if at all possible.

Don't use unspecified arguments. C++, like ANSI C, allows you to cling to C's wild and woolly past, by declaring functions that take unspecified numbers and types of arguments, the classic example being

```
void printf(char *, ...);
```

This is a cheesy leftover from the Cretaceous era. There are very few functions indeed that need to have an interface like this. If you want to be able to omit arguments, for example, you can use default arguments or function overloading (both defined below). Unspecified arguments come from hell.

Do use default arguments, but cautiously. A better technique than unspecified arguments is default arguments. You can specify default values for arguments that are only used sometimes. This is especially handy in constructors. For example,

```
TView::TView(TVPoint itsSize, TVPoint itsLocation,
  TView *itsSuperView = NIL);
```

which can be called either with three arguments or with two. This can help you avoid that agonizing decision as to whether to include an option or not. However, be sparing; clearly, long strings of defaults can make it hard to figure out what's going on. Furthermore, you can only leave off arguments at the end, not the middle, so if you have ten defaults and someone wants to specify the last one, they must specify the preceding nine as well. This sort of defeats the idea. Having more than two default arguments is a bad idea, and even two is questionable.

Also remember that for both default arguments and function overloading, having too many versions of the same function decreases the safety provided by type-checking, and makes it more likely that you will accidentally call a different version from the one you intended to call.

Function Name Overloading

C++ also lets you overload function names, by letting two functions (member or nonmember) have the same name as long as the types of their arguments differ. This feature is useful when you want to have different versions of the same function; they should all be related. For example, you may want to have a constructor that takes lots of options, as well as one that is simple to use. Also, you may want to make functions that take different types. Examples include:

```
Rectangle::Rectangle(Point leftTop,
  Point rightBottom)
Rectangle::Rectangle(short top, short left,
  short bottom, short right)
void TPort::MoveTo(short, short)
void TPort::MoveTo(Point)
TComplex TComplex::Add(TComplex)
TComplex TComplex::Add(int)
```

This can be very useful but also can cause problems.

Don't unintentionally use the wrong argument type. The biggest problem is the unintentional use of the wrong argument type when overloading, which defines a new function. If TView has a member function

```
TView::Print(const TPrintRecord *)
```

and you define a subclass where, intending to override this function, you declare

```
TMyView::Print(const TStdPrintRecord *)
```

or

```
TMyView::Print(TPrintRecord *)
```

or even

```
TMyView::print(const TPrintRecord *)
```

because you forgot the type of the original argument (or misspelled the name), C++ assumes you don't want to overload the original function and simply declares it as a new function. You have not overridden the original; it's still available. The latest version of CFront will warn you about the first two cases, but not the last.

Also remember that, as mentioned earlier, the more variants a function has, the easier it is to call the wrong one unintentionally because the arguments you supply just happen to match another variant.

Watch your overrides. If you have an overloaded member function (whether virtual or not), and you override it in a derived class, then your override hides all overloaded variants of that member function, *not just the one you overrode*. Thus, if you want to override an overloaded member function, you must override *all* of the overloaded variants. C++ treats the overloaded function as a single entity; the scope resolution rule for C++ is to find the first class that has any function with that name defined, then look for a match based on argument type. The C++ team at AT&T believes this is the correct rule; their reasoning is that an overloaded set of functions is really just one function with a bunch of variants, and that you should not be naming functions with the same name unless they are really the same function.

An example that illustrates this behavior follows:

```
class A {
public:
  void Foo(long);
  void Foo(double);
};

class B: public A {
public:
  void Foo(double);
};
```

```
B bar;
bar.Foo(2);
```

The call actually winds up calling B::Foo(double) after coercing the integer argument to double.

On a positive note, CFront will warn you if you override some but not all of a set of overloaded member functions. For details, see the 1985-1989 paper discussed in the "Background Reading" sidebar, and the reference manual.

Don't abuse function overloading. Function overloading can be abused. Functions should not have the same name unless they basically perform the same operation, as in the preceding examples. If that is the case, then having the functions identically named can be a great help in reducing the number of things a programmer must remember.

Operator Overloading

Another fun C++ feature is the ability to define operators for your own classes. If you define a fixed-point data type, C++ lets you define the standard arithmetic operators for it, which makes code a lot easier to read.

Use operator overloading only where appropriate and clear. Operator overloading also has tremendous potential for abuse. Defining the + operator for fixed-point numbers helps clarify code. Defining it as set union is also fairly clear. Defining => to mean "send a message" is crazy. Operator redefinition only helps when the new function is similar to the standard meaning of the operator; otherwise, it just confuses people. An example is C++'s streams facility, which redefines < and > as output and input operators. This confuses a lot of people.

If you like, use functional syntax to call a base class's operator. C++ occasionally delivers a pleasant surprise. One example is the syntax for calling overloaded operators. Of course, you can use the usual inline operator syntax; that's why C++ has operator overloading. The surprise is that you can also use functional syntax, which is sometimes essential, especially for calling a base class operator. Here is an example of a subclass operator using the base class's operator:

```
const TWindow& TWindow::operator=(const TView &v)
{
  this->TView::operator=(v);
  return *this;
}
```

(The explicit this-> is actually unnecessary here but was included for clarity.) In this example, TWindow has a base class TView, and we want to be able to assign a TView to a TWindow by just copying the TView part and leaving the rest of TWindow alone. To do this, we want to use TView's assignment operator. The functional notation here is the only way to do it. The pleasant surprise was that this notation is allowed.

Type Coercion

Use type coercion selectively. Like so many C++ features, type coercion can either clarify or obfuscate your code. If a type coercion seems "natural," like the coercion between reals and integers, then providing a coercion function seems like a good idea. If the coercion is unusual or nonsensical, then the existence of a coercion function can make it very hard to figure out what's going on. In the latter case, you should define a conversion function that must be called explicitly.

In general, coercion operators are useful in a way similar to operator overloading, and the same guidelines make sense.

Define type coercion rules for C++ to use. C++ will automatically coerce one type to another, but only if there is a direct way of doing so. In other words, if a coercion is defined from type A to type B, C++ will use it automatically where appropriate. It will *not* concatenate coercion operators if there is not a direct coercion. So even though a coercion may be defined from type A to type B, and type B to type C, C++ will not automatically coerce type A to type C (you can do it explicitly via casts, though).

There are two ways of defining type coercions for C++ to use: constructors and type coercion operators. They are appropriate under different circumstances. Note that since all coercion operators must be member functions of some class, it is not possible to define a coercion from one nonclass type to another nonclass type. Also note that if more than one function is defined to perform the same coercion, they cannot be used implicitly or via a cast, since an ambiguity exists as to which to call. They can still be invoked explicitly.

If you have a constructor with a prototype that looks like any of the following:

```
TargetClass::TargetClass(SourceType)
TargetClass::TargetClass(SourceType &)
TargetClass::TargetClass(const SourceType &)
```

then C++ will use it to convert from SourceType to TargetClass where appropriate. This form is useful when (1) the target type is a class (it can't be used for a primitive target type), and (2) the author of the target type wants to provide a coercion. If either of these conditions don't hold, you can use the second form of type coercion.

If the source type is a class, you can define a member operator function to perform the coercion. These operators have prototypes that look like

```
SourceClass::operator TargetType()
```

TargetType may be either a primitive type or a class. It need not be the name of a type; it can be any type specifier (as long as it does not contain array of [] or function () forms. Those must be handled via a typedef). This form is appropriate when the target type is not a class, or the source code for the target type is not available (that is, the coercion is being provided by someone else).

Encapsulation and Data-Hiding

Make explicit use of public, private, protected. C++ thoughtfully allows you to leave out the private keyword in several places. Don't: it decreases C++'s well-known clarity. Class definitions should always explicitly state the visibility of their members and/or base classes. Write it like this:

```
class TFoo: public TBar, private MBaz {
public:
  public members;

protected:
  protected members;

private:
  private members;
};
```

Your public interface should come before your protected interface, and since your private interface is only necessary to make the compiler happy, it should be last.

Use no public or protected members that aren't functions. Always make all member variables private. (It's OK to make functions protected or public. In fact, classes that don't are very boring.) You can provide access functions to get and set your variables if you want (although you should think about exporting a more abstract interface instead). If you're really concerned with performance, you can make those functions inline (but see "Inline Functions," earlier). Remember, don't compromise for the sake of performance *until you have numbers* to base your decision on!

Understand what "protected" really means. What the "protected" access mode means is not completely clear from Bjarne's various books and papers, so we will attempt to clarify the issue.

When a member of a class is declared protected, to clients of the class it is as if the member were private. Subclasses, however, can access the member as if it were declared private to them. This means that a subclass can access the member, but only as one of its own private fields. Specifically, it *cannot* access a protected field of its parent class via a pointer to the parent class, only via a pointer to itself (or a descendant). Here are some examples:

```
class A {
protected:
```

```
    void Bar();
};

class B: public A {
  void Foo();
};

class C: public B {
...
};

void B::Foo()
{
  A *pa;
  B *pb;
  C *pc;

  pa->Bar();     // Illegal: A::Bar() is "private"
  Bar();         // OK: "this" is of type B*
  pb->Bar();     // Also OK
  pc->Bar();     // Also OK
};
```

Protect constructors for abstract base classes. It's frequently useful to have a class that is not meant to be instantiated as an actual object, but only to be used as a base class for other classes. Examples include classes such as TApplication or TView. Such classes are called *abstract base classes*. If you want to enforce this status, you can make it impossible to instantiate such a class by making all of its constructors protected. In that case, the object cannot be created by itself, but only as part of a derived class.

In addition, there is a way to declare a member function abstract (that is, to require that it be overridden in descendants); this is called a *pure virtual function*. A class with such a member function cannot be instantiated, nor can any descendant class, unless all such functions are overridden. The syntax for this is as follows:

```
class Foo {
public:
  virtual void Bar() = 0;
};
```

You can also declare some (but not all) of the constructors for a class protected if you want those constructors to be used only by derived classes. The class can still be instantiated using the constructors that are public.

As a shortcut, declare private base classes. When you declare a base class private in C++, the derived class inherits all of its members as private members. This means that the derived class is *not* considered a subtype of the base class, even though it is a subclass. You cannot pass a pointer to an object of the derived class when a pointer to the base is expected. This lets you inherit the behavior of a class without inheriting its type signature.

Since the derived class is not a subtype, it doesn't have an "is-a" relationship with the base class. Why not just make it a member, then? This is what you would normally do. However, if you need to reexport most of the functionality of the base class, you would have to write wrapper functions in your derived class that turned around and called the member class functions. Instead, you can use this slimy shortcut.

By making the class a private base class, you don't inherit the type signature, but you do inherit the functionality, which can be made selectively visible without having to write wrapper functions. If A is a private base class of B, and B wants to make A::Foo() visible, then write the following in the declaration of B:

```
...
public:
  void A::Foo();
```

which makes Foo() visible to clients of B.

Use friends sparingly. Friend classes and functions are another C++ feature. Needless to say, they are a breach in the safety of types and in the integrity of the data abstraction provided by classes. If you have friends, you're probably doing something wrong (like taking frequent showers).

About the only time this feature should be used is when implementing binary operators that can't be member functions. Another circumstance is a set of tightly related classes (an example from

Bjarne's book is matrices and vectors). Generally, however, avoid friend classes and functions.

Hide implementation classes by declaring them incomplete. Sometimes a public class (one that you export to clients) must refer to a class that is only used in your implementation. How do you avoid exposing the implementation class? If the only reference is a pointer, then you can declare the implementation class as an incomplete class:

```
class TImplementation;

class TInterface {
...
private:
  TImplementation *fHidden;
};
```

This also works if your member functions have arguments of type TImplementation * or TImplementation &. If you have actual TImplementation objects as fields, though, you must include the full declaration of TImplementation.

Don't expose yourself. The most important thing to remember is not to expose your implementation to either your clients or your subclasses (which are really just another kind of client). If you do so, you are tying the hands of those who must enhance your code.

It is very important to make sure that your class acts like a black box. The interface you export to clients and subclasses should reflect precisely what they need to know and nothing more. You should ask yourself, for every member function you export (remember, you're not exporting any data members, right?), "Does my client (or subclass) really need to know this, or could I recast the interface to reveal less?"

If you find that the interface to your class consists mostly of functions to get and set your private data members, you should ask yourself whether your object is really defining an abstract enough interface. The key is to think about the abstraction that your object represents and how clients view and use that abstraction, not how it is implemented. This is possibly the hardest thing to do in object-based design, but is also one of the biggest advantages and has the biggest long-term payoff.

See Alan Snyder's paper. For an excellent discussion of the issues involved in data abstraction, encapsulation, and typing, see Alan Snyder's paper "Encapsulation and Inheritance in Object-Based Programming Languages" in the 1986 OOPSLA proceedings.

Virtual Functions

(Almost) all member functions should be virtual. Virtual functions are pretty inexpensive. Because of this, any class that is intended to be used in a polymorphic fashion (that is, a pointer to a subclass may be passed where a pointer to the class is expected) should have all of its functions virtual. It's hard to guess in advance which functions may be overridden in the future (although private functions can't be, and so need not be virtual).

You should only use nonvirtual functions where you are very sure that the class (or this particular aspect of it) *will never have a subclass*. An example is a fixed-point data type, which is self-contained, or a graphics point, or other similar classes.

The assignment operator is also a special case. Assignment isn't inherited like other operators. If you do not define an assignment operator, one is automatically defined for you; it consists of calls to the assignment operators of all of your base classes and members (this is discussed in the 1985-1989 paper mentioned in the sidebar "Background Reading"). It's OK to make your assignment operator virtual, but it's only useful under rather specialized circumstances. A virtual function call will be generated for a virtual assignment operator only when the left-hand side of an assignment is a reference or a dereferenced pointer.

(Almost) all destructors should be virtual. What the !@&#%! is a virtual destructor, you ask? And well you might, because this is actually something you should never have had to worry about. What do you think happens here?

```
class A {
  ~A();
};

class B: A {
  ~B();
};

A *foo = new B;
delete foo;
```

B::~B gets called, then A::~A, right? Wrong! Only A::~A gets called! Isn't that special? For the right thing to happen, you must declare your destructors virtual. For example,

```
virtual ~A();
virtual ~B();
```

If you do this, the right destructors will get called. Needless to say, *any* class that has a virtual member function, inherits one, or is used in a polymorphic fashion *must* have its destructor declared virtual, or horrible things will happen.

Be careful when you call virtual functions in constructors and destructors. If you call a virtual function from a constructor, be aware that the version of the function that corresponds to the constructor will be called, not the version that would normally be called. For example, if A has a method foo, B is a subclass of A, and B overrides foo, a call to foo from A's constructor calls A::foo, not B::foo. A call to foo from B's constructor does call B::foo. This is sufficiently confusing that it is best not to call a virtual function from a constructor at all. Naturally, this only applies to virtual functions of the object whose constructor is running; virtual functions of other objects (including those of the same class) are perfectly fine (unless they in turn call one of your virtual functions).

If you think about it, it doesn't make sense to call virtual functions from constructors and destructors. Since base class constructors are called before derived class constructors, and base class destructors are called after derived class destructors, the object is in a partially valid state. If a virtual function overridden in a derived class is called from the base class constructor, it may access derived class features that have not been initialized. Similarly, if it is called from the destructor, it may access features that have already been destroyed.

Use virtual functions the right way. If you are coming from the non-object-based programming world, a word about use of virtual functions might be in order. Virtual functions should be used whenever you want to have more than one implementation of the same abstract class. They allow the system to defer the decision on which function to execute until run time.

The right way to use virtual functions is to structure them around well-defined abstractions. If someone is to override a virtual function, they must have a clear definition of what the function does, even if they only call the inherited version after a little bit of processing.

The *wrong* way to use virtual functions is via a "come-from" mechanism like some Macintosh trap patches. Don't override a virtual function because "I know it's called from over here with these parameters." Needless to say, this wreaks havoc with the data abstractions that are one of the major benefits of object-based programming. This is why the function must have a definition that is clear in terms of the object it belongs to, without any reference to its possible callers. If you override a function, the override must make sense in terms of the definition of the function itself.

Multiple Inheritance

Multiple inheritance is a fairly new feature in object-based languages. To understand it better, look at Figure 1. In the single inheritance class hierarchy on the left, each class has only one parent. By contrast, in the multiple inheritance class hierarchy on the right, a class can have more than one parent. Note, for instance, that TAirplane inherits from both MFlyingObject and MVehicle.

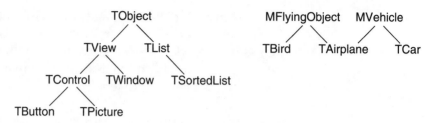

FIGURE 1
Single inheritance vs. multiple inheritance.

Use in a controlled fashion. With multiple inheritance, there is great potential for designing a confusing class hierarchy that resembles a spaghetti bowl. Here are some guidelines for use of multiple inheritance.

We start by artificially partitioning classes into two categories: base classes and mix-in classes. To distinguish the two, base class names begin with T (for example, TView), and mix-in class names begin with M (for example, MEditable). Base classes represent fundamental functional objects (like a car); mix-ins represent optional functionality (like power steering).

The first guideline is: A class can inherit from *zero or one* base classes, plus *zero or more* mix-in classes. If a class does not inherit from a base class, it probably should be a mix-in class (though not always, especially if it is at the root of a hierarchy).

The second guideline is: A class that inherits from a base class is itself a base class; it cannot be a mix-in class. Mix-in classes can only inherit from other mix-in classes.

The net effect of these two rules is that the base classes form a conventional, tree-structured inheritance hierarchy rather than an arbitrary acyclic graph. This makes the base class hierarchy much easier to understand. Mix-ins then become add-in "options" that do not fundamentally alter the inheritance hierarchy.

Like all guidelines, this one is not meant to be hard and fast. Multiple inheritance can and should be used in other ways as well if it makes sense. The fundamental thing to keep in mind is that people (including programmers) are better at understanding regular structures than arbitrary acyclic graphs.

As part of multiple inheritance, C++ contains a new feature called virtual base classes. The trouble is, if both B and C are subclasses of A, and D has both B and C as base classes, then D will have two A's if A is not virtual, but only one A if it is. This is a very confusing situation, and no matter which alternative you choose, programmers will have a hard time understanding it. To avoid getting into a situation like this, follow the preceding guidelines for use of multiple inheritance. And incidentally, using virtual bases presents another problem: once you have a pointer to a virtual base, there's no way to convert it back into a pointer to its enclosing class.

It's OK to have multiple occurrences of a base. Sometimes the same base class (it should be a mix-in) will occur more than once as an ancestor of a class. It doesn't hurt to have a base class twice (aside from wasting space because of multiple pointers to the virtual function table) and if you need to cast back from the base class pointer to something else you may not have a choice, but it's really only useful to have a base class twice if data members are associated with it.

Part 3: Design Issues

In this part you'll find a discussion of general problems of programming in C++.

Working in a Value-Based Language

C++ has a different object model from Object Pascal or Smalltalk. The most fundamental difference is that whereas Object Pascal and Smalltalk are reference based (that is, like Lisp, assignment means copying a pointer), C++ is value based. By this we mean that classes in C++ are treated just like primitive types, whereas in Object Pascal objects are treated very differently from primitive types. This is actually a benefit, since all types in a C++ program are handled in the same style, as opposed to the multiple styles in Object Pascal. (Smalltalk, like C++, is also self-consistent.) There are some implications for your C++ programming style, however.

Don't use pointers unless you mean it. Pointers should be used in C++ in the same way you would use them in plain C or plain Pascal; that is, when you really want multiple references to the same object, or a dynamic data structure. If you really just want to pass something by reference to avoid copying, then you can use a reference rather than a pointer (see below). In fact, you can even pass a class by value if the copying overhead isn't too high and you don't care about polymorphism (for example, the class has no virtual functions).

Don't allocate storage unless you must. In a reference-based language like Object Pascal or Smalltalk, all objects must be heap allocated. In C++, it's better to treat values the same way you would in C. For example, instead of defining a Clone operator, overload the assignment operator; instead of allocating and returning an object, have the caller pass one in by reference and set it. This allows your classes to be treated just like primitive types, and in the same style. In general, leave storage allocation up to the class client.

By doing so, you can make use of one of C++'s unique features: the ability to have automatic and static objects, and objects as members of classes. No matter how clever or efficient a storage allocator we have, it can never be as fast as allocating an object on the stack, or as part of another object. If an object can be local to a function, there is no storage allocation overhead. Many objects have very localized scope and do not need to be allocated on the heap.

There is one exception to the rule about allocating an object and returning a pointer: you must do this when the type of the returned object may vary. Anytime a function must choose what type of object to return, the function must allocate the object, not the caller.

It's still all right for the caller to allocate storage even when the type of object being passed in may vary, since references, like pointers, can be used polymorphically (that is, you can specify a TSubFoo& to an argument of type TFoo&). The key question is whether the caller or the function must determine the type. In the former case, leave allocation to the client; in the latter, the function must allocate the object on the heap and return it.

Summary: pretend everything is a primitive. In summary, you should design your classes so that using them is just like using a primitive type in C. This will let the client use them in a style that is "natural" for C. In cases where you wish to avoid copying, pass arguments by reference. Use pointers only when you want a truly dynamic data structure, or when polymorphism demands it (note that references allow for polymorphism also, since they are really just a different kind of pointer).

Background Reading

Bring yourself up to date. You've just finished reading Bjarne Stroustrup's book *The C++ Programming Language* (Prentice-Hall, 1987) and you're feeling pretty smug. You've finally got C++ nailed.

Wrong.

You still have one more reference to read: the paper "The Evolution of C++: 1985 to 1989." This paper is included with the AT&T C++ *Selected Readings* manual, which is available in conjunction with MPW C++.

At least one statement made in earlier versions of the paper (which were titled "The Evolution of C++: 1985 to 1987") is wrong. The order of execution of base class and member constructors and destructors is determined by their declaration order, not by the order in which calls are made to such constructors in your constructor's header. This is a change to the language that was made after the 1985-1987 paper was written; see the 1985-1989 version for a full discussion.

Other books that give a good discussion of features that are new in C++ 2.0 are *The C++ Primer* by Lippman (Addison-Wesley, 1989) and *The C++ Answer Book* by Hansen (Addison-Wesley, 1990). The latter book not only discusses 2.0 but also gives solutions to all of the problems in Stroustrup's book.

Finally, look for Bjarne's own updated manual, *The Annotated C++ Reference Manual* (with Ellis, Addison-Wesley) to be published later this year.

Read up on ANSI C. If you were whelped on good ole Kernighan and Ritchie C, you may have a few surprises in store for you. There have been several changes to the language as part of the ANSI standardization process. If you learned C a while back, it might be a good idea to brush up on ANSI C. We highly recommend the second edition of Kernighan and Ritchie (*The C Programming Language*, Prentice-Hall, 1989), which has appendixes that detail the differences between the original language and the ANSI version. Another good book is *C: A Reference Manual*, 2nd ed., by Harbison and Steele (Prentice-Hall, 1987). For purists, the ANSI C draft and rationale are available from ANSI itself (Draft Proposed American National Standard for Information Systems—Programming Language C, 1988, ANSI Doc No X3J11/88-159).

Study object-based design. Doing a good job of object-based software design requires more than just learning an object-based language. The whole point of object-based languages is to permit a different approach to software design. This approach takes time and energy to learn. Without spending that time and energy, it's not possible to gain the full benefits of the approach.

That's why you should read *Abstraction and Specification in Program Development* by Liskov (McGraw-Hill, 1987) and *Object-Oriented Software Construction* by Meyer (Prentice-Hall, 1988). The first book does not discuss object-based design per se, but it does cover the topic of data abstraction, an important component of object-based design, very well. The second book is a little pedantic in places, but has many, many good suggestions and ideas in it. Reading both is hard work (especially since both are based on obscure languages), but will help you a great deal.

One example of an issue that *Object-Oriented Software Construction* covers quite well is the question of whether to use a class as a base (inherit from it) or a member (include it as a field). As Bertrand Meyer notes, the distinction is whether the new class can act as an instance of its base class (that is, it "is-a" object of that type) or uses an instance of the class (it "has-a" object of that type). For example, an automobile "is-a" vehicle, but it "has-a" engine. For good discussions of this and other issues, read the book (this particular discussion starts on page 333).

Brian Wilkerson's "How to Design an Object-Based Application," in this issue of *develop*, is a good language-independent introduction to object-based design. You should find the design techniques presented in his article useful in your own work.

Taking the time to learn how to design with objects may be painful (after all, we're all working as hard as we can already), but it can make a big difference in the quality of the system when it's done. Every extra minute you take to improve the design now will pay off in easier maintenance and enhancements later.

Pointers Versus References

C++ provides two very similar mechanisms for passing references to entities. One is the familiar pointer from classic C; the other is a new concept, the reference. Pointers are declared as follows:

```
TFoo *fooPtr;
```

But references are declared like this:

```
TFoo &fooRef;
```

A pointer must be dereferenced to access what it points to, but a reference can be used as is, and acts as a synonym for the object it refers to, both for fetching and storing. This makes it similar to other highly refined mechanisms, such as FORTRAN's equivalence statement (or VAR parameters in Pascal). The entity to which a reference refers may only be set when the reference is created; in this respect it is somewhat like a const pointer that gets a virtual * put in front of it wherever it is used, and puts a virtual & in front of the expression from which it is initialized. Here are two illustrative examples:

```
void Bump(int *ip)
{
   *ip += 1;
}
Bump(&j);
```

```
void BumpR(int &i)
{
  i += 1;
}
BumpR(j);
```

There are certain circumstances where references are mandatory, for example, overloading the assignment operator. In other cases, either a pointer or a reference can be used. The question is, which should be used when?

References should be used when a parameter is to be passed "by reference," as in Pascal. This means that the called function is going to forget about the argument as soon as it returns. A regular reference should be used if you are going to modify the argument (TFoo &), and a const reference should be used if you are not going to modify it but don't want the overhead of call by value (const TFoo &).

Pointers should be used when the function you are calling is going to retain a reference (an alias) to the object you are passing in, such as when you are constructing a dynamic data structure. An example is putting an object into a MacApp TList: the TList retains a pointer to your copy of the object. The explicit use of pointers lets the reader know that aliasing is occurring.

By using pointers and references appropriately, you can increase the readability of your code by giving the reader hints as to what is going on.

Portability

Don't make assumptions. The Macintosh is the best personal computer in the world, but there are times when you'll want to run your code on a different machine. For example, you might have access to a CRAY or a VAX. Don't make assumptions that are only valid for the 680x0 family of processors. For example:

- Don't assume that int and long are the same size.
- Don't assume that longs, floats, doubles, or long doubles can be at any even address.
- Don't assume you know the memory layout of a data type.

- Especially don't assume you know how structs or classes are laid out in memory, or that they can be written to a data file as is.

- Don't assume pointers and integers are interchangeable. Use void * if you want an untyped pointer, not char *.

- Don't assume you know how the calling conventions are implemented, or indeed any detail of the language implementation or run time.

ANSI specifies the following about C's built-in types. This is all you can safely assume:

- unsigned chars can hold at least 0 to 255. They may hold more.

- signed chars can hold –127 to +127. They may hold more.

- chars may be either unsigned chars or signed chars. You can't assume either. Therefore, don't use char unless you don't care about sign extension.

- shorts can hold at least –32,767 to 32,767 (signed) or 0 to 65,535 (unsigned).

- longs can hold at least –2,147,483,647 to 2,147,483,647 (signed) or 0 to 4,294,967,295 (unsigned).

- ints can hold at least –32,767 to 32,767 (signed) or 0 to 65,535 (unsigned). In other words, *ints cannot be counted on to hold any more than a short*. int is an appropriate type to use if a short would be big enough but you would like to use the processor's "natural" word size to improve efficiency (on some machines, a 32-bit operation is more efficient than a 16-bit operation because there is no need to do masking). *If you need something larger than a short can hold, you must specify long.*

If you need exact information, you can use the symbols defined in limits.h. or float.h. Remember, though, that the values of these symbols can change from processor to processor or compiler to compiler, within the limits just defined (for more information, see the ANSI C specification).

It's very easy to write nonportable code, and it takes some vigilance to avoid it. It's well worth the effort, however, the first time you port to a different processor, or try to use a different compiler.

Pick a canonical format for messages and data files. Remember that AppleTalk networks connect to non-Apple computers such as the Intel-8x86 based MS-DOS machines. Thus, if you write or read any data in a context where it might go to or come from a different CPU, you have to worry about formats. Such situations include reading or writing disk files, or sending data over a network (or even over NuBus). The other CPU might even have a different byte order! The only solution to this problem is to pick a canonical format for your messages or data files.

Just because you have a canonical format doesn't mean you must pay a big overhead every time you access your data. An alternative is to perform the translation to or from canonical format at a predetermined time. For example, outline fonts might have a certain canonical format, which may not be convenient for a particular processor to deal with. However, they can certainly be converted to a convenient local format when the font is installed.

Don't use (gasp!) naked C types. Another way to make your life miserable is to use primitive C data types in your declarations. This is a bad idea, since if the implementation ever changes you have to do a lot of editing by hand. It's much better to declare a type (via class definition or typedef) that represents the abstract concept you want to represent, then phrase your declarations that way. This lets you change your implementation by simply editing the original type definition. Think of these types as giving your data physical units, like kilograms or meters/second. This prevents you from accidentally assigning a length to a variable with type Kilogram, catching more errors at compile time.

So instead of

```
long time;
short mouseX;
char *menuName;
```

use (for example)

```
typedef long TimeStamp;
typedef short Coordinate;
class TString { ... };
```

```
    .
    .
    .
TimeStamp time;
Coordinate mouseX;
TString menuName;
```

It's OK to use a raw C type under certain circumstances, such as when the quantity is machine dependent, or when it can be characterized as (for example) a small integer. Otherwise, though, it's best to give yourself flexibility down the road.

Two ANSI C header files, StdDef.h and Limits.h, contain useful definitions. Here are two of the more useful ones:

```
size_t
```

The type returned by the built-in C sizeof function. This is useful for representing the sizes of things.

```
ptrdiff_t
```

A type that can represent the difference between any two pointers.

The astute reader has noticed that these names do not conform to our guidelines. In the interest of clarity, however, we deem it better to use the names as defined by the ANSI C committee.

Another item worthy of note: if a data type is unsigned, declare it unsigned; this helps avoid nasty bugs down the road.

Error Reporting

Returned error codes are (ironically) a very error-prone technique. MacApp's standard is to use exceptions: a structured technique for reporting exceptions back to a function's callers.

Unfortunately, the exception scheme does not handle an important case: an exception that occurs in a constructor. Handling this properly requires compiler support, since any base class and/ or member constructors that have already been called must have their corresponding destructors called; only the compiler can know this. Until we get an official C++ exception scheme, you must handle this problem on a case-by-case basis.

Signaling an exception in a destructor is not a good idea, since any destructive behavior that has already taken place probably cannot be reversed. Don't do it.

Conclusion   We've covered a lot of ground in this article. Don't feel bad if you didn't understand every point we tried to make. It took us years of working with objects before we figured out what virtual base classes were good for! As you use C++ in your own work, think about the rules we've laid down and see if they aren't applicable to your own situation. Come back and read these guidelines every so often, just to refresh your memory. And finally, don't be shy about formulating some guidelines of your own!

David Goldsmith has been at Apple for four years, and now focuses his energies on future system software. He has also worked on MacApp and the Macintosh Toolbox (during the inception of System 6.0). He received an MA in physics from Harvard in 1980, and since has worked for Wang, Mosaic Technologies, and as a contractor for Lotus. For him, the thrill of the job is "making computers available to people whose lives don't revolve around computers." His main interest outside the office is his family, with its new member, eight-month-old Jane. He also enjoys reading and listening to classical music.

"Hackerjack" Palevich is our local meerkat handler (look that one up in *National Geographic*!). He has a degree in computer science from MIT, where his "Thesis of Terror" was a prelude to his video game days at Atari. Two years at Apple have landed him in video conferencing and screen sharing. As the son of an American diplomat, he's lived in some pretty interesting places (Berlin, Poland, Laos, Greece, Maryland, and Cupertino). He didn't buy an Apple II in the eleventh grade, and has regretted it since. His interests include filmmaking, animation, and aerobics. He claims to be halfway a nerd, but only his wife knows for sure. He also likes to tell stories, so we're not sure that any of this is really true.

The Complete Symantec C++ Development Environment

NOW THAT YOU'VE WORKED WITH A SCALED-DOWN version of Symantec C++, you'll want to upgrade to the full version. The complete Symantec C++ development environment lets you take advantage of the powerful features and capabilities that have made Symantec's THINK Languages the leading development tools for the Macintosh. This chapter will describe some of those features, including:

- The Project
- The Editor
- Libraries
- Fast turnaround

- Source-level debugging
- Inline assembler
- Object-oriented programming
- The THINK Class Library
- Scripting and Apple Event support

You're familiar with some features of the Symantec C++ environment from working with the special version of the product included with this book. In the full version of the product, however, you can take advantage of many additional features, such as an enhanced project window, full source-level debugging capabilities, and an inline assembler. The THINK Class Library provides object-oriented building blocks for writing Macintosh applications. Other powerful new features include an optimizer for even tighter code, a class browser for object-oriented programming, full ANSI compatibility, and Apple Event support for customization. In addition, with the complete version of Symantec C++, you can build your own double-clickable applications.

Special Upgrade Offer

Symantec will upgrade owners of *Learn C++ on the Macintosh* to the complete Symantec C++ development environment for a special price. See the back page for further details and an upgrade coupon.

Overview of the Symantec C++ Environment

Symantec C++ is a unique development environment for the Macintosh. It features very fast C and C++ compilers, a resource compiler, a faster linker, an integrated text editor, an auto-make facility, and a project manager that holds all the pieces together. Because the editor, the compilers, and the linker are all components of the same application, the THINK Project Manager knows when edited source files need to be recompiled.

Symantec C++ is a complete, integrated environment, not just a C++ compiler for the Macintosh. Traditional development environments consist of three separate applications: the editor, the compiler, and the linker. It is up to you to create your source files with a text editor, run each file through the compiler, and finally, link all your object files. In Symantec C++, the project manager oversees the operation of the compilers, the linker, and the editor. They all work in concert as part of the same application. This way, the project manager knows when you've edited a file. The appropriate compiler produces object code that the linker can put together in an instant. Then the project manager can launch your program. And because Symantec C++ is still running, it can launch the source level debugger, so you can debug your program.

You can run your program from Symantec C++ as you work on it. Your program runs exactly as if you had launched it from the Finder, not under a simulated environment. If you use MultiFinder or System 7, your program runs in its own partition while Symantec C++ remains active, so you can examine and edit your source files as you watch your program run.

With Symantec C++ you can build Macintosh applications, desk accessories, device drivers, and any kind of code resource. The standard C libraries include all the functions specified in the ANSI C standard, as well as some additional UNIX operating system functions. The C++ libraries include IOStreams, a flexible expandable class library for doing input and output, and complex, a library that enables you to do mathematic operations with complex numbers.

Writing a program in Symantec C++ is like writing a program in any other development environment. You create your source files, compile them, then link the object code to create an executable file. The difference is that in Symantec C++, you use the same application to do all of this.

The Project

The project is at the heart of the Symantec C++ development environment. It takes over the functions of several other files in traditional development environments. The project holds the object code of all your compiled source files and maintains the dependencies and connections among them. It keeps track of files that need to be recompiled or that depend on an edited #include file. The project also lets you assign different compilers to different files. This means that you can have C, C++, and even resource files in the same project. If you're using the source level debugger, the project keeps track of the information that the debugger needs.

Figure H.1 shows a sample project window. It contains a list of all the files that comprise your program. To the right of each file name is the size of that file's object code. To the left of each file name is the "bug" column that Symantec C++ adds to the project window when you choose the Use Debugger command. Symantec C++ generates debugging information for files that have gray diamonds next to them.

FIGURE H.1

bullseye++ ᴨ	
❋ Name	**Code**
▽ **Segment 2**	**9640**
◆ bullMenus.cp	632
◆ bullseye.cp	456
◆ bullWindow.cp	178
CPlusLib	1690
MacTraps	6680
▽ **Segment 3**	**28192**
ANSI++	28188
Totals	**38410**

Rather than producing a separate binary object code file, Symantec C++ keeps all object code in the project document in ready-to-link form. Because the project document knows all the files that make up your program (including header files), it can keep track of changes. When you edit a source file, the project manager marks it for recompilation. When you edit an #include file, the project manager marks all the files that use it.

The Editor   Once you've created a project document, the next step is to add your source files. Symantec C++ source files are standard text files, so you'll be able to use existing source files. The Symantec C++ editor uses standard Macintosh editing techniques, so you're familiar with its basic operation. It also provides some features that help you edit source code. Its search facilities include a pattern-matching option based on Grep, and a multi-file search that looks for strings in any file in your project.

Figure H.2 shows a sample search dialog from Symantec C++.

FIGURE H.2

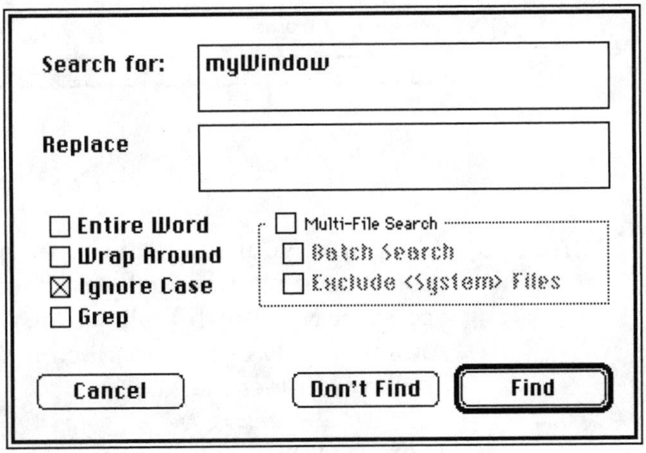

```
┌─────────────────────────────────────────────────┐
│                                                   │
│   Search for:   ┌─────────────────────────────┐  │
│                 │ myWindow                    │  │
│                 └─────────────────────────────┘  │
│                                                   │
│   Replace       ┌─────────────────────────────┐  │
│                 │                             │  │
│                 └─────────────────────────────┘  │
│                                                   │
│   ☐ Entire Word     ┌ ☐ Multi-File Search ·····┐ │
│   ☐ Wrap Around     │ ☐ Batch Search          │ │
│   ☒ Ignore Case     │ ☐ Exclude <System> Files│ │
│   ☐ Grep            └·························┘ │
│                                                   │
│   ┌──────────┐      ┌──────────┐ ┌╔══════════╗┐ │
│   │ Cancel   │      │Don't Find│ │║  Find   ║│ │
│   └──────────┘      └──────────┘ └╚══════════╝┘ │
│                                                   │
└─────────────────────────────────────────────────┘
```

You can open as many files as the memory in your Macintosh will allow, and each file appears in its own edit window. Although you usually create and open source or header files, you can also use the Symantec C++ editor to open any text file.

Holding down the Option key as you click in the title bar of the project window brings up a pop-up menu containing the names of all the #include files used in the project. (See Figure H.3.)

FIGURE H.3

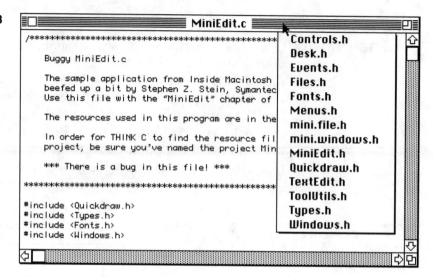

```
/***************************************    Controls.h
                                           Desk.h
    Buggy MiniEdit.c                       Events.h
    The sample application from Inside Macintosh    Files.h
    beefed up a bit by Stephen Z. Stein, Symantec   Fonts.h
    Use this file with the "MiniEdit" chapter of    Menus.h
    The resources used in this program are in the    mini.file.h
    In order for THINK C to find the resource fil   mini.windows.h
    project, be sure you've named the project Min   MiniEdit.h
    *** There is a bug in this file! ***           Quickdraw.h
                                                    TextEdit.h
 ***************************************             ToolUtils.h
                                                    Types.h
#include <Quickdraw.h>                               Windows.h
#include <Types.h>
#include <Fonts.h>
#include <Windows.h>
```

Libraries

Along with your source files, you must add your libraries to the project document. Virtually every program you write will need to access the Macintosh Toolbox. You can call any Macintosh Toolbox routine exactly as it's described in *Inside Macintosh*. The code for Toolbox routines marked:

```
[Not In ROM]
```

as well as the glue code needed to call some of the other Toolbox routines is in the MacTraps and MacTraps2 libraries.

Your Symantec C++ package also includes several other libraries you can use in your programs. The ANSI library contains the standard ANSI functions defined in the ANSI standard. The UNIX library contains UNIX system functions, including memory calls. The IOStreams library contains flexible expandable C++ classes for doing input and output. The complex library contains C++ classes for manipulating complex numbers. You can use these libraries when you port code from other systems. You can also create your own libraries in Symantec C++.

Fast Turnaround

Symantec C++ lets you run your program directly from the environment. With the single command Run, the project manager automatically recompiles the source files that are new or have changed, and loads any unloaded libraries. Then the Symantec C++ linker links all your code together instantly. In this one step you accomplish in seconds what used to take several minutes or longer.

The project manager launches your program as if you had double-clicked on it from the Finder. This way, you know exactly how your program will behave in actual conditions. If you're running under MultiFinder or System 7, the project manager launches your program in its own partition. Since Symantec C++ is still running, you can look at your source files while your program is running.

Source-level Debugging

To help get your program working correctly, you can use Symantec C++'s source level debugger. The Symantec C++ debugger lets you debug your code the way you wrote it: in C or C++. You can set breakpoints, step through your code, debug objects, examine variables, and change their values while your program is running. You can set conditional breakpoints that stop execution only when certain conditions are true. You can debug inline functions and templates. And because the debugger runs under MultiFinder, you can edit your source files while you're debugging.

The debugger windows show you the source of your program and the values of your variables. The Source window (see Figure H.4) contains the source text of your program, the debugger's status panel, statement markers, the current statement arrow, and the current function indicator. The title of the Source window is the name of the source file.

The Source window shows the source text of your program. When you start the debugger, this window shows the file that contains the main() routine of your application. The top of the Source window has a six-button status panel. These buttons control the execution of your program. The column of diamonds running along the left side of the source text are **statement markers**. Every line of your program that generates code gets a statement

FIGURE H.4

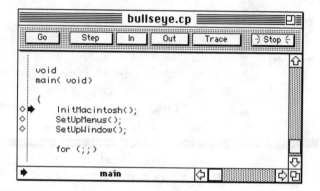

marker. You can set breakpoints at these statement markers. When your program is running, the debugger stops execution just before a breakpoint. You can set three kinds of breakpoints: simple breakpoints, conditional breakpoints, and temporary breakpoints.

The black arrow to the right of the statement markers is the **current statement arrow**. This indicator shows you the **current statement**, the one the debugger is about to execute. When you start your program, the current statement arrow is at the first executable line of your program.

The source debugger uses the space at the lower left of the Source window for the name of the **current function**. When you click here and hold the mouse button down, the debugger displays a pop-up menu that shows the call chain—the names of the functions that were called to get to the current function.

The other debugger window is the Data window. (See Figure H.5.) In this window you can examine and set the values of your

FIGURE H.5

variables. The Data window is modeled after a spreadsheet. You can type variable names into the entry field (left column), then press the Return or Enter key. When your program is running, the variable value will appear in the right column.

Inline Assembler

Symantec C++ lets you use assembly language in your C and C++ programs. You can use the built-in inline assembler for assembly language in your source files, or you can use object files generated by other assemblers. Symantec C++ works within the compilers to produce object code. You can use instructions for the Motorola MC68000 and MC68020/030/040 processors and for the MC68881 floating-point coprocessor. You can refer to variables and functions within assembly language routines. Your C and C++ routines can go to labels in the assembly routines and vice versa.

Object-Oriented Programming (OOP)

Symantec C++ provides a selection of tools for object-oriented programming. The very fast C++ compiler lets you write object-oriented programs using the powerful C++ language. The C compiler includes object-oriented extensions that allow you to write object-oriented programs using extensions to standard C. The THINK Class library allow you to write object-oriented Macintosh programs very quickly by providing a set of classes that implement a standard Macintosh application. The THINK Class library is included in both C and C++ versions. The integrated class browser allows you to navigate your object-oriented programs quickly.

Object-oriented programming is a compelling choice for many programmers today and the built-in OOP capabilities of Symantec C++ make it accessible to you whether you're a novice or more advanced professional.

The THINK Class Library

Macintosh programming is not hard to learn, but it requires mastering some new concepts and many operating system routines. To make learning Macintosh programming easier, Symantec C++ comes with the THINK Class Library.

The THINK Class Library (TCL) is a collection of classes that implement a standard Macintosh application. The TCL takes care of things like handling menu commands, updating windows, dispatching events, dealing with MultiFinder, maintaining the Clipboard, and so on. The TCL takes care of the common Macintosh interface, so you can concentrate instead on your program's functionalism.

Scripting and Apple Event Support

The Symantec C++ project manager provides scripting support. This means that you can automate complex or repetitive tasks performed in Symantec C++ using scripts written or recorded using third-party products like Frontier (Userland) or AppleScript (Apple).

The project manager also links with Symantec's THINK Reference, an online hypertext guide to the Macintosh Toolbox. Extensive information on any Toolbox routine can be brought up with just a double-click.

Symantec C++'s interface to Apple's SourceServer source control system makes team programming and version control easy and reliable. The ToolServer interface allows you to use a rich set of MPW programmer utilities from the Symantec C++ environment.

The project manager's third-party editor support means that you can use your favorite programmer's editor instead of the one that comes with Symantec C++, without giving up the benefits of an integrated environment. The project manager and the third-party editor communicate through apple events, so the project manager can still keep track of which source files have been edited.

Why Upgrade?

As you can see, the full version of Symantec C++ offers a host of features not included in this special book-version of the product: the project document, libraries, full source-level debugging, inline assembler, object-oriented programming, the THINK Class Library, and more. As you develop your skills as a Macintosh programmer, you'll want the power and flexibility the Symantec C++ development environment offers. Plus, you can upgrade to the complete version for a special price. See the coupon at the back of the book for details.

Appendix I

Bibliography

1. "Unoffical C++ Style Guide," David Goldsmith and Jack Palevich, in *develop, The Apple Technical Journal*, Issue 2, April 1990, Apple Computer, Inc., Cupertino, CA.

2. *The C++ Programming Language*, 2nd ed., Bjarne Stroustrup, 1991, Addison-Wesley Publishing Company, Reading MA.

3. *C++ Primer*, 2nd ed., Stanley B. Lippman, 1991, Addison-Wesley Publishing Company, Reading MA.

4. *Advanced C++: Programming Styles and Idioms*, James Coplien, 1992, Addison-Wesley Publishing Company, Reading MA.

5. *Elements of C++ Macintosh Programming*, Dan Weston, 1990, Addison-Wesley Publishing Company, Reading MA.

6. *C++ Programming with MacApp*, David A. Wilson, Larry S. Rosenstein, and Dan Shafer, 1990, Addison-Wesley Publishing Company, Reading MA.

7. *Inside Macintosh*, Volumes I–V, Apple Computer, Inc., 1991, Addison-Wesley Publishing Company, Reading MA.

8. *Inside Macintosh*, Volume VI, Apple Computer, Inc., 1991, Addison-Wesley Publishing Company, Reading MA.

9. *New Inside Macintosh*, Apple Computer, Inc., 1992–1993, Addison-Wesley Publishing Company, Reading MA.

10. *Macintosh Human Interface Guidelines*, 1992, Addison-Wesley Publishing Company, Reading MA.

11. *Macintosh C Programming Primer*, Volume I, 2nd ed., Dave Mark and Cartwright Reed, 1992, Addison-Wesley Publishing Company, Reading MA.

12. *Macintosh C Programming Primer*, Volume II, Dave Mark, 1990, Addison-Wesley Publishing Company, Reading MA.

13. *Macintosh Pascal Programming Primer*, Volume I, Dave Mark and Cartwright Reed, 1991, Addison-Wesley Publishing Company, Reading MA.

14. *Learn C on the Macintosh*, Dave Mark, 1991, Addison-Wesley Publishing Company, Reading MA.

15. *The C Programming Language*, 2nd ed., Brian Kernighan and Dennis M. Ritchie, 1988, Prentice-Hall, Englewood Cliffs, NJ.

16. *Macintosh Programming Secrets*, 2nd ed., Scott Knaster, 1992 Addison-Wesley Publishing Company, Reading MA.

17. *How to Write Macintosh Software*, 3rd ed., Scott Knaster, 1992, Addison-Wesley Publishing Company, Reading MA.

Index

!, 40, 173
!=, 40, 173
#, 44
#define, 44
#include, 44, 65, 223
%, 37, 173
%=, 37, 173
&, 35, 37, 71, 173, 310
&&, 40, 173
&=, 37, 173
'\n', 241
( ), 173, 183, 186–190, 201
( )( ), 188
*, 35–37, 173, 211–212
*/, 45, 54
*=, 37, 170–173
+, 32, 35, 37, 170, 173–174
++, 35–36, 39, 173–174
+=, 37, 173
, (comma), 40, 173
^, 37, 173
~, 37–38, 109, 173
-, 35, 37, 173
--, 35, 39, 173–174
-=, 37, 173
->, 30, 35, 101, 173, 183, 194–198, 311
->*, 173
., 35, 100–101, 173
.*, 173
/, 37, 173
/*, 45, 54
//, 54
/=, 37, 173
:, 112

::, 85–88, 104, 173, 310
;, 42
<, 40, 173
<<, 37, 55–62, 173, 229–234
<<=, 37, 173
<=, 40, 173
<fstream.h>, 227
<stream.h>, 227
=, 36–37, 173, 183, 198–203
^=, 37, 173
==, 40, 173
>, 40, 173
>=, 40, 173
>>, 37, 55–56, 62, 173, 229–234, 308
>>=, 37, 173
?:, 39, 173
[ ], 173, 183, 190–193
\, 26, 37
\", 27
\', 27
\?, 27
\a, 27
\b, 27
\f, 27
\n, 27
\r, 27
\t, 27
\v, 27
\\, 27
|, 173
|=, 37
|=, 173
||, 40, 173
…, 43–44

A

Abstract base classes, 412
Abstract class, 158, 307
Access codes, 111–113, 307
Access functions, 113, 307
Address differences, 60, 71
Ambiguities, 270
   multiple-root example, 271–274
   nonVirtual source code, 272–274
   virtual base class, 274–280
   virtual source code, 277–280
AND, 38, 40
ANSI C, 421–422
   keywords, 42
   operators, 37–42
Apple Programmers and Developers Association
   (APDA), 300, 391
Apple Technical Journal, The, 391, 439
AppleLink, 303
Application framework, 299, 307
argc, 43
Argument names, 393
Arguments, 405–406
argv, 43
Arithmetic operators, 37
arrayPtr, 248
Array(s), 29–30
   automatic initialization, 30
   of parameters, 43
   pointers, 35–36
   range checking for, 190
   templates, 248, 255
Arrow operator, 194–198
Assignment operators, 37, 415
Assignment statement, 86, 190, 281–282
Assignment, initialization versus, 280
Assignment, memberwise, 199, 310
auto, 34, 42
Automatic initialization, 30
Automatic objects, 99, 307
Automatic type conversion, 32–33, 51

B

Backslash, 26, 27
Backspace, 27
badbit, 311
Base class, 307
   and constructors with parameters, 147–153
   inheritance, 134
   root, 260, 310
   virtual, 274–280
Bedrock, 301
Bell, 27
Binary operator, 37, 40
Bits, 220–221, 311
Bitwise logical operators, 37–38
Bounds checking, 255–256
break, 42
Buffered, 209
Built-in operators, 164, 173
Bundling, 96, 307

C

C code, running under C++, 50
   automatic type conversion, 51
   function prototypes, 50
   scope changes, 51–53
C programming, 21–24
   comments, 45
   functions, 43–44
   literal constants, 24–28
   operators, 37–42
   preprocessor directives, 44–45
   statements, 42
   summary, 45
   variables, 28–36
C Programming Language, The, 45, 421
C++ Primer, The, 305, 421, 439
C++ programming, 47–50
   comment marker //, 54
   default argument initializers, 64–68
   function name overloading, 75–79
   inline functions, 88–90

input and output, 55–63
new and delete operators, 79–85
new features, 54
reference variables, 68–75
scope operator, 85–88
summary, 91
C++ Programming with MacApp, 439
Call operator ( ), 186–190
Call-by-reference, 74
Carriage return, 241
case, 42
Case
    functions, 216–217
    global variables, 86
    scientific notation, 239
cerr, 55
    buffered version, 209
char, 24, 28–29, 42
Character constants, 26–27
Character-based interface, 208
cin, 55, 61–63, 209
class, 97, 250, 308
Class declaration, 97, 133
    See also Base class; Derived class
Class derivation, 133, 308
Class functions, 104
    constructor, 104–107
    destructor, 109–110
    parameters, 107–108
Class libraries, 299–301, 308
Classes, 97–98
clear( ), 221, 225
clog, 209
close( ), 226–228
Colon, 112
Comma operator, 40, 173
Command key, 14
Command-line arguments, 43
Comments, 45
    markers, 54
Conditional operator, 39, 173

const, 42, 398, 400–402
    qualifier, 34
    and reference types, 281–282
Constant names, 395
Constructor, 104, 141–147
    adding parameters to, 107
    with parameters, 147–153
Constructor function, 308
cont source code, 58–60
continue, 42
Control character, 216–217
Control Manager, 298
Coplien, James, 439
Copy constructor, 286, 308
Copyright notice, 392
cout, 55, 209
Curly braces, 42
Current function, 436
Current object, 101–102, 308
Current statement, 436
Current statement arrow, 436

D

Data member, 100–103, 308
    access codes, 111–113
Data-hiding, 410–415
Debugging, 435–437
dec( ), 241
Decimal constants, 24
Declaration, 53, 308, 404
    class, 97, 133
    function, 43
    static, 266
    template instantiation, 250
    union, 31
Decrement operator, 35, 39, 173–174
default, 42
Default argument initializers, 64–68, 308
Default arguments, 405–406
Definition, 53, 308
Delete operator, 79, 103, 173, 183, 186

Derivation chain, 142, 271, 308
Derived, 279
Derived class, 131, 308
   constructors and destructors, 141–147
   inheritance, 134–141
   overriding member functions, 154–158
   parameters, 147–153
   summary, 159
Destructor, 109–110, 141–147, 308
   virtual, 415–417
develop, 7, 304, 391, 439
Dimension, 29
do, 42
double, 26, 29, 42
Double quotes, 27–28

E

Edit menu, 297
Editor, 433–434
Ellipsis, 43–44
else, 42
Encapsulation, 410–415
End-of-file, 212, 241
ends( ), 241
enum, 28, 42, 398
Enumerations, 28
EOF. *See* End-of-file
eofbit, 311
Equals operator, 198–203
Errors, 427
EXCLUSIVE OR, 38
Explicit typecasting, 51
Exponent, 25
extern, 34, 42
Extract, 12–13
Extraction operator, 55, 173, 229–234, 308

F

failbit, 311
Fields, 30
File-opening modes, 218
fill( ), 241, 237
Find Text dialog box, 18

fixed, 240
flag( ), 236
float, 26–29, 42, 175
Floating-point constants, 25–26
flush, 240
Font, 17–18
for, 42
Formal parameter list, 249–251, 309
Formatting output, 234
   example, 237–239
   flags, 235–237, 239–240, 309
Formfeed, 27
free( ), 79
friend, 119–128, 413–414
Function(s), 43–44
   access codes, 111–113
   argument names, 395
   arguments, 405–406
   case, 216–217
   memberwise initialization, 286
   name overloading, 75–79, 309, 406–408
   overload matching rules, 79
   prototypes, 43, 50
   templates, 251–253

G

get( ), 210–212
get pointer, 215, 218
getline( ), 213
Getter function, 113, 309
Global variables, 86, 402–403
Global variables names, 395
goodbit, 311
goto, 42
Graphical user interface, 296

H

Header files, 44
Hex numbers, 239
hex digit, 216–217
hex( ), 241
Hexadecimal constants, 24
Horizontal tab, 27

I

I constructor, 311
Identifier, 29
if, 42
if-else statement, 39
ifstream class, 216–220
ignore( ), 213
Increment operator, 35–36, 39, 173–174
Inheritance, 134, 309
    protected access code, 136
    class derivation example, 136–141
    See also Multiple inheritance
init source code, 283–284
Initialization, automatic, 30
Initialization, memberwise, 284–292
Initialization versus assignment, 280
    const and reference types, 281–282
    init source code, 283–284
    member initialization list example, 282–284
Inline, 88, 309, 403–404
Inline assembler, 437
Input and output, 55
    iostream and objects, 63
    iostream input, 60–63
    iostream output, 57–60
Insertion operator, 55, 309
Inside Macintosh, 302, 434, 439
Instantiation, 250, 252–253, 311
int, 24, 28–29, 42
Integral constants, 24–25
Integral type, 24
Interface guidelines, 296, 309
Interface vocabulary, 296
ios::, 218
iostream, 55, 205
    character-based interface, 208
    classes, 208–209
    close( ), 226–228
    customizing, 228–234
    formatting output, 234–240
    get( ), 210–212
    getline( ), 213
    ifstream, 216–220, 226–228

    ignore( ), 213
    input, 60–63
    istream, 209–210
    istrstream, 241–244
    manipulators, 240–241
    and objects, 63
    ofstream, 217–220, 226–228
    ostream, 209–210
    ostrstream, 241–244
    output, 57–60
    peek( ), 214
    put( ), 214
    putback( ), 214
    read( ), 228
    reading data from a file, 217–219
    seekg( ), 215
    seekp( ), 215
    state bits, 220–226
    strstream, 242–244
    summary, 244
    utilities, 215–216
    write( ), 228
isalnum( ), 216–217
isalpha( ), 216–217
iscntrl( ), 216–217
isdigit( ), 216–217
isgraph( ), 216–217
islower( ), 216–217
isprint( ), 216–217
ispunct( ), 216–217
isspace( ), 216–217
istream, 209–210
istrstream, 241–244
isupper( ), 216–217
isxdigit( ), 216–217
Iterator function, 190

K

Kernighan, Brian, 421, 440
Key (Command), 14
Keywords, ANSI C, 42
Knaster, Scott, 304, 440

L

Learn C on the Macintosh, 45, 440
Left bit shift, 38
Left-justify, 238
Libraries, 434
Lippman, Stanley, 305, 421, 439
Literal constants, 24
    character, 26–27
    enumerations, 28
    floating-point, 25–26
    integral, 24–25
    string, 27–28
Local variables names, 86, 395
Logical operators, 40
long, 24–26, 29, 31–32, 42
long double, 26, 29
Lowercase, 216–217

M

Macintosh C Programming Primer, 303–304, 440
Macintosh Human Interface Guidelines, 309, 440
Macintosh Pascal Programming Primer, 440
Macintosh Programming Secrets, 304
Macintosh Programming Secrets, 304, 440
Macintosh Toolbox, 297–299, 309
MacTraps library, 298
main( ), 43, 127, 279
malloc( ), 79–80
Manipulators, 240–241, 309
Matching rules, 78–79
Member functions, 100–103, 309
    operator overloading, 166–167
    overriding, 154–158
Member initialization list, 268, 281–284, 309
Member names, 395
Member selection operator, 194–198
Memberwise assignment, 199, 310
Memberwise initialization, 284, 310
    example, 286–292
    function, 286
    memberWise source code, 287–292
Memory allocation, 79–85, 183
Menu Manager, 297

N

Naming conventions, 395
new, 99, 173, 183
new handler, 81
New Inside Macintosh, 439
new operator, 79–85, 186
Newline, 27
newTester source code, 83–85
nonprivate, 134, 135
NOT, 40
NULL byte, 27
NULL constant, 27
NULL, 81, 211, 241

O

Object, 265, 310
Object programming, 93–95
    access and privacy, 111–114
    class functions, 104–110
    classes, 97–98
    creating an object, 98–100
    data members, 100–103
    deleting an object, 103–104
    example, 114–119
    friend, 119–128
    member functions, 100–103
    pointer, 99
    struct, 96
    summary, 128
objects, 97
Object-Oriented Programming (OOP), 437
oct( ), 241
Octal constants, 24
ofstream class, 217–220
Open Project, 19
Operands, 176

M (continued, second column top)

Multidimensional arrays, 29–30
Multiple inheritance, 310, 417–419
    example, 260–265
    multInherit source code, 262–265
    static members, 266–270
Multiple overloading functions, 167

Operator(s), 37, 173
  arithmetic, 37
  assignment, 37, 415
  bitwise logical, 37–38
  built-in, 164, 173
  call, 186–190
  comma, 40
  conditional, 39, 173
  decrement, 35, 39, 173–174
  equals, 198–203
  increment, 35–36, 39, 173–174
  insertion, 55, 309
  logical, 40
  precedence of, 41–42
  relational, 40
  sizeof, 41
  subscript operator, 193
Operator overloading, 161–166, 310, 408–409
  call operator, 186–190
  equals, 198–203
  member selection operator, 194–198
  multiple overloading functions, 167
  new and delete, 186
  operator versions, 176
  overloadable and nonoverloadable, 173–174
  overloader overloading example, 177–183
  overloading an overloading function, 176
  summary, 204
  using a member function, 166–167
OR, 38, 40
ostream, 209–210
ostrstream, 241–244
Overloading
  function template, 253
  functions, 78–79, 176, 407–408
  source code, 76–78
  See also Operator overloading
Overriding function, 154

P
Parameters
  arrays of, 43
  adding to constructor, 107–108
  base classes and constructors with, 147
  constructors with, 147–153
  formal list, 250
Parentheses, 182
Passed by reference, 424
peek( ), 214
Pointers, 35–36, 99, 419–420
  get, 215, 218
  put, 215, 243
  smart, 194–198, 311
  versus references, 423
Pound sign, 44
Precedence of operators, 41–42
precision( ), 240–241
Preprocessor, 397–398
Preprocessor directives, 44–45
Preprocessor pass, 44
Printable ASCII character, 216–217
private, 111–114, 136, 231, 410–415
Project, 310, 431–432
Project file, 13, 310
Project menu, THIN C++, 18–20
Project window, 15, 310
Projector, 394
protected, 113, 136, 410–415
Protection, 265
protoTester source code, 66–68
public, 111–114, 136–139, 265, 410–415
Punctuation characters, 216–217
Pure virtual function, 412
Push button, 298
put( ), 214
putback( ), 214
put pointer, 215, 243

Q
Qualifier, 34
Question mark, 27
Quotation marks, 27–28

R
Radio buttons, 298

Range checking, 190
Read only memory (ROM), 297, 310
read( ), 228
readMe, 219–220
Rebuild desktop file, 14
reference, 72, 281–282
Reference variables, 68–75, 310
References, 423
register, 34, 42
Relational operators, 40
Remove Objects, 19
Return, 27, 42
Right bit shift, 38
Root base class, 260, 310

S

scientific, 239–240
Scope, 51–53, 310
Scope operator, 85–88, 266, 310
scopeTester source code, 87
Scripting, 438
Scroll bar, 298
Scrolling, 5
seekg( ), 215
seekp( ), 215
Self-extracting archive, 12
Set Tabs & Font dialog box, 18
setf( ), 235–236, 241
Setter function, 113, 310
short, 24, 29, 31–32, 42
showbase, 239
showpoint, 239
showpos, 239
signature, 76, 311
signed, 28, 42
Single quote, 27
Single-byte backslash characters, 26–27
sizeof( ), 41–42, 52, 173
Smart pointer, 194, 311
smart.Ptr, 194–197
smartPtr source code, 195–198

Source code file, opening, 204
Source-level debugging, 435–437
Space, 216–217
sprintf( ), 241
State bits, 220, 311
Statement markers, 435
Statements, 42
    assignment, 86, 190, 281–282
    friend, 119–128
    if-else, 39
    sizeof, 52
    typedef, 31–32
static, 34, 42, 266–268
Static initialization, 403
Static members, 266–270, 311
Storage-class specifiers, 34
strcpy( ), 199–201, 288
String constants, 27–28
Stroustrup, Bjarne, 305, 421, 439
strstream, 242–244
struct, 30, 32, 42, 96
Subscript operator, 190–193
switch, 42
Symantec C++, 429–431
    editor, 433–434
    inline assembler, 437
    libraries, 434
    Object-Oriented Programming (OOP), 437
    project, 431–432
    scripting, 438
    source-level debugging, 435–437
    THINK class library, 437–438
    upgrade offer, 430

T

Tabs, 17–18
Templates, 248–250, 311
    defining an object using, 250
    example, 254–260
    formal parameter list, 249–251
    function, 251–253

instantiation, 250, 252–253, 311
    source code, 255–260
Terminator, 42
Ternary operator, 39
THIN C++, 9–11
    features, 16–20
    installing, 12–13
    testing, 13–16
THINK class library, 437–438
THINK Reference, 302–303
this, 102–103, 202, 267
tilde, 109
tolower( ), 216–217
toupper( ), 216–217
Two-stage construction, 106, 311
Two-stage initialization, 110
Type, 29
Type coercion, 409–410
Type names, 395
Typecasting, 34
Typedefs, 31–32, 42

U

Unary operator, 37, 39
Unbuffered, 209
union, 31, 42
Unions, 31
Unofficial C++ Style Guide, 304, 439
unsetf( ), 235–236
unsigned, 28, 42
unsigned int, 25
unsigned long, 25
Upgrade offer, 430
Uppercase, 216–217, 239
User Interface, 295–296
Utilities, I/O, 215–216

V

Variables, 28
    arrays, 29–30
    automatic initialization, 30
    automatic type conversion, 32–33
    const qualifier, 34
    global and local, 86–88, 402
    pointers, 35–36
    reference, 68–72, 310
    storage-class specifiers, 34
    structs, 30
    this, 103
    typecasting, 34
    typedefs, 31–32
    unions, 31
Vertical tab, 27
virtual, 154–156, 276
Virtual base class, 274–276, 311
Virtual functions, 275, 415–417
virtual source code, 277–280
void, 42
void pointer, 33
volatile, 34, 42

W

Weston, Dan, 439
while, 42
while clause, 36
while loop, 220, 222, 234, 243
White space, 210, 235, 241
width( ), 237–239, 241
Wilkerson, Brian, 422–423
Wilson, David, A., 439
Window Manager, 298
write( ), 228
ws( ), 241

Next on your reading list from Addison-Wesley...

Learn C on the Macintosh®, by Dave Mark, 450 pages, $34.95, ©1991.

Macintosh® C Programming Primer, Volume I, Second Edition: Inside the Toolbox Using THINK C™, by Dave Mark and Cartwright Reed, 656 pages, $26.95, ©1992.

Macintosh® C Programming Primer, Volume II: Mastering the Toolbox Using THINK C™, by Dave Mark, 496 pages, $24.95, ©1990.

Macintosh® Pascal Programming Primer, Volume I: Inside the Toolbox Using THINK Pascal, by Dave Mark and Cartwright Reed, 544 pages, $24.95, ©1991.

These and other Addison-Wesley computer titles are available wherever computer books are sold, or by calling Addison-Wesley's order department at (800) 358-4566 or (617) 944-3700, 9 a.m. to 5 p.m., EST.

 **SYMANTEC.™**

Put Your Learning to Work with Symantec C++ for Macintosh.™

Buy Symantec C++ for Macintosh for $299

and save 40% off the retail price of $499!

Symantec C++ is the ultimate development environment for the Macintosh. Featuring an extremely fast C++ compiler, an even faster linker, a multi-window text editor and a powerful source-level debugger, Symantec C++ gives you the power to develop any Macintosh application, desk accessory, device driver or code resource.

- **Superior Code Generation:** Symantec C++ compiles faster than any other C++ compiler without compromising code quality. The global optimizer further refines code size and speed of your executable program.

- **Complete Integration:** All the tools - editor, compiler, optimizer, linker, debugger and browser are fully integrated for unsurpassed turnaround time from idea to completed program.

- **Object Oriented Programming:** The THINK™ Class Library provides the C++ building blocks for writing your programs, including all the components for Macintosh user interface such as windows, menus and controls.

--- --- --- --- --- --- --- --- --- --- --- --- --- --- --- --- --- ---

Order Form - Symantec C++ Special Offer

☐ Please send me Symantec C++ for Macintosh for $299 plus $8 shipping. Please add state tax.

☐ Check ☐ Visa/MC/AX#: _____ Exp Date: _____

Name: _____ Company: _____

Street: _____ Phone: _____
(No P.O. Boxes, Please.)
City: _____ State: _____ Zip: _____

Country: _____

Please mail check or credit payment to: Symantec Fulfillment Center, Attn: Symantec C++ Addison Wesley Offer, PO Box 22335, Denver, CO. 80222-0335. Telephone orders: (800) 228-4122, Please allow 2 weeks for processing your order.

State Sales Tax: 3%(CO), 4%(GA, MI, NY), 4.5%(VA), 5%(AZ, IN, IA, MA, MD, OH, WI), 5.725%(MO), 6%(CT, DC, FL, NJ, PA), 6.25%(IL, TX), 6.5%(MN, WA), 7.25%(CA). Canada (7%). Please also add local sales tax in AZ, CA, GA, NY, OH, TX, WA, WI.

Offer good in US and Canada only. Units not to be resold. All payments must be in US dollars and checks must be drawn on a US bank.

THINK, THINK C and Symantec are trademarks of Symantec Corporation. ©1993 Symantec Corporation. All rights reserved.